THE ARCHITECTURE OF WREN

KERRY DOWNES

THE ARCHITECTURE OF WREN

First published by Granada Publishing 1982
This edition published by Redhedge 1988

British Library Cataloguing in Publication Data

Downes, Kerry
    The architecture of Wren. — 2nd ed.
    1. England. Buildings designed by Wren,
    Sir Christopher, 1632–1723. Architectural
    features
    I. Title
    720'.92'4

ISBN 0-9513877-0-7

Filmset and printed in Great Britain by
BAS Printers Limited, Over Wallop, Hampshire

FOR MARGARET

CONTENTS

LIST OF TEXT FIGURES

LIST OF PLATES

NOTE TO THE READER

Exploration showed that the only practical way of keeping this book in print was to take personal charge of the whole business. I am sorry to disappoint those who wanted the *ignis fatuus* of a complete and massive "standard work", but I believe that others will still find this book useful as what it was meant to be.

Ideally a new edition would have been re-set and in the modern integrated fashion, but this was not economically feasible. My thanks are due to Messrs. William Collins who, having returned the British rights to me, made available the original films, thus helping to pass on the economy to the reader. It has, however, been possible – and indeed it was necessary – to make some additions and corrections to the text. A good reason for placing them in this Note is that they are more usefully seen at the front than tucked away at the end; the real reason, however, is again economic: a little re-arrangement released sufficient space for what was needed without disturbing the rest of the original.

The following paragraphs contain, arranged in order by page number of the main text, supplementary material of two kinds, corrections of errors and notices of new information or references.

5 The Royal Society was actually established before the end of 1660.

11 Wren was not sole architect to St Paul's until his appointment under the Royal Warrant of 12 November 1673; clearly the Dean had nobody else in mind.

12 n.34 For Wren's patent as Surveyor, 28 March 1669, see BM MS. Lansd. 698.

18 n.48 Wren's signature on a document of 29 June 1711 in the Harley Papers (BM MS. Loan 29/217, f.602) is so shaky and spidery as to suggest not the weakness of age but some sort of clinical trauma, otherwise unrecorded and effectively concealed by his colleagues and family. Such a misfortune would have given point to veiled contemporary references to his failing powers.

20 n.61 For the problem of longitude and other matters of number see J. A. Bennett, *The Mathematical Science of Christopher Wren* (Cambridge, 1982).

29 The 'modern' Oxford architecture of Wren's youth, from his own college, Wadham (1610–13) to the chapel of Brasenose (1650s), contributed more than has been recognized to his architec-

tural formation. See the introductory essays in the exhibition catalogue, *Sir Christopher Wren*, Whitechapel Art Gallery, 1982, where Wren's attitudes to intuition and to architectural detailing are also further discussed.

33 Two eye-witnesses to Wren's model for the Sheldonian wrote that the building was also to be used for performing plays, and presumably they wrote what they had been told. H. M. Colvin's imaginative attempt (*Unbuilt Oxford*, London, 1983, 13–20) to reconstruct the design on this basis – with no visual evidence – evades the dilemma of provision between a stage and a ceremonial entrance. In 'Wren and Sheldon', *Oxford Art Jnl*, VI/1 (1983), 45–50, Charles Saumarez Smith shows the degree to which the 'progressive' aspects of the Sheldonian were not only understood in Oxford but also by no means universally approved.

46 For an illustrated catalogue of the St Paul's collection of drawings for the Cathedral, see now K. Downes, *Sir Christopher Wren: the Design of St Paul's*, London, 1988.

48 Unusually, the shells over the small doorways in Pl. 21 are an identifiable borrowing from Palladio, as pointed out by John Harris. They appear (enclosing busts) as overdoors in the elevation detail for the Palazzo Chiericati (*Quattro Libri*, Bk. II, 7).

52 n.126 The 'preliminary' drawing of the First Model appears to be, as suggested by J. Summerson (*Burlington Mag.*, XCVII, 1955, 120), an eighteenth-century copy or reduction. Thomas Worsley of Hovingham, Surveyor-General of Works from 1760 to 1778, may well have had access to Wren drawings then remaining in the Office of Works and now lost.

69 Wren's subsequent secretiveness is confirmed by a direction in the Minutes of the St Paul's Commission (Guildhall MS. 11770); the executive committee, of which the architect himself was an active and no doubt guiding member, instructed him on 12 October 1676 to bring the 'Design of the Church' to be locked up in the office, keeping a copy for himself. The attempts of printmakers to publicize the design show the success of this policy; the dissemination of the design among the builders was, without a complete model, effected more by individual detail models than by drawings. See Downes, *Design of St Paul's* (above, note to 46).

72 n.159 The Lincoln Cathedral Library was re-opened in 1988 after a sensitive restoration, including the revival of the original light grey marbling with *trompe-l'œil* bevel-revealed panels. Wren's autograph report of 1676 (now in the Lincoln Record Office) lists rates for gilding, painting in flat 'stone colour', veined black or white marbling, rance marbling, cedar, walnut and 'Indian wood' graining. It is in the category of *advice* rather than either *direction* or *design*.

76 n.164 The Hampton Court fire of 1986, which started in an apartment over the south state rooms, has exposed previously unknown aspects of the construction, including Wren's use of iron in the top storey, where the floor is partly supported by beams and partly hung from the roof trusses by iron rods (information by courtesy of the Hampton Court staff of English Heritage).

77–8 Wren can be allowed rather more time between the Warrant and Definitive designs. To judge by modern procedures, the former may have lain on an official desk for up to a year before the signature of 14 May 1675. At the latter end, the supposed foundation-laying of June 1675 seems to be fictitious, and the start of work must date from the connection of a water supply from the New River Company's main on 17 July (*Wren Soc.* XIII, 64). The contracts signed by the masons on 18 June did not become legal until confirmation by the Commission on 15 July.

80 Confirmation that rustication was originally intended comes from new study not only of the sequence of drawings but also of the engravings of around 1700. Wren's authorized prints, titled *Ex autographo architecti*, show no rustication and the drawings on which they were based showed none either (compare Pl. 58). But William Emmett's pirated prints (see p. 116 and n.241) were made from the building up to roof level and show rustication; for the unbuilt dome and west towers Emmett relied on 'leaked' copies of Wren's drawings.

81 and n.247 See now R. A. Beddard, 'Wren's Mausoleum for Charles I and the Cult of the Royal Martyr', *Architectural History*, XXVII (1984), 36–49.

82 Wren's forward planning of work at St Paul's was due not only to mistrust. There were sound statical reasons for building all four legs of the dome concurrently, to maintain equal loading on all of them; the Commission's Minutes (see above, 69) show that the King's authority to proceed west of the choir was obtained in March 1676. The build-

ing accounts also show that Wren created a rolling programme, in which each trade moved gradually from east to west and was succeeded by the next one; thus continuity of work could be ensured for the various building firms over many years.

83 n.179 The spectre of the 'missing model' for St Paul's, although revived by G. Beard, *The Work of Christopher Wren* (1982), – a work whose use requires caution – still has no basis in fact.

85 The distinctive decoration of the *upper* transept ends was not executed, and perhaps not designed, before their construction in the early 1690s.

90 The Evelyn reference is to n.197.

97 A tour of the surviving Tudor kitchens and other offices at Hampton Court reveals not only their vast extent but also the logistical advantages for the architect of retaining them as against the disruption to the whole household which would have accompanied their rebuilding.

103 n.216 See now K. Downes, 'Hawksmoor's House at Easton Neston', *Architectural History*, XXX (1987), 50–76.

111 n.231 Parts of the sashes have recently been found at St Paul's (communication from Robert Crayford).

114 n.236 The claim (*Architects' Jnl*, 15 June 1988, 24–5) that Hawksmoor's drawings 'may well reflect Wren's own thinking' has as little foundation in reality as any other recent attempts to validate or invalidate schemes for the St Paul's area as either in or out of accord with Wren's intentions.

PREFACE

Over ten years ago, in prefacing a work now out of print, I expressed a vague hope of writing a large book on Wren; the pages that follow will show how far, if not why, I have changed my mind. The convenience of having 'everything under one cover' is illusory, and for a useful book other priorities are higher. This is primarily a book about Wren's architecture, and his achievement in the sciences is only discussed in that context. There has never been a good collection of photographs of Wren's buildings, let alone one designed, as this is, to be analytical and comparative. There is still much to say about the character of the man and his architecture, and I believe I understand them better now than I did a decade ago. In a few places, however, I felt I could not improve on the earlier book and therefore incorporated paragraphs without notice.

Of many debts, my foremost in scholarship is to Sir John Summerson, in production to Moira Johnston. From the former not only have I received advice, encouragement and example over many years, but so often in re-exploring the Wren material I have found his discreet signposts showing that he has already been that way. The latter not only commissioned this work but accepted and defended my idea of what it should contain. In this respect I should explain that, although it is now scheduled to appear in Wren's 350th anniversary year, the coincidence was not originally intended and results from unforeseen and unavoidable delays.

Many of my observations and conclusions arose from the recurrent needs of teaching, and I would thank those generations of students at Reading and elsewhere who have heard, discussed, and helped whether consciously or not to refine what is presented here. Particular thanks are due among former students to John Bold and Peter Smith, and to Jane Hoos for her observations on Hampton Court. Among colleagues, new material has come from John Harris in respect of Tring, from Gerald Cobb on the history of the City churches, and above all from Robert Crayford, who has generously allowed me to refer to some of his still unpublished detailed studies of St Paul's.

Beachcombers should note those aims which I did not entertain. Not every building is equally discussed or illustrated, and some are not represented at all, and in general I have concentrated on those that interest, move or puzzle me. Drawings are discussed only in relation to executed buildings or to the development of Wren's ideas. Like him, I have been cautious of novelty; rather have I concentrated on the evidence already before me. I have also been selective in the provision of accessories: the notes are a minimal guide to sources used, the bibliography is restricted, and the list of works does not include every projected design or minor commission.

I am again grateful to those who have actively or passively facilitated photography; also, among custodians in particular, to the staff of the Codrington Library at All Souls and the Guildhall in London, and to Reginald Williams of the British Museum Print Room. Acknowledgement for the reproduction of photographs or originals is gratefully made to the Warden and Fellows of All Souls (Plates 2, 6, 20, 21, 56, 57, 58, 74, 165); Visitors of the Ashmolean Museum, Oxford (1); British Museum (22); Courtauld Institute of Art (47, 48); Department of the Environment (162); Guildhall Library (59, 71, 131, 132, 142); National Monuments Record (23, 28, 30, 31, 34, 35, 37, 38, 41, 46, 70, 71, 88, 91, 93, 94, 95, 96, 101, 107, 112); Thomas Photos, Oxford (44); Westminster City Libraries (161); Yale University, Art and Architecture Library (133). Figure 16 is based on drawings in the RIBA Drawings Collection; where it is of interest, sources for other figures may be deduced from the notes.

Finally, and most of all, my wife discussed the problems, first heard and then read the drafts, and prepared the typescript; the book owes so much to her acute ear, eye and judgement, her companionship on expeditions, in despair and in discovery, as well as to her success in maintaining normal life during the various stages of authorship. To her it is affectionately dedicated.

Department of History of Art
University of Reading
February 1982

I   PROMISE

The memorial tablet to Sir Christopher Wren (1632–1723) over his grave in the crypt of St Paul's, the Cathedral of London which he designed and saw to completion, carries the words, *Si monumentum requiris, circumspice* (if you are expecting his monument, look around you). Funerary inscriptions of the time, modelled on those of ancient Rome, are usually more concerned with the rank and the achievements of the person commemorated than with his personality, and no neater or more appropriate epitaph could have been chosen than this reference to what was both the largest and the greatest accomplishment of an architect who was also a distinguished anatomist, geometrician and astronomer.

The construction of St Paul's is copiously, almost completely, documented by surviving records including the detailed building accounts, and we know a good deal about the several designs which, over a period of nine years, preceded the final one. We know less about the architect. The deficiency is not so much in the datable events of his life – of which many are known – as in where he lived, what he and his family were like as people, many of the personal details which, if known, give us the feeling we have met a historical figure. It is, however, one of the tasks of the biographer, the historian or the art-historian, to look beyond the evidence apparent around him and to make the most – but not too much – of even the smallest clues he can find. Something more than a chronicle of Wren's life and actions should therefore be possible.

Wren's son Christopher (1675–1747) compiled, and his grandson Stephen published in 1750, not a biography but a collection of memoirs including transcripts of many original documents. *Parentalia*, as it was entitled, concerns chiefly Sir Christopher's scientific and architectural career, but the first two-fifths of the folio volume is about his father, also Christopher (1589–1658), Dean of Windsor, and his uncle Matthew (1585–1667), Bishop of Ely. The architect's son began work on the compilation during his father's last years, but he was a devoted apologist rather than a skilled writer or a systematic biographer. There were many questions which he no doubt intended to ask his father, but, as often happens, circumstances did not allow him to do so; there were also matters which his father could no longer recall clearly, if at all, and some on which the son misunderstood what he was told. Within these limitations, however, *Parentalia* is a valuable, indeed a unique source of information about Wren's works.[1] Although, as his son explained to a correspondent in 1739, the architect's papers were first drafts, generally 'blotted and interlined',[2] some of the letters and other documents printed there are not known from any other source.

We have several likenesses of of Sir Christopher, including one superlative one in the bust that Edward Pierce made of him about 1673, the year he became truly established both socially – by knighthood – and artistically – by the 'Great Model' design for St Paul's. This bust remained in the family until 1737 when the younger Christopher gave it to the Ashmolean Museum in Oxford (Plate 1). Pierce was a good carver and a competent portraitist, but on this occasion he produced a masterpiece which has been called the best sculpture from an English hand in the seventeenth century.[3] Pierce was perhaps inspired by what Wren could have told him of Bernini's *Louis XIV* at Versailles, executed while Wren was in Paris; certainly the personality of his sitter also led Pierce to surpass his usual standard. Wren, as we know from other evidence, was small in stature[4] and had the wiry liveliness that sometimes attends those who were delicate as children but survive into a hearty old age; there seems to be no record, other than Wren's own, of his meeting in 1665 with Bernini, who was also a small, lively man but twice the Englishman's age. Pierce gives us truly a 'speaking likeness' of the kind for which the great Italian sculptor was renowned, in which the lips are about to part in speech and the sharp features and alert expression portray an acute observer of all around him, as if Wren is interviewing those who look at his image and is learning far more in the exchange than he gives away. Such a man must have chosen his words well and sparingly – the labour his son found in his manuscripts is consistent with this – and it is the more regrettable that we know so little of his conversation. In a letter printed in *Parentalia*, Thomas Sprat recalls a discussion with Wren 'on the Subject of the Wit of Conversation'. Wren seems to have maintained that women were better speakers than men because they were 'less disturbed with busy Thoughts . . . quicker and readier for new Impressions, they talk more of circumstantial Things, they sit longer together, and . . . keep their feet warmer and drier, and go less into the moist and open Air'. This account of domestic discussion of inessentials, sheltered from the damp, might appear to exemplify what is now called male chauvinism, but it is clear from the context that Wren and Sprat valued the contribution of the distaff side to the play of words and ideas. But as Sprat's stolidly clear prose gives no clue to the character of the discourse he sought to rehearse, we are thrown back on imagination.[5]

Wren's power with words is evident from the few letters and the various reports which survive, some of which will be quoted in due course. Flowery locutions were distasteful to him, but his vocabulary was rich and his choice of words was exact and epigrammatic. In the 1670s the diary of his colleague and friend Robert Hooke (1635–1703) records the range and frequency of his conversation, since in those years they were in almost daily contact over both scientific matters and the building of the City churches. But Hooke's diary itself, unlike those of Pepys and Evelyn, is so abbreviated as rarely to give more than the topics, and occasionally the outcome, of a discussion: 'Agreed not' for example. We know that Wren was generous with ideas, and made many suggestions in scientific matters which he left others to develop.[6] He must also have been generous with his time to those who, in whatever walk of life, came to him for his advice. We know that he was liberal to his architectural assistants; the greatest, Nicholas Hawksmoor (1661–1736), who became an architect of genius, looked back all his life with pride to the values and the training he received from Sir Christopher. But Wren's son draws no character of his father in *Parentalia*, and we know least of all about his private life. His two marriages produced several children, but he married late, at the age of 37, and was widowed for the second and last time at 48.

His first wife, Faith Coghill, was four years his junior and they had probably known each other since childhood; she died of smallpox in September 1675 and their only surviving son was Christopher, the author of *Parentalia*. In February 1677 Wren married Jane Fitzwilliam, the daughter of Lord Fitzwilliam of Lifford, in the Chapel Royal;[7] she bore him two children, Jane (died 1702) and William who was mentally handicapped but lived well into middle age. The second Lady Wren died in October 1680, and we know of no other involvements either later or earlier. It is perhaps easy therefore to think of Wren as a cold, even monastic, intellectual who married when and because he thought it important rather than from any deep emotion. But people are not what they seem from a *curriculum vitae*. We have no intimate diary of Wren's, and if we did not have those of Hooke and Pepys we should have no idea at all that Hooke, another cool intellect, used to sleep with his housekeepers, including his niece, or that the righteous public servant Pepys, jealous equally for his respectability and for his wife, engaged in sexual experiments with dubiously pretty women in carriages and upper rooms. We can only say that what little is known of Wren's intimate life was quite normal for his time.

What was far above the norm was his intelligence. When John Evelyn called him a 'Miracle of a Youth' in 1654 he was an Oxford MA and Fellow of All Souls. The writings and the working models of his early teens, signs of precocity known and interpreted only by his family, had already given place to a reputation among the learned scientific thinkers of the day. When, ten years later, Evelyn met him again in Oxford, his praise had risen to 'incomparable genius', the emphasis being on the adjective to give the specific meaning reserved nowadays for the noun. By 1664, at 32, Wren held an Oxford chair and an international reputation; he was not only a founder member of the Royal Society but also had the attention of its first patron, Charles II, in both scientific and architectural matters. He had already lived through the glorious and the abject years of Charles I, the Civil War, the Commonwealth and the Restoration. None of these events left him untouched. Bishop Wren, his uncle, was imprisoned from 1642 until 1660 for his support of Archbishop Laud's High Anglicanism and of the King. His father's Deanery at Windsor was twice ransacked by Cromwellian soldiers and the family became refugees with the Dean's son-in-law William Holder, who was appointed Rector of Bletchingdon, between Bicester and Oxford. The Restoration brought the release of his uncle but no guarantee of political stability in either the shorter or the longer future, and the architect was to live through the Revolution of 1688, the succession crises of 1702 and 1714 and the Jacobite rising of 1715 before finally losing his appointment as Surveyor of Works in 1718 in a mean 'reorganization' generated by party, not national politics, and by greed and envy rather than by idealism. His capacity to survive in office so far, and his dignified letter of retirement (p. 20), bear witness to his intellectual strength as well as to the stoic values inculcated in him by his father and his teachers.

Christopher Wren was born on 20 October 1632 at East Knoyle, Wiltshire, of which his father was the Rector;[8] later a house became available at Windsor on Dr Wren's appointment as Dean. On account of his poor health young Christopher was first educated at home, by a private tutor, William Shepheard, and by his father, who was a man of varied interests which included architecture. There survives inaccessibly at Shirburn Castle Dean Wren's copy of Sir Henry Wotton's *Elements of Architecture* (1624) annotated in his hand with a care which, according to the compiler of *Parentalia*, was habitual.[9] The notes include the criticism that the pre-Fire Christ Church, Newgate Street in London, was practically all window, 'fitter for a stage than for a church', an observation on Wotton's statement that any room other than a church might be well lit, 'devotion more requiring collected than defused spirits'. Sir Christopher's observation and use of light were to be more complex. The Dean also noted his invention of the serpentine river 'to reduce the Current of a Mile's length to the Compass of an Orchard' to the benefit 'of all Purposes, either of Gardenings, Plantings, or Banquetings, or airy Delights, and the multiplying of infinite Fish in a little compass of ground'. There is no evidence that this ingenious anticipation of the landscape garden, both useful and decorative, was constructed anywhere, but the volume also contains a note and a diagram of what *Parentalia* calls 'a very strong Roof made by him at Knoyle'.[10]

Among the Dean's papers was also found a prediction, since all the numerical letters in the Latin alphabet make 1666 (MDCLXVI), of 'some ominous Matter' in that year.[11] Such divinations and chronograms were a favourite game of the time, and a belief in the possibilities of the unknown was no more nor less unscholarly than the current interest today of serious scientists in 'black holes' or extra-sensory phenomena. Seventeenth-century discoveries in astronomy had shown that the sky could no longer be regarded as a concentric series of immutable crystal spheres, but as late as 1680 Evelyn, commenting on the sighting of a comet, wrote, 'What this Portend . . . God only knows . . . I pray God avert his Judgments; we have had of late severall Comets, which though I believe appear from natural Causes, & of them selves operate not, yet . . . may be warnings from God'.[12]

From 1641 to 1646 the boy Wren was strong enough to be a boarder at Westminster School, where he completed the traditional grounding in the Classics under the headship of the famous educationist Dr Richard Busby. In 1642 he marked his birthday by addressing a letter in Latin to his father, with the precociously elegant subscription *E Musaeo meo* (from my Study). In 1645 the anniversary gifts were an essay on the rise of rivers and a *Panorganum Astronomicum*, a machine which, according to the dedicatory Latin verses, showed both the movements of the stars and of the sun through the year, and the phases of the moon.[13] Wren first learned mathematics from his sister's husband, the Rev. Dr William Holder;[14] after he left Westminster he continued his studies privately and with Sir Charles Scarburgh.[15] Scarburgh was both a mathematician and an anatomist, and Wren made for him cardboard working models of muscles. When he went up to Oxford in 1649[16] the youth's achievements also included a mechanical weather recorder, a device for writing in the dark, a deaf-and-dumb alphabet (speech was one of Holder's interests), and a treatise on spherical trigonometry. He received his BA in 1651 and his MA two years later and then spent four years in research as a Fellow of All Souls. In 1657 he was appointed Professor of Astronomy at Gresham College, the City of London's university college in Bishopsgate; subsequently the college was occupied by the army after Cromwell's death, and Wren returned to All Souls. After the Restoration Gresham College re-opened, but the following year Wren gained the Savilian Chair of Astronomy at Oxford and a Doctorate of Civil Law. However, 1661 was to be a turning point for quite different reasons.

The twelve years since Wren first entered Wadham College were not only a period of concentrated study and research and continued inventiveness, for the remarkable qualities of whose results we have to rely largely on contemporary estimates. A university brings together good minds in a whole world of different fields, and Wadham, under the leadership of its Warden, John Wilkins, was the birthplace of a discussion group of varied specialists including Wren. An important feature of the group was that, in the troubled political and religious atmosphere of the 1650s, it included without discord committed supporters of both the Royalist and the republican cause. From about 1658 meetings were also held in London, and late in 1660 they were regularly constituted into a society. Charles II, whose intelligence far exceeded his formal education and who was interested in learning as well as novelties, accepted the patronage, thus establishing the Royal Society in 1661.

The King took a keen interest in the Society in its early years; in his own laboratory at Whitehall he probably went no farther than schoolboy science, but he did also commission, in the Restoration year itself, a large telescope to stand in the Privy Garden.[17] The telescope and the microscope had begun recently to open up new worlds outside and inside that accessible to the naked eye, and Wren came more particularly to his patron's notice through the use of both instruments. In the summer of 1661 he completed at Charles's request a set of enlarged drawings of microscopic creatures; these do not survive but they must have been like those engraved a few years later (*Micrographia*, 1665) by Wren's colleague Hooke. At the same time Wren used telescopic observations to make a relief model of the earthward side of the moon, which he presented to the King mounted on a pedestal with an inscription saying that one orb (the earth) was not enough for his greatness.[18] There is a curious parallel to this in the mount designed by Bernini for his bust of Louis XIV, which was to have stood on a terrestrial globe with the motto,[19] *picciola base* (a small base [for such a figure]): for the first time the scale of the planetary system began to be realized.

There is a consistency, as Sir John Summerson has pointed out, through nearly all Wren's recorded work of this period, as well as most of his boyhood efforts.[20] Whether in the study of weather, or of the very small or the very distant, in an instrument to write a copy at the same time as the original, or in anatomy, he was concerned with drawings, models and mechanisms, with an evident delight in things that not only worked but could be seen to work. Wren's interest in sundials was no exception; dialling or gnomonics was, like perspective drawing, map-making and stereotomy (the mathematics of cutting stones for vaults), an application of projective geometry, which was not to become a securely based science for at least another century. Clearly from boyhood until the design of the towers of St Paul's after 1704 Wren liked drawing and was good at it, retaining into his seventies a hand that was orderly, precise, expressive and unshaken. It was not an impossible step or even a very large one from drawing, mechanisms, dissections and experiments in blood transfusion to the total visible realization of ideas in architecture. *Parentalia* includes in a list of inventions exhibited by Wren before 1660, 'New Designs tending to Strength, Convenience and Beauty in Building': these are the three aims of architecture according to the ancient Roman writer Vitruvius, so even at this date Wren's concern with building was wider than one of engineering.[21] It is hardly conceivable that his father had not talked with him about architecture in general and about Windsor Castle, Westminster Abbey and Wadham College in particular. But the first specific architectural connection of which we know anything is datable to 1661. That September an expedition was prepared to commission the fort at Tangier, which had been ceded to Britain as part of the dowry of Charles II's Queen, Catherine of Braganza. Wren received a letter from his cousin Matthew Wren, Lord Chancellor Clarendon's secretary, asking him as a renowned geometrician to go out to supervise work at Tangier. Christopher had 'no Inclination to accept, being not then so consistent with his Health, but humbly prayed his Majesty to allow of his Excuse, and to command his Duty in England': this is, according to *Parentalia*, our only record of the exchange, which links with it a letter from Thomas Sprat in Oxford to Wren in London.[22] Sprat told him that the Vice-Chancellor had asked him why the Professor of Astronomy was absent 'so long after the beginning of the Term' and that the excuse Sprat made for him was the King's command in the matters of the fortifying of Tangier and – far more significant for the future – the repair of old St Paul's. *Parentalia* dates the letter 1663 without day, but this was a bad guess: the mention by name of the Vice-Chancellor, Dr Richard Bayley, places it in the autumn of 1661 since Bayley resigned the following summer.[23] We know also that in mid-October 1661 Dr John Barwick, the new Dean of St Paul's, started to restore liturgical services to the old cathedral;[24] this, rather than the Royal Commission for that purpose, dated 18 April 1663, must indicate Wren's first involvement with the building.

The inducement in the Tangier invitation was a promise: the reversion of the Surveyorship of the King's Works whenever the Surveyor, Sir John Denham, should die. It has generally been assumed that this promise meant no more to King Charles – for it did not, so to speak, cost him anything – than had his appointment of Denham immediately after the Restoration. Denham's qualifications for the post had been hardly strong: he was a good administrator but (according to Evelyn) 'a better poet than architect'. He probably never designed a building himself, and perhaps most significantly he had given loyal and extraordinary service to the King in exile. Charles was a master of expediency in matching what he had to dispose of with the demands he had to meet. But he was also as hard a judge of men as he was a soft one of women, and was shrewd enough to be able to see in Wren qualities of which the latter was still scarcely aware, and to recognize that Wren would prove to be a better architect at any rate than Denham. Moreover, by the autumn of 1664 Wren and the King were probably making designs for Whitehall (p. 43).

Meanwhile Wren returned to discharge his Oxford duties, holding the chair in name at least for twelve years; in 1662 he lectured on spheres, on Easter and on navigation,[25] and the following year he drew the illustrations for his friend Thomas Willis's book, published in 1664, on the anatomy of the brain. But already the business of architecture began to occupy progressively more of his thoughts. In 1663 his first two works in architecture were initiated; appropriately the commissions were from a relative and a friend and the buildings were in Cambridge and Oxford (Plates 5, 11). It is customary to see in Pembroke Chapel and the Sheldonian Theatre, as first works, a hesitant and amateurish quality, and this view goes with an unexpressed assumption that they were designed overnight or by leafing through Serlio and other architectural books almost as one would choose goods from a mail order catalogue. It will be argued later that such a view of their style is not consistent with Wren's later work, and neither is the corresponding idea of their genesis consistent with Wren's character. At present it is only necessary to point out the importance for these buildings of the delay between the events of 1661 and their commencement. In 1699 Vanbrugh seems to have undertaken the design of Castle Howard without premeditation, but that was characteristic of him and he could rely on Hawksmoor's help; neither Wren's character nor his resources were at all similar.

While he was in prison Bishop Matthew Wren, Christopher's uncle, vowed that if he survived to see the Crown and Episcopacy restored he would commission a new chapel for Pembroke, his old college at Cambridge. *Parentalia* omits the chapel from the list of Sir Christopher's Cambridge work, and only mentions it in the life of the Bishop, but this would only allow serious doubt about its attribution if *Parentalia* were a systematic record.

In 1663 Wren was also designing a more complex building, the theatre in Oxford named after its instigator, Gilbert Sheldon, who gave it to the University on his appointment that year as Archbishop of Canterbury. His pious aim was to remove the predominantly secular and partly ribald degree ceremonies from St Mary's

Church to a purposely built structure. Wren showed a 'model' of the Theatre at a Royal Society meeting on 29 April 1663, and was asked to provide for the archives an account, which does not survive, of 'the whole frame of it'. The exhibition of the model indicates not only the Society's wide interests – not then confined to the natural sciences – but also the probability of consultation. The foundation stone was not laid until more than a year later, and in October 1664 Evelyn convinced himself that Wren accepted his advice 'in some particulars', which suggests that even when site work was well advanced the design above ground was still fluid.[26]

On 22 June 1665, three months before the consecration of the Cambridge chapel, Wren wrote to Ralph Bathurst, a member of the Wadham group in the 1650s and recently elected President of Trinity College, Oxford, about his design for a new range of lodgings in the college garden (p. 44). The most important reference in the letter, however, is to 'Mons. Mansard, or Signor Bernini, both which I shall see at Paris within the fortnight'. There is scattered information in letters about Wren's stay in France; when Evelyn wrote to him on 4 April he knew the visit was intended, and mentioned the possibility of contacts. The first report of his presence is from a correspondent late in August, to the effect that he had been well received and had met Bernini and seen both his design for the Louvre and the bust of Louis XIV.[27]

Wren had probably left England, as he intended, about the end of June, when the prudent were beginning to desert London on account of the spread of the plague. The only surviving letter from Wren himself is undated but was written in the early autumn; he meant then to leave France at Christmas, but he may not have done so since he is first mentioned as back in England early in March 1666. During a visit of six months or more, scientific contacts as well as an introduction to the English Ambassador, the Earl of St Albans, smoothed his entry into French cultural circles. His letter, however, is largely about the places he visited and contains a list of the principal French artists and architects. 'My business now', he wrote, 'is to pry into Trades and Arts', and he referred to a written work then 'on the Anvil', no doubt for the Royal Society and perhaps never finished: 'Observations on the present state of Architecture, Arts, and Manufactures in France'.

From his previously declared intention of meeting François Mansart, the senior and most distinguished French architect of the day, and Bernini, the architect of Pope Alexander VII, to his later desires expressed in his letter of bringing back 'almost all France in Paper' – engravings and perhaps drawings – Wren's travels appear to have had one primary purpose. The arrival of Bernini to make designs for completing the Louvre, abandoned the day after he returned to Rome, may have influenced the timing of the trip, but Wren must have realized that Italian and French books and the architecture of Inigo Jones and his followers could teach him no more. With the notable exceptions (p. 46) of Jones's Banqueting House at Whitehall (Plate 4) and his colossal Corinthian portico at St Paul's (Fig. 21A), truly classical architecture in England was mainly domestic in both purpose and scale. The dissolution of the monasteries under Henry VIII had left in most places a surplus of churches. Charles I had failed to rebuild Tudor Whitehall as a Renaissance palace; of Charles II's attempt to do so at Greenwich, to the design of John Webb, the single block ever built was just rising through the scaffolding. Wren was perhaps a bad traveller; certainly he never went abroad again and in 1698 urged his son, then in France, to weigh carefully whether going on to Italy was worth the cost and rigours of the journey for 'the seeing of fine buildings' and being able 'to say hereafter that you have seen Rome, Naples and other fine places'.[28]

But in the summer of 1665 the seedling planted out four years previously had grown so far that Wren knew, not that he would abandon the sciences – for he never did so – but that he would embrace architecture with a commitment such that the seeing of fine buildings was essential; indeed Evelyn's April letter, offering him a copy of his translation of Fréart's *Parallel*, is written as to an architect.[29] In Paris the scale as well as the richness and modernity of the Louvre and Tuileries Palaces was new to him, and he was no less impressed by the organization of the vast building works there and the convenience and size of the *quais*, the embankments between which the Seine flows through Paris. The feminine atmosphere of the early Versailles displeased him on account of its 'Works of Filgrand and little Knacks' but yet the palace 'call'd me twice to view it'. He was struck in the Marble Court there by the 'Mixtures of Brick, Stone, blue Tile and Gold'; the French sense of texture in exterior architecture made a lasting impression on him. 'Bernini's Designs of the Louvre I would have given my Skin for, but the old reserv'd Italian gave me but a few Minutes View' which he 'had only time to copy . . . in my Fancy and Memory'. It would be twenty years before they worked their way to the surface in his own style. Le Vau's College of the Four Nations, across the river from the Louvre and still building, influenced him in a similar way.[30]

The masonry fronts of Paris streets were as new to Wren as they had been to a traveller like Evelyn two decades earlier, for English cities were still full of wood-frame façades with plaster infilling. He saw most of the country houses between Liancourt near Senlis to the north and Fontainebleau to the south of the capital. When he left England he had never seen a dome, for there was none to see, and those of the Jesuit Church (now St Paul-St Louis), the Oratoire, the Sorbonne, the Val-de-Grâce, the church of the Visitation and the never finished St Anne-la-Royale by Guarini, introduced him to a form which excited both the artist and the engineer in him, although at the time he cannot have foreseen the opportunities which calamity would offer him to build domes himself.

Less than two months after he was reported back in London, in May 1666, Wren the architect was unequivocally revealed in a new report to the St Paul's Commission with a proposal for building a new crossing capped by a tall dome. In referring there to the domes he had seen in Paris, 'constructed by the best Artists French and Italian', he not only described his 'daily conference with them and observing their Engines and Materials' but claimed to have himself 'promoted this geometrical part of Architecture yet farther [so that] the raising of Materialls may yet be more facilitated so as to save in the lofty Fabricks very considerable part both of the Time and Labourers hire'.[31]

In the basest estimation Wren was a brilliant intellectual with friends in high places and a great deal of good luck. Four months after his report, the question of how unstable the old cathedral had become was answered abruptly by the Great Fire which, between 2 and 5 September, engulfed the whole City of London leaving three quarters of it in ashes and parts of St Paul's no more than a quicklime quarry.

II OCCASION

On or about 11 September 1666 Wren gave the King a plan for rebuilding London:[32] a totally new plan with new regular streets and broad avenues instead of the alleys and lanes which made up the greater part of the old City. The drawing out of a fair copy would have taken many hours, and Wren's promptness must indicate not only the speed with which he was able to attack a problem when necessary but also a degree of forethought about the planning of cities. One feature of his plan, a broad quay all the way from the Temple on the west to the Tower of London on the east, resulted immediately from his experience of Paris the previous year, as well as less directly from the experience of men like Evelyn, who had also seen the canal and quay systems of the Netherlands. Evelyn too had written pamphlets on the traffic and smoke problems of the City, and submitted his own rebuilding plan, as did Hooke and at least three others, some days after Wren's.

Parentalia states that Wren was ordered by the King to make a plan whose realization was thwarted by the avarice and stupidity of the citizens; this story seems to have been taken from Hawksmoor, who was a small boy at the time of the fire but in the 1710s and 1720s developed a grudge – not at all unique among architects – against City fathers in general, seeing in them the chief impediment in the way of architectural utopia.[33] In fact there was nothing official about any of the plans, and the City was of necessity rebuilt on the old street plan, with minor improvements, since London must be restored as quickly as possible or else cede primacy to some new city, on another site, free from London's restrictive and jealously guarded privileges. However, since planning and building had as yet no permanent bureaucracy the first step was a rebuilding commission, appointed early in October 1666 and consisting of three architects chosen by the King – Wren, Hugh May and Roger Pratt – and three by the City – Hooke, Peter Mills (the City Surveyor) and the mason Edward Jerman. Their work was administrative and supervisory, and new buildings were financed by private or (for example the Livery Companies' halls) corporate enterprise. There were two notable exceptions to this procedure: special commissions were set up to rebuild the parish churches and St Paul's Cathedral, and since there could be no monetary return on those buildings Parliament legislated for a tax on coal, already the principal fuel of London, to pay for them. Wren was now made sole architect of St Paul's; for the churches he had overall responsibility and the particular help of Hooke.

These matters were not formalized until 1670. In the meantime London had had to deal with the hard winter of 1666–7 and a war with the Dutch, while the clergy at St Paul's slowly realized that the ruins could not even temporarily be patched up into a place of worship. The Wren who in 1670 saw the construction of a wooden model of his first design for the cathedral, and the commencement of the parish churches, was a very different person from the Wren who, a week before the Fire, had viewed the old cathedral and had argued, against some of his companions' opinion, that the leaning piers of the nave were not an ingenious medieval perspective compensation but a sign of danger. He had gained in experience and in status. In 1668 he wrote a long report on Salisbury Cathedral for his old Oxford friend Seth Ward, who had become its Bishop. He also designed a new chapel and cloister for Emmanuel College, Cambridge, for which much of the money was provided by William Sancroft, Dean of St Paul's. The spring of 1669 saw his appointment as Surveyor of the King's Works on the death of Sir John Denham,[34] the summer the solemn inauguration of his Sheldonian Theatre at Oxford, and December his marriage to Faith Coghill at the Temple Church. The last of these events, whatever the depth of Wren's feelings, marked the end of the institutional life of the single academic; the middle one made public his first large building and one of his most experimental; the significance of the first lay not merely in the command it gave him of all royal buildings south of the Scottish border and the prestige of that command beyond the limits of the Office of Works, but also in the fact of his appointment over the heads of two senior architects who were, on the evidence available to themselves at any rate, better qualified for the post.

One was John Webb (1611–72) who as the pupil, draughtsman, and later hand and even eye of Inigo Jones was the nearest for his time to a trained professional architect and had been brought from early retirement to design the new palace at Greenwich. The other, Hugh May (1621–84), who may have learned painting from Sir Peter Lely, acted as a secret agent for the King in exile – which gave him some direct knowledge of Continental architecture – and had risen from the Paymastership of the Works, his reward at the Restoration, to the Comptrollership, the second post in the establishment. In this office he had since 1668 kept a check or control on Denham's expenditure, which was not difficult; but he had also for much longer made up for some of Denham's deficiencies as a designing architect, as well as building up a private practice. There is an almost total dearth of documents about May, except for his handsome portrait at Audley End and occasionally his flamboyant signature, but from both contemporaries' opinion and the evidence of his buildings he was a knowledgeable and talented architect. Charles II recognized his worth by giving him, in compensation for the Surveyorship, a considerable additional salary.

The 1670s were for Wren a decade of manifold activity, which can be glimpsed in the diary of Hooke, who was in almost daily contact with him. This decade encompassed all his married life and saw the commencement of his most admired building, Trinity Library, and of his cathedral successively to two different designs. The foundations of fifteen parish churches in 1670–1 were followed by another sixteen before 1680. In 1673, having been encouraged to think more grandly of St Paul's, he made the design recorded in the surviving Great Model, which was completed to a length of 20 feet the following year. In 1673 too he resigned his Oxford chair of Astronomy in acknowledgement of his commitment to another discipline in another place, and received his knighthood. In 1675, after the Great Model design had been staked out on the site and then rejected by the clergy, he redesigned St Paul's twice more and work began. The following year Trinity College Library in Cambridge was begun and the monument to the Great Fire was finished. In 1677 he was Vice-President, in 1681 President, of the Royal Society, while from 1679 he was on the committee of the Hudson's Bay Company.

Most of Wren's activity was in an area bounded by the Tower, Westminster, the River Thames (often the fastest as well as the smoothest highway) and the northern fringe of London about a mile from the river. To be in the country one need only cross that boundary, or take a coach to the fresh air of Hackney or Kensington, but we do not know how often Wren did so. He travelled in the 1680s to Chelsea and in the 1690s to Hampton Court on account of work in progress there, and we know of some other excursions. But he is only known to have visited the Trinity Library site once, in its first year; after that the Cambridge mason Robert Grumbold came to see him in London. It is difficult to draw conclusions from records of the 'Riding Charges' he received in the Royal Works, for like Wardrobe Money and Christmas Allowances they were a recognized way of augmenting the officers' salaries to offset inflation, and corresponded therefore to the provision today of a company car rather than to an expense account paid against submitted bills.

As Surveyor of Works Wren had an official house in Scotland Yard, which was then a group of courtyards and buildings to the north of Whitehall Palace and was the headquarters of the Office of Works. While it was not unusual for the officers to let their official residences and live elsewhere, Wren appears to have spent a good deal of his time at Scotland Yard, partly perhaps because it was convenient to keep an eye on Court and Palace, partly also because its atmosphere was not too different from that of the Deanery at Windsor or the Oxford colleges. There is a local tradition that he lived on the South Bank across the Thames from St Paul's where he could watch the progress of the cathedral, but that is a story more picturesque than probable, and the identity of the supposed residence, marked now by a cartouche – not a County of London 'blue plaque' – has silently been transferred within living memory from one Bankside house to another.[35]

Whitehall itself was a rambling series of buildings, estimated to contain two thousand rooms varying in date from the original York House of the late middle ages to the constant and endless series of additions made since the Restoration. The more important buildings, including the Great Hall and Chapel, were of masonry, but considerable portions of the palace were little more than terraces of houses with wood frames filled in with lath and plaster. Indeed, additions of this kind were still being made in the 1670s after Parliament had outlawed timber building in the city of London; it is not surprising that Whitehall had a serious fire in 1691 and a terminal one seven years later. The 1698 fire left little of the palace usable except the Cockpit offices on the west side of the street, backing on to St James's Park, and Jones's Banqueting House. Whitehall remains today synonymous with the administration of government, but William III's disinclination to live there had set a precedent and the palace was not rebuilt. Apart from the works of art destroyed in the fire the most regrettable losses were the Chapel and gallery built by Wren in 1685–7 for James II. These had a notable place in Wren's architecture, but they were also significant as a gesture of James's Roman Catholicism and his political arrogance and, at the same time, of his acceptance that Whitehall was an architectural problem, as it would continue to be until the traumatic solution of the fire.

Charles II had earlier shown the same acceptance. He had been a boy of seven or eight when Jones first submitted to his father designs for a modern palace, regular and symmetrical in plan and elevations and, like the Banqueting House, classical in the range and understanding of its vocabulary of detail. In exile Charles II had been able to acquire some notion of the actuality of such a great waterfront palace in the spreading though still unfinished buildings of the Louvre and Tuileries. As early as 1661 (a dated drawing) Webb, who had drawn out Jones's design and subsequently made others of his own, was again considering Whitehall,[36] although he had then no post in the Works; neither had Wren in the autumn of 1664 when he made a design for duplicating the Banqueting House and linking the two buildings by a portico (p. 43). By then Webb's King Charles building at Greenwich was under construction, but by 1669 Charles, constrained by not only the perennial money problems of the Stuarts but also the economic consequences of the Great Fire of London, abandoned Greenwich. At the same time, at the commencement of Wren's Surveyorship, a detailed survey of the Whitehall buildings was ordered, in such detail as to imply not the prospect of their replacement but the necessity of their maintenance.[37]

Wren's first building as Surveyor was the new Custom House in the City, for which he produced characteristically a solution to aesthetic and functional problems alike (Plate 22). In 1670 he was in charge of the addition of a new apartment at Hampton Court, about which not very much is known since it was destroyed in Wren's own rebuilding of 1689.[38] But when, five years after appointing Wren as Surveyor, the King considered himself again able to support a major palace project, the work was entrusted not to Wren but to May.

Windsor Castle had for long been in the care of a separate Works establishment, of which May was appointed Comptroller in 1674. Over the next decade, the last of his life, May produced a remarkable neo-Norman remodelling of the Upper Ward of the castle, a new range on the north side (the Star Building), and a set of state apartments – King's Side, Queen's Side, each with its staircase, St George's Hall and state chapel – whose decoration, by a team led by the painter Antonio Verrio and the carver Grinling Gibbons, echoed in iconography, rivalled in richness and surpassed in bold illusionism the contemporary interiors created at Versailles for

Charles's cousin Louis XIV. May was older than Wren and already known as a designer of great houses, and in the Windsor staircases he showed considerable spatial imagination. The King may have consulted Wren, but in any event the latter had more than enough in the 1670s to occupy him and to keep him daily in London. Thus it was not until about 1682 that he was called on for large-scale secular projects, at Chelsea Hospital and Winchester Palace (Plates 114, 160).

The building of the Royal Hospital at Chelsea was begun in 1682; today it still serves its original purpose as a home for retired soldiers. The project combined philanthropic ideals with royal patronage and prestige; the concept, though not the design, of the buildings was directly based on the Hôtel des Invalides in Paris founded by Louis XIV in 1670, drawings of which were sent to the Duke of Monmouth, Charles's natural son, in 1678. Wren contributed to the project his services for nothing (as he did at Trinity Library in Cambridge and Greenwich Hospital) although in 1693 the Treasury awarded him a gratuity of £1,000 as a way of making it clear that he, and not Lord Ranelagh, had been in charge of the building.[39] Construction proceeded rapidly, although Chelsea was only completed, including the side courts added for James II, in the reign of William and Mary.

At Winchester in 1683 the foundations were laid for an edifice which had some design features in common with Chelsea and was in plan recognizably indebted to Versailles. Winchester had been the Saxon capital of England, but in the last years of his reign Charles II's motives for building there were neither the support of his authority by claiming continuity with Alfred and Canute nor, as may have been the case when he began Greenwich twenty years earlier, the precaution of a residence to the seaward of London in case the nation rejected him as it had his father. It was reported at the time that the building, which Charles wanted to be finished with the greatest speed possible, was intended as a hunting lodge in the neighbourhood of the New Forest,[40] but nobody who had seen the extent of the plan could believe that. For Winchester was to be a complete palace, on the axis of the medieval cathedral and linked to it by a new straight street. The resemblance to Versailles was surely intentional; the site's advantages were distance from Westminster and the eye of Parliament, coupled with proximity to the Solent and easy access to the secret emissaries from France on whom Charles's policies increasingly depended.

Winchester was virtually abandoned upon Charles's death on 6 February 1685. Twelve months earlier May had died, and Wren had been allowed both to assume responsibility for Windsor, where the work had been completed, and to leave the Comptrollership vacant. The latter arrangement was potentially disastrous since it gave the Treasury no check on the Surveyor's conduct. However, there is no evidence that Wren acted improperly; he was capable both of deploying his staff to use the best of their abilities and of saving the Crown money where the expense of a post seemed unnecessary.

Charles II died a Roman Catholic, keeping on his deathbed an often renewed promise he had as often found it impolitic until then to fulfil. His brother James II, blessed with more scruples but less political sense than Charles, paraded his Catholicism from the moment of his accession. He heard mass publicly at Whitehall a week after his accession, and commissioned the ostentatious Chapel which was first used at Christmas 1686. Since May, whose experience with Windsor would have been appropriate for this task, was no longer alive, it fell without question to Wren. The result was short-lived, for almost as soon as it was completed the Chapel was closed for alterations and it was not used between James's flight from England in the autumn of 1688 and the fire of 1698 which destroyed it. Records are scanty, but Evelyn's famous notice of it was favourable in spite of his horror at the restoration of Popery which it was intentionally made to symbolize. The fire also destroyed the other new buildings associated with the Chapel: a new gallery facing the Privy Garden and a staircase which gave access to the royal gallery pew in the Chapel as well as to the south end of the Banqueting House (Plate 161).

As his reign progressed towards the final breakdown of relations between king and nation, James carried on a policy of appointing Catholics to official posts, and Wren seems to have felt himself in some danger of losing the Surveyorship when in May 1687 he wrote to a kinsman: 'wee are bound to our good behaviour uncertain wch. way the next wind may tosse us, wee are afrayd of being absent from our charge, & therfore watch as those who travell in suspected places'.[41] However, either his tact or his intellectual reputation, as well as his innocence in secular politics, helped him to weather this crisis as well as the subsequent one of the Revolution of 1688. In the first year of their reign William and Mary commissioned not only the enlargement of Kensington House but also the rebuilding – total in the first scheme, partial in the final one decided on in the summer of 1689 – of Hampton Court. Wren's humbler duties at this time included the design of (according to Narcissus Luttrell's description) an 'itinerant house for his majestie to carry into Ireland, for him to lye in, in the field; it is to be taken into peices and carried on two waggons, and may be quickly fixt up'. No more is known of this portable headquarters from which William directed his military campaign, but from what we know of Wren's ingenuity it may well have anticipated some of the comforts of the modern trailer home.

As the head of an office which was concerned with Crown buildings from the design of a new palace through the arrangements for a royal funeral and the staging for a state trial in Westminster Hall down to the painting of railings and the paving of the street at Charing Cross, Wren's attention and his signature were called for in a constant succession of small matters affecting Crown buildings, land or interests; the manuscript known as 'Court Orders' in the Soane Museum is a record of many of these between 1669 and 1695.[43] Wren was able to deal with a large amount of administrative work because he was good at delegating and quick at grasping a problem and deciding on a course of action.

In the autumn of 1694, at an age when today a senior public servant would be thinking about retirement to the chairmanship of a company or corporation, Wren became engaged in a new venture, the Royal Hospital for Seamen at Greenwich, intended to be the counterpart – and in appearance the rival – of Chelsea. Like Chelsea, Greenwich Hospital (whose buildings now house the Royal Naval College) combined philanthropy, focused by the casualties after the battle of La Hogue in 1692, with the patronage of the Sovereigns. William and Mary granted the site of Greenwich Palace, including Webb's abandoned King Charles Building, on 25 October 1694, and according to Hawksmoor, who later wrote a pamphlet about the Hospital,[44] Queen Mary took a particular interest in the project until her death from smallpox at the end of the year. Wren served on the Royal Commission set up for the project and on both the initial Grand Committee and the Fabrick Committee which built the Hospital. As architect to the fabric he gave his services without fee, although he had the paid assistance of Hawksmoor, as his personal clerk from the commencement of work in 1696 and as Clerk of Works from 1698. Hawksmoor was by then an architect in his own right with considerable experience, and he seems to have been given a free hand in some parts of Greenwich as well as helping Wren in the early design stages; however, Wren was in overall control as firmly as he had been over the City churches in the 1670s.

Of two other projects which occupied Wren in 1698 only one succeeded: the repair of the north transept of Westminster Abbey, which was, with the collaboration of William Dickinson, a considerable and not unsympathetic work of restoration, although a less 'correct' one than that of Gilbert Scott and Pearson which replaced it in the 1880s. Wren was Surveyor to the Abbey from 1698 until his death, and *Parentalia* credits him with the design of the west towers as well as the unexecuted spire over the crossing. The towers that were built, however, in 1734–45, were designed by Hawksmoor who succeeded Wren in charge of the building.

The other 1698 scheme was produced with great care and great optimism as well as, like the 1666 London plan and the designs for Hampton Court in 1689, with great speed. Whitehall burned down on 4 January 1698, and on 3 March Narcissus Luttrell reported that the King had shelved the matter of rebuilding until Parliament should provide a supplementary vote to pay for it. Parliament never looked like doing so, and never did, and Wren's large plans and elevations, for two different designs, must have been completed in those two months. We know from Luttrell also that Wren had surveyed the site a fortnight after the fire, and an outline survey appears as the basis of the larger of Wren's plans.[45] The drawings (Plate 165) are meticulously detailed in pen and ink and shaded in wash, and some scholars have been tempted to see in them the hand of a younger man such as Hawksmoor. However, the vocabulary of design is unequivocally Wren's, and draughtsmanship was always an activity in which Wren enjoyed the exercise of his skill.

In 1697 the choir of St Paul's was opened; Parliament decided to withhold half of Wren's salary as Surveyor to the Cathedral until the completion of the whole building, which still lacked both dome and towers. This gesture was as misguided as it was mean, for Wren's constant concerns were not only the supply of materials and maintenance of standards but also the completion of the whole. The time scale of a great and complex building is quite different from that of a design on paper, and Wren would produce the definitive designs for dome and towers when they were needed, in about 1703–04. The last stone of the lantern was placed in 1708 by his son Christopher, who had been born the year building began;[46] in 1711 the cathedral was officially declared finished and Wren was able to recover his arrears of salary.

Of course at 78 he was less active; equally he was less occupied than he had been in the 1670s and 80s. In 1705[47] he had given advice on the project to build a palace in Woodstock Park for the Duke of Marlborough, the victor of Blenheim, but the obvious architect for the job, and the Duke's choice, was John Vanbrugh, who was gaining for himself the primacy as a designer of great houses previously held by May and then William Talman (1650–1719). At the height of her favour at court, the Duchess of Marlborough convinced herself that she had secured Wren to design her London house over the wall from St James's Palace; she mistrusted all architects but believed she had found one as amenable as he was distinguished. In fact Sir Christopher seems to have outwitted her by turning over to his son the commission for the excessively plain Marlborough House the Duchess wanted.[48]

'The little old man', as a correspondent described Wren to the Duchess at this time, may have hoped that this delegation would help to gain for his son the succession as Surveyor of Works when his own retirement became inevitable. His hope was not widely shared: certainly Vanbrugh and, less realistically, Hawksmoor, would have liked to prove themselves in that high office. Hawksmoor, who had served Wren since 1679 or 1680, never had the opportunity; Vanbrugh, who by his own industry made himself a professional, and had influential friends, was once offered the post, probably by Lord Carlisle in 1715, 'but refus'd it', as he later wrote, 'out of Tendernesse to Sr Chr: Wren'.[49] In the end, when Wren was told in 1718 that his services to the Crown were no longer required, he was succeeded by William Benson, who had as much political influence as Vanbrugh and none of his architectural talents. With a King (George I) absent for much of the year in Hanover, the Royal Works entered a period of mediocrity; within fifteen months Benson's dangerous incompetence was established, but another nonentity succeeded him. Wren's dismissal through the intrigue of Benson marked the end of an era in English architecture, but it also ended almost fifty years of influence, which his critics had come to see as his architectural despotism, and nearly three decades of attempts, sporadic at first but finally concentrated, to discredit him.

William Talman had, possibly through the agency of the Earl of Portland,[50] been appointed in May 1689 to the post of Comptroller of Works which had been unfilled for the five years since May's death. Talman was beginning to establish a country house practice in place of that of May, whose pupil he very possibly had been. Talman was ambitious and arrogant, as well as talented, and by 1702 he had a number of successful commissions to his credit and an equal number of aggrieved and dissatisfied patrons to his debit. During his first year in office Talman made the most of a collapse in the new building at Hampton Court, in which two workmen were killed and several injured, to discredit Wren; he failed to do so, and William

III supported the authority of his Surveyor.[51] In 1699 Talman petitioned the Treasury for the Comptrollership at Windsor which Wren had held since May's death; again he was unsuccessful and the number of friends on whom he could rely was dwindling. When in 1702 Vanbrugh, who had replaced him as architect of Castle Howard, the 3rd Earl of Carlisle's Yorkshire palace, managed through Carlisle's influence also to replace Talman as Comptroller, Wren cannot have been sorry.

Talman's attacks were personal and motivated above all by the desire for his own gain; subsequent allegations certainly had some objective substance. In 1704 Vanbrugh, taking his Comptrollership very seriously, found irregularities in the use of the Patent Officers in undertaking contract work on Crown buildings; he 'made severall attempts upon Sr Chr. Wren to perswade him to redress it himself' and, finding Wren tolerant to the point of evasion, wrote to the Treasury. He then asked Wren why a mason named Hill had not replaced the Queen's Master Mason in the work at Kensington Orangery; Wren replied that Hill 'was a Whimsicall Man, and a piece of an Astrologer, and would Venture upon nothing till he had considered the Starrs, . . . and therefore had refus'd the Work'. Vanbrugh did not think Wren 'has any Interest in his part of it' but also reminded the Treasury that 'those Fellows' had prevailed on Wren to appoint, against both his own inclination and the Treasury's direction, an unreliable drunkard to a clerkship. Vanbrugh was nevertheless well disposed to the Surveyor.[52]

In 1709 the Duchess of Marlborough found that Wren 'from his age was imposed upon by the workmen',[53] and four years later Thomas Archer, seeking the post of Comptroller (which Vanbrugh had for political reasons temporarily lost) referred to 'frauds and abuses . . . so great that by the price of work set out by the Queen's servants the whole nation, but more particularly the city of London, is a great sufferer, and the Queen herself . . . is extremely imposed upon'.[54] *Frauds and Abuses at St Paul's* had been the title of a pamphlet published the year before by the Residentiary Canon of St Paul's, Dr Francis Hare. His allegations were largely conjectural and motivated by pique that Wren, with sixty years' experience, knew best in matters both of the cathedral and of architecture in general. Others replied to the pamphlet, and the battle exhausted itself when the libels reached absurdity.[55]

Meanwhile the philosopher 3rd Earl of Shaftesbury, writing early in 1712, had strongly attacked the decline of public architecture 'thro' several Reigns . . . under the Hand of one single Court-architect'; Wren's architecture was for Shaftesbury the equivalent of Louis XIV's politics and ought to be equally distasteful to the enlightened British nation. Now both Wren's competence and his taste were under fire, and his salaries and privileges were benefits to be coveted.[56] The prescription for a new British style, written only in negative terms by Shaftesbury as anti-French, anti-Baroque and anti-Wren, was filled positively by Colen Campbell's *Vitruvius Britannicus* of 1715, which in the guise of a picture-album of contemporary British architecture proclaimed a revival of the style of Inigo Jones with the *Quattro Libri dell'Architettura* of Andrea Palladio as its holy book. A balustrade was added to St

Paul's against Wren's wishes by the new Commission of 1717, because the Banqueting House had one: Wren commented that 'ladies think nothing well without an edging'. After the accession of George I, in the winter of 1714–15, Vanbrugh and Lord Halifax had devised a new Board of Works, on which Wren sat as Surveyor although, with no casting vote, he presided in name only. The Board's minutes are uneventful since little work was in progress, but Wren's survival depended on the good will of his colleagues. Between the first meeting on 6 May 1715 and Benson's dismissal in July 1719 Vanbrugh made 224 attendances out of a possible 250; at first his zeal is explicable by his part in the reform and his concern for Wren, subsequently by his mistrust of Benson.[57]

By March 1719 Vanbrugh's case against Benson was sound enough to be presented to the Treasury, but one unforeseen effect of its receipt there seems to have been that Wren, who had retired to a house on the Green at Hampton Court, was asked for his comments on 'mismanagement [by] the late Commissioners of the Board of Works'. His reply to the Treasury of 21 April expressed both concern and surprise, pointed out that he had had no power in the Commission, and ended: 'as I am dismiss'd, having worn out (by God's mercy) a long life in the Royal Service, and having made some figure in the world, I hope it will be allow'd me to die in peace'.[58]

1719 is also the date of the first draft of *Parentalia*,[59] which the younger Christopher probably compiled at Wroxall Abbey in Warwickshire which his father had bought for him in 1713 (perhaps out of the arrears from St Paul's) and to which he had retired in 1716 after losing the Chief Clerkship in the Office of Works.[60]

We know even less about Sir Christopher's retirement than about his earlier life, but he does not seem to have died of boredom. The draft of *Parentalia* contains a copy of a letter he wrote in 1714 to the Royal Society to accompany a solution – evidently in his opinion a definitive one – of the problem of determining longitude at sea. An efficient marine chronometer was not built for another twenty years – by John Harrison – and neither the nature nor the fate of Wren's invention, which he presented in cypher, is known.[61]

Wren died on 25 February 1723. Newspapers refer to his funeral and burial on 5 March in the crypt of the great cathedral he had lived to see completed. The earliest published account of his death, in Ward's *Lives of the Gresham Professors* (1740), states that he caught a cold on the way from Hampton Court to stay in the house he leased, after his dismissal, in St James's Street. Subsequent accounts are more detailed, and perhaps embroidered: possibly on the basis of family tradition Elmes says in 1823 that he died in his chair taking a nap after dinner. A year later Christopher was using the London house; there were many financial and legal matters to clear up.[62] In the mid 1720s he commissioned fifteen engravings of St Paul's and other buildings as (according to Vertue) a trial run for a more complete edition of his father's work.[63] He retained the architect's library and the largest single collection of his drawings, many of which are now in Wren's second college,

All Souls. Few great figures attain immediate and unbroken appreciation without temporary eclipse. Christopher's programme of publication seems to have been poorly supported, and with his own health failing he laid aside the *Parentalia*, for whose publication in 1750 we are indebted to *his* son Stephen, who is often wrongly credited with its composition.

The early Georgians could not ignore St Paul's, through which Wren was famous even if not celebrated. His immediate influence was principally on those he taught, especially Hawksmoor, and on the early work of James Gibbs, whom he befriended when in 1709 the young Scottish architect arrived in London fresh from the Roman studio of Carlo Fontana. Gibbs's steeples at St Clement Danes, St Mary-le-Strand and St Martin-in-the-Fields are descendants more direct than Hawksmoor's towers from the Wren churches.

The earliest panegyric of Wren is probably Hogarth's in the *Analysis of Beauty* (1753), calling him the 'Prince of architects' and praising especially the steeples and the outside of St Paul's; the interior could not compare, for want of decorative painting and sculpture, with St Peter's in Rome. Hogarth's sympathy was exceptional for its day, and without any influence from Wren he shared the latter's distinction between the absolute laws of nature and the empirical ones of the arts (p. 27).

There is a story about an English nobleman discovering the beauty of St Stephen Walbrook through an engraving of it in Italy; more profound was the interest in the dome of St Paul's shown by Parisian architects in the third quarter of the eighteenth century, especially in relation to the construction of Soufflot's Ste-Geneviève. Both visually and structurally the dome of the United States Capitol in Washington, DC, is much remoter from St Paul's. In general, American colonial architecture was based on books and memories, and Gibbs's *Book of Architecture* (1728) inspired a number of 'Wren' steeples in the eastern United States. Improbable claims have also been made for Wren as the author of such buildings as William and Mary College in Williamsburg. While Wren may have given advice or cast an eye over a project in more cases than we know, the criterion for his authorship must lie in the consistency of his mind rather than in the persistence of his name.

III QUALITY

Wren is a *famous* architect: he is one of the few members of his profession of whom almost everyone has heard. Undoubtedly this distinction is due in the first place to his good fortune in the commissions he obtained, since St Paul's Cathedral and his work at Hampton Court are known to every tourist, while the Great Fire of 1666 gained him a mention in the most elementary history text-books, as the Royal Society member who rebuilt the City churches as well as St Paul's. But fame, in the sense of being known to all men, is not identical with historical greatness – Nell Gwyn is famous, but Charles II or William III are, at least arguably, historical figures of large calibre. And that is not all. The decisions and the actions of a statesman or a commander are facts of history; they belong to the past, and in the present we can know them only through their description, their depiction, or their consequences. The same limitations *may* apply to the work of artists, some of whom led interesting or dramatic or picturesque lives, and there is a level of general knowledge at which Van Gogh is better remembered for cutting off his ear than for painting sunflowers. On a more serious plane, and among Wren's contemporaries, the architecture of Hugh May is now very difficult to discuss, since most of it has been destroyed or altered and can only be imagined from descriptions and drawings. May's connection with Windsor Castle is historically as important as Wren's with Hampton Court, but because almost no traces of it survive it is relatively little understood, while to the sightseer it is unknown. Whatever their particular destination or function, works of art, including architecture, are much more to be looked at than read about, and the person who has begun to look at architecture is interested in the architect's work. Questions arise to do with quality and meaning: does this building please or impress or overawe us? Is it good, or even great, architecture? And if we move from the artefact to the mind that conceived it, was he a great, or at least a good, architect? The proper meaning of *appreciation* is the attempt to answer such qualitative questions, which are as likely to be asked by the reader about Wren as are quantitative or factual ones about who he was, what he did and when.

It may be a by-product of his very fame, or of the failure of confidence which overtakes the English in face of their artistic heritage, that makes the answers to such questions so elusive in the case of Wren. Certainly phrases like 'this lovely Wren church' or 'historic Wren house' are clichés which seem to pre-empt all discussion, although usually they are employed to indicate that the repair or the acquisition of the building concerned will be costly. For many twentieth-century writers the architect of St Paul's was famous, therefore he was great, and for those who find his style on occasion lacking in elegance the deficiency is pardonable in the light of his assumed greatness. Some writers on the other hand, with a greater awareness either of the achievements of Renaissance and seventeenth-century architecture, or of the critical standards of the century that followed Wren's death, have considered it necessary to submit his work to stricter critical assessment. In doing so, they have found that the peculiarly individual character of Wren's mind and his art fares somewhat indifferently in comparison with Michelangelo or Mansart, and equally so by the canons of taste of Georgian England. It is neither frivolous nor cynical to mention that Michelangelo and Mansart had the advantage, like grand opera and *haute cuisine*, of being foreign, although ironically even in his lifetime Wren began to be attacked for being aesthetically un-British. It has been suggested that his artistic greatness lies in his versatility, in the range of architecture he produced, in its quantity, or in the manner in which he 'made himself into a great architect'.[64]

In his classic essay *The Mind of Wren* (1936)[65] Summerson argued that Wren missed true greatness because his scientist's intellect clipped the wings of his imagination. The character of Wren's talent has already been examined, and Abraham Cowley (1618–67) is one example of a poet whose muse apparently deserted him under the early Royal Society's pressure for the rationalization of English language and literature. Summerson's analysis remains significant in showing the extent to which Wren's intellect formed his artistic personality, one very different from those of Hawksmoor and Vanbrugh in the next generation. But the idea that, had that personality been different, Wren could have been a better architect, or one more like Hawksmoor and Vanbrugh, or the implication that he ought to have been, cannot be sustained by the same kind of argument.

The view commonly held in the Georgian era that Wren had lacked Taste was one which the architect's son tried hard to refute in *Parentalia*, and in a sense Wren's admirers have ever since been making excuses for him. If there is any significance in the continued search for excuses and explanations, it must be that those modern scholars who have been most critical of Wren still believe him to be a better artist than such criticism might imply: there are faults, after all, to be found in Shakespeare, Rembrandt and Bach, and to deny this does them no service.

During the first quarter of the eighteenth century, the period in which Georgian Taste came to be formulated, it was also realized by literary critics that Shakespeare should be judged by the rules of his own time since those either of a later age or of Antiquity might be inappropriate. Aesthetic judgements have always depended on 'rules', arbitrarily formulated or adopted, as a means of giving the authority of reasoned thought to what ultimately are personal preferences. During the sixteenth century, however, the importance of rules in architectural aesthetics was greatly enhanced, not only by the development of book printing, which created rather than satisfied a demand for books of directions, but also through the belief of Renaissance architects and theorists (who inherited a late-medieval preoccupation with systems and rules) that Antique architecture was based on a set of rules whose rediscovery would provide the key to the new architecture of the Renaissance. This belief was mistaken, stimulated but not substantiated by the precepts of Vitruvius, the only Classical writer on architecture whose writing has survived; by the time this was realized, a system of Renaissance rules had been invented to supply the deficiency and give substance to the authority of Antiquity.

Wren was a self-taught architect, as Inigo Jones had been half a century earlier, but whereas Jones came to building from painting Wren's approach was that of a scientist who could draw well and who believed that he could tackle any kind of problem to which he chose to apply his mind, brilliant by nature and disciplined by study and experience. Much of what he needed to know could be found in books, and the rest must be learned by asking people expert in their own fields. In addition to knowledge of both the structural and the visual sides of architecture, he needed not only the confidence that he could design buildings but also a basis of evidence, from his own and others' estimation, without which that confidence would be illusory. While in 1661 or even 1665 he might be seen as an intellectual of such brilliance that it would be foolish not to consult him on a problem like the future of St Paul's, there seems to have been no period at all in which he was considered an amateur: it was accepted that his professionalism could and did range from one sphere of activity to the next. This transition was undoubtedly easier and less remarkable in the middle of the seventeenth century than in a later period, for several reasons. First, architecture itself was not yet a profession in the sense that, for example, law, medicine and the church already were professions. Secondly, the dichotomy which so worries twentieth-century society, between the culture of science and technology and that of arts and letters, would have been unthinkable in Wren's day: indeed, it is a gross modern over-simplification to say that Wren was a scientist who became an architect. Thirdly, the emphasis placed by Renaissance theorists on the gentlemanly and intellectual status of the architect, as distinct from the master-mason, actually made it more acceptable for an academic figure to take up architecture than it was for even an experienced master craftsman.

From the start, then, contemporaries took Wren the architect as seriously as he took himself. If even his earliest works, Pembroke College Chapel and the Sheldonian Theatre, should not be called amateurish, neither should ignorance or incompetence be held to account, in a man with Wren's understanding of knowledge and proficiency, for those idiomatic features of his buildings which would be unwarrantable in the eighteenth century. But Wren's career lies firmly in the seventeenth century, and like Shakespeare he and his age need, as far as the limitations of the historical process allow, to be seen as they were. Wren's departures or 'lapses' from the expected were deliberate; they had meaning for him and there is meaning to be found in them for us. They are important because they can be seen to be idiomatic and consistent. Certain formal themes or devices recur through an artist's work that are peculiar to him; they may simply reflect the way he sees things or they may be so obsessive as to dominate his whole production. In either case the constancy with which they appear shows that they are not accidental in their nature.

That is not to say that either their invention or their recurrence is the result of deliberate and conscious thought. Indeed we are all familiar with the ways in which the mind produces ideas. Some ideas seem to arise spontaneously, as prehistoric bones rise to the surface of a tar pit or as driftwood is washed up on the beach, and we can take them up or throw them back. The deliberate search for ideas, inspiration, memory or solutions, on the other hand, seems to be amenable less to conscious control than to the kind of trick we use in attempting to see faint stars in the sky by looking away from them. It is when we relax our concentration and let the mind wander for a moment that the answer is likely to flash into view. Artists, writers and thinkers have developed all sorts of mental devices, as well as physical ones like sketching, walking about, meditation, drawing on graph paper, playing Wagner on the piano, or repeating a formula or a routine, in order to trap and retain fleeting ideas. But ideas, even if retained, are no more than raw materials for a work of art which, considered in formal terms, is a structure of ideas, combining a kind of framework or armature with the many small events which it supports and to which it gives location, order and relationship. The unique quality we call an artist's style derives, in perhaps equal measure, from the individuality of the ideas his mind produces and from the idiom of the framework on which he puts his ideas together. This idiom, which we call his sense of form, is the product not only of heredity and experience but also of training and practice.

Wren claimed in his inaugural lecture of 1657 at Gresham College that geometry and arithmetic, as 'the only Truths that can sink into the Mind of Man void of all Uncertainty',[66] preceded logic as the basis of all human activity and the key to all disciplines, and while an inaugural lecture is not an occasion for understating one's case there is no reason to suppose that he ever abandoned his claim. In the undated notes on architectural theory which appear in *Parentalia* as 'Tract I' he stated that both firmness and beauty depended on geometry, that geometrical figures are beautiful, and that geometry was the universal criterion of beauty. He went on to warn the architect against 'Novelties, in which Fancy blinds the Judgment',[67] a sentiment not too far from the Royal Society's attempt, in the words of its first historian Thomas Sprat, 'to separate the knowledge of Nature from the colours of Rhetorick, the devices of Fancy or the delightful deceit of Fables'.[68] Wren's motto of *Numero Pondere et Mensura*[69] (by number, weight and measure) reflects what is commonly held to be a scientist's attitude, one which leaves little room for imagination. That attitude, however, pertains rather to a mechanic, and St Paul's Cathedral was not designed by a mechanic. Wren wrote from Paris that 'Building certainly ought to have the Attribute of eternal, and therefore [be] the only Thing incapable of new Fashions'.[70] If, however, he ever wondered whether it might be desirable or possible to drain architecture of everything fanciful, accidental, unconscious or irrational, his own works must have shown him otherwise.

In fact Wren did not claim that fancy simply blinds the judgement, but that it does so in novelties. It is as if he were echoing, although he cannot have known it, the stricture of Inigo Jones on the 'composed ornaments [that] Proceed out of the aboundance of designers and wear brought in by Michill Angell and his followers [which] in my opinion do not well in sollid Architecture'.[71]

The operation of Fancy could be dispensed with entirely only by reducing design to a formula; the inhuman repetitiveness of the honeycomb is the extreme example of such reduction, but it is to be found in some of those constructions of mankind which do not merit the title of architecture because they have nothing to communicate either to the senses or to the emotions or to the intellect. Something like it indeed is not far from the surface in the Greek Doric temple. In architecture as in music, regularity and repetition (rhythm) are essential to the aesthetic structure; not only to the bearing of loads and the fabrication of materials but also to the sense of order we expect, whether consciously or not, in buildings. The architect cannot work outside their limitations any more than speech can dispense with grammar and syntax. What will vary, among different artists working in the same medium, is the balance between intellect and intuition, both in the artist's personality and style and in the beholder's or hearer's response. Without entering into an involved attempt to define the terms, it is fair to say that in 'classical' art qualities of intellect are foremost: rationality and balance, the avoidance of extremes, components which even in complex relationships are clearly perceptible. In 'romantic' art, on the other hand, qualities of intuition seem to predominate: free imagination, the cultivation of the irrational and the extreme, total effects in which the constituents are subordinate to the whole and even may not be separately perceptible. The despatch and the receipt of the message are not always identical, for emotive effects are often produced by calculated measures, while conversely intellect or reason may be the target for irrational attack. Although 'classical' and 'romantic' only became polarized as aesthetic alternatives in the nineteenth century the two sides of creativity which they represent are as old as the history of art; they are implied for example in Pliny's distinction between representing things as they are and as they seem to be.[72] Caravaggio at the beginning of the seventeenth century was instanced as a painter of appearance not of essence, and the distinction lies behind those we now make in seventeenth-century art between the Classical and the Baroque.

Critics and theorists as well as artists in the century of Caravaggio and Wren were very much aware of the duality of style and intention, and this duality is reflected in the distinction Wren draws in *Tract I* between 'two Causes of Beauty, natural and customary'.[73] *Nature* may suggest to us, in relation to art, the romantic irregularity of natural things like cliffs, oak trees, apples, streams or clouds, but in the seventeenth century minds as diverse as the scientist Galileo and the architect Borromini identified Nature with geometry, the regular Nature of crystalline structures, the perpetuation of species and the symmetries of growth, the effects of gravity and the cycles of the weather. For Wren beauty from Nature is rational: it is 'from Geometry, consisting in Uniformity (that is Equality) and Proportion'. Beauty from custom on the other hand involves memory, intuition and emotion and is not rational. It is associative, being 'begotten by the Use of our Senses to those Objects which are usually pleasing to us for other Causes, as Familiarity or particular Inclination breeds a Love to Things not in themselves Lovely'. To Wren at the lectern, the sometime Savilian Professor of Astronomy, 'always the true Test is natural or geometrical Beauty', perhaps not merely on principle but also as a refuge or sanctuary from the novelties and dangers of the imagination. For in customary beauty 'lies the great Occasion of Errors; here is tried the Architect's Judgment', that faculty liable to be obscured by Fancy.

Wren proceeds to a special case of his general distinction: 'Geometrical Figures are naturally more beautiful than other irregular', and the word 'naturally' is taken up in the next phrase: 'in this all consent as to a Law of Nature'.[74] Here then is a clue to the basis not only of his theory of beauty but also of his approach to design. The laws of God concern the spirit, and their infringement injures the spirit: the punishment is perceptible only to the moral, not the physical senses unless, as happened in Biblical times, it was made visible as a lesson. The laws of a society are subject to sanctions and are also capable of alteration, by the society's choice or acquiescence. The laws of logic concern the intellect; they are unalterable and infringement also concerns the intellect, resulting in an erroneous conclusion. The laws, or rules, of aesthetics – the precepts for example of Renaissance theorists and the supposed rules of the Ancients – are not laws in any of these senses, being rather rules of thumb or habits of thought which have been hallowed by tradition or by the reputation of their promulgators. Their infringement may be tasteless, but every artist is free, if he wishes, to defy, adapt or re-write them.

The laws of nature again are different from any of these: 'in this all consent as to a law of nature'. Fire burns, weights fall, the sun rises, and without the supervention of *super*-natural forces such laws are inevitable and immutable. The arch and the dome, far from defying gravity, depend on its properties as much as on those of materials. The scientist knows that, whether he is investigating them in 'pure' science or seeking to utilize them in 'applied' science, he can only work within the laws of nature. The New Science which the Royal Society did not invent but practised was new because it aimed to take nothing for granted, accepting only what could be counted, weighed, measured or observed: on its crest are the words *Nullius in verba* (On the words of no man). The Royal Society embraced the descriptive as much as the experimental sciences, but with the same attitude. The old Aristotelian explanation could no longer be accepted that, for example, things fall because they have a quality of heaviness; it was the rejection of such ideas which led to Newton's formulation of the law of gravity, as well as to the realization that invisible things like air also have weight. Wren and his contemporaries did not distinguish between pure and applied science, and the development of the barometer, in which he played a considerable part, was as much an advance in pure knowledge as a means towards new kinds of measurement and experiment. The Royal Society did not use the word 'science' for its work, but the term 'experimental philosophy': experiment was the basis of its whole activity. It was also of very great importance for Wren's architecture.

In the sciences experiment either shows that expectation is correct or incorrect or answers questions like 'how much, how far, how fast, how many?'. In the first category it helps to formulate and clarify natural laws, in the second it may do no more – but cannot do less – than acknowledge laws that are already formulated. For an intelligence such as Wren's it was evident, however, that in artistic matters there were no comparable laws and therefore the experimental procedure to which he was accustomed could not have the same function. A totally geometrical and regular architecture, 'void of all uncertainty', would ultimately be both inhuman and unscientific, because natural laws extend also to those responses of the eye and the brain upon which either reasoning or intuitive appreciation depends. These responses are intimately connected with the sense of order already mentioned, and thus the limitations of regularity and rhythm are, through the psychology of perception, intimately connected with natural laws. In the design of architecture, therefore, experiment can only be a process of trial and error, in which the accidents of a particular situation are assessed – but not proved or disproved – in relation to the perceptive process. We do not know that Wren followed this line of argument; nevertheless there are indications, both in his buildings and drawings that he did not aim at a totally geometrical and regular architecture, and in his writings also that he gave considerable attention to the beholder's responses. That is to say, there is evidence of more than one sort, that he looked for a balance between intellect and intuition. The 'lapses' in his architecture, which have already been mentioned and will later be considered in more detail, were one factor in this balance; another was his concern with the visual effect of architecture on the beholder. This concern is nowhere better seen than in the long sequence of designs he made before reaching the final appearance of the dome and towers of St Paul's, but he also expressed it in writing, both in his report of 1668 on Salisbury Cathedral,[75] in which he praised the medieval architect who 'knew better that nothing could adde beauty to light', and in a passage in *Tract I* on perspective.[76]

'The Architect', he wrote there, 'ought, above all Things, to be well skilled in Perspective', and it is clear, not only from the absence of perspective drawings from his office but also from his argument, that he was thinking of the ability to visualize rather than to draw. For, as he explained, what looks well in an elevation may not do so in a model 'especially when there are many Angles and Projectures'. Even a model is an imperfect guide to what is built, 'because a Model is seen from other Stations and Distances than the Eye sees the Building'. The architect should distinguish also, he continued, between things to be seen near at hand which 'may have small and many Members, be well furnished with Ornaments, and may lie flatter' and those to be seen at a distance; again 'for Objects whose chief View is in Front, and for those whose chief View is sideways', different criteria apply.

The first works in architecture of Brunelleschi precede those of Wren in the 1660s by 250 years. By about 1675 Wren's style had reached a stage of development – notably in Trinity College Library at Cambridge – analogous to the High

Renaissance of the early sixteenth century; by the 1690s his architecture could not be considered old-fashioned in comparison with his Roman contemporary Carlo Fontana. From another point of view, Inigo Jones's Whitehall Banqueting House, completed in 1622, was England's first 'Renaissance' building in the sense of an understanding of a whole design rather than the piling up of individual details (Plate 4). It was startlingly new, and its message was not fully absorbed into English architecture until the 1660s. When Wren was an undergraduate at Oxford half-way through the century, 'modern' architecture was for him that of his own college, Wadham, which had been built and completed as a new foundation in 1610–13 (Plate 3). Oxford is notable for the late survival of both the stylistic features and the craft techniques of late Gothic stone-masonry, and while the Wadham buildings profited in symmetry and regularity from singleness of design and execution the windows contain Gothic pointed tracery. But the central frontispiece between hall and chapel is quite typical for its date of the attitude to the Classical orders which was only to be superseded with the Banqueting House. The orders are placed in their correct sequence ascending in richness from Doric to Ionic, Corinthian and Composite, and their parts are reasonably close to Antique orders in detail and proportion. On the other hand, they bear little relation either to the rest of the façade or to Classical building types, or even to late-medieval castellated gateways from which the central feature is ultimately descended. The designer, presumably the mason William Arnold, has in fact provided a series of shelves on which the orders as examples of a learned art are displayed, much as are the statues of King James I and the founder Nicholas Wadham and his wife.

The speed and proficiency with which English architecture caught up with that of France and Italy during Wren's career are largely due to three factors: the length in time of the Renaissance, spanning by then in its broadest stylistic sense two and a half centuries, meant that its architecture was now the rich common language in western Europe; secondly, when early in the seventeenth century the Renaissance idea of the architect as a gentleman and scholar finally reached England it became not only possible but desirable for that common language to be absorbed; thirdly the development of architectural publishing and especially of reproductive engraving made its absorption much easier at such a distance from Italy. Wren's own style passed, in a manner of speaking, from Brunelleschi to Carlo Fontana in one life-time; his mind, however, was not of a kind to comprehend any discipline without question. In the spiritual and moral spheres he seems to have accepted implicitly the values of his father and uncle: episcopacy and monarchy, piety and royalty. But in all other branches of knowledge, whether sciences or arts, he was committed to a return to first principles. The architectural literature of the Renaissance, as much as any other body of knowledge, could be of service to him only in so far as he had established its authority for himself. What the books told him he could only verify by experiment. He was indeed fortunate in that first friends and later the accident of fire gave him the opportunity to construct experiments in the branch of learning he had come to recognize as properly his own.

IV EXPERIMENT I

The list of Wren's works consists almost entirely of churches, palaces and public and scholastic buildings. Although two country houses can be attributed to him with some security, and his influence on the architecture of great houses may have been stronger than is generally believed, he did not develop a private-house practice. The direction of his career may have been determined by patronage and the Great Fire, but with hindsight we can say that most of his buildings are, because of their function and location, *public* demonstrations of those unalterable mathematical truths on which he set so much value.

This is true of his first work.[77] Pembroke College Chapel is a modest building in scale and has a kind of privacy in that it belongs to the college and can only be entered from the college court. But the west end of the site fronts Trumpington Street, one of the main thoroughfares of Cambridge; Wren's façade thus cannot be seen from anywhere within the college, and offers no link between the private space it encloses for worship and the public space from which it is seen. In the very place where we most expect an entrance, there is none (Plate 11).

The architectural profession was not yet established, and the design of a building was commonly the result of agreement between builders and users; the architect who was not himself a master craftsman was still something of a novelty in England in 1663, as he had been two hundred years earlier in Italy when Leone Battista Alberti, a scholar writing on architecture for other scholars, recommended to his readers the kind of experienced mason on whom he himself relied. At Pembroke there were four parties: Bishop Wren, who gave the money; his nephew; the College led by the Master, who were to use the Chapel; those who were to build and decorate it. The surviving contracts for the structure and the woodwork were agreed between the College and the craftsmen and do not mention either the patron or Wren, who was the farthest removed from the work. A wooden model was made, which survives in the College, though in a damaged state, well enough to show, besides the roof construction, the identity and location of all the external features of the completed building including the three-light Venetian window at the east end, the arched side windows with architraves resting on brackets, and the niches and pilasters of the west façade. Much of this detail has become detached from the model, and what remains shows that it was never executed with sufficient precision to be a guide to the carver. Thirty years ago students were cautioned against interpreting the word 'model' in seventeenth-century documents as more than a drawn design; this caution still holds good, but nevertheless a growing number of specific mentions of wooden models has come to light. Both Wotton in 1624 and Roger Pratt in 1660 recommend the construction of a model to make a record of the design available to all those concerned with the building.[78] It was indeed a substitute for elaborate drawings and a guide to the way the different parts and aspects of the building fitted together. For details of the ornament the craftsmen might be left to make their own designs, given verbal prescriptions, or furnished with either three-dimensional patterns or particular drawings such as those Wren is known to have prepared in the 1670s for Trinity College Library. In that instance we know of no model but we do have a set of drawings in Wren's hand complete enough for the whole building to have been constructed by correspondence.[79]

Since we know nothing of Wren's brief as architect at Pembroke, the absence of a street door, the hexagonal bell turret and indeed other features may have been imposed on him as well as the choice of site; however, this building has enough in common with the works that followed it to be discussed as the fruit of a commission in which choices were open to the architect and the outcome was deliberately attained. On the other hand, his brief may have been limited in a quite different way.

The interior of the Chapel is a single cell lit by tall windows on either side, with a deep coved and fretted plaster ceiling of a kind, and a decorative refinement, that by 1660 were not uncommon in *domestic* architecture. Until 1880 when George Gilbert Scott added a chancel arch and a fifth bay, moving outwards the original east end wall, the room had been symmetrical; only its fittings and the triple window over the altar distinguished one end from the other. It would in any case be reasonable to suppose that both the ceiling and the woodwork in Wren's first building were designed, not by him, but by the specialists who were to carry them out: Wren's contribution then could have been to design the structure and the exterior elevations of a simple space. This supposition becomes the more likely when we consider that the College immediately commissioned a west gallery which broke the symmetry, and very soon an organ in the gallery which, although smaller than the present one which replaced it in 1707, obscured much of the west window he had provided (Plate 14). Even today an architect has no control over the way his building may be cluttered for use after completion. Wren can hardly have been pleased either by the placing before 1688 (the date of Loggan's engraved view) of a large lozenge-shaped clock face – since removed – on the façade immediately above the main window.

In the design of churches Italian Renaissance architects in general were so much concerned with internal spaces that often they drew plans of interiors without showing the outside walls at all. The design problems of the façade were different, frequently the inverse of the interior, and could often be deferred. In Pembroke Chapel, as far as the beholder is concerned, interior and exterior are separated to an even greater extent by the indirectness of the route between the street front and the interior. It has become fashionable to see architecture as 'space', but in some past

31

ages this concept was alien even to architects. There is no reason to believe that at this stage in his career Wren saw his design as a unity: rather it must have appeared to him, as it still does to us today, as an interior space with side and end walls. The same multiplicity or fragmentation is indeed apparent in other early works.

Wren's major statement at Pembroke is thus the public one, to the street. Here are to be found Corinthian pilasters and a pediment, the characteristics of a temple front, applied to the end wall. Alberti had assumed the identity – or rather the confusion – of the Antique temple with the Renaissance church, to the extent that he used the word *temple* for both indiscriminately, and since Wren can hardly have dreamed from thin air an elevation with so many and such authentic temple-like features it is legitimate to look for his sources. An obvious one seems to be the small ruined temple at Tivoli illustrated by Serlio in Book III of his *Architettura*; however, since Serlio gives both an elevation and a plan, it would have been unequivocally clear to Wren that the Tivoli façade had a door taking the whole width of the middle bay, and that its pediment front projected from the wall of the *cella* with four full columns forming a proper portico.[80]

We know that Alberti also introduced, in his church of S. Andrea in Mantua, the fusion of the temple front with the Roman triumphal arch; although Wren is unlikely to have known Alberti's church (which is later in date than his book) the combination of motives was available to him through the general repertory of sixteenth-century architecture. The pilastered single-arch triumphal structures also illustrated in Serlio are as appropriate as the Tivoli temple both to the appearance of Wren's design and to its peculiar lack of any entrance; the arch is actually closer in feeling to Wren's round-headed window. Moreover he knew that he was designing a monument to both his uncle's personal liberation from captivity and the restoration of the monarchy. Since a simple copy of an ancient façade would not give him what he needed it is reasonable that both images, and probably others, should be in the back of his mind.

The Sheldonian Theatre's ceremonial foundation stone was laid on 26 July 1664 after a long period of preliminary work. The University of Oxford was negotiating with the City for the site in March 1663,[81] and Wren's initial design was under development by then if not before, since on 29 April he showed a model of it to the Royal Society.[82] It is impossible to say with certainty what that model, for which the carver William Bird was paid £10, represented, but as it was returned to Oxford[83] it probably served a similar purpose to the Pembroke Chapel model and gave information about the whole structure rather than merely about what is usually considered its most 'scientific' feature, the roof construction.

The delay between the spring of 1663 and that of 1664 was perhaps due not only to academic dilatoriness and financial uncertainty but also to Wren's care in preparing for the project, since once work started in earnest its progress was even and unbroken to its completion in time for the opening ceremony on 9 July 1669. The surviving acquittance book records mainly payments for days worked and materials supplied and thus says less about the chronology of the building than we should like; it shows, however, that the masons worked through the winters in the lodge built for them, dressing stone in readiness for setting in the spring when the danger of frost damage to fresh mortar was past.[84] For Wren's second commission the Theatre is indeed remarkable. It is far more ambitious than Pembroke: large, complex and full of innovations. In designing a building for whose function there were no obvious precedents Wren interwove archaeology, technology and Baroque illusionism with a fresh response to new problems of order both functional and visual. These problems concerned in particular lighting, seating, roofing and the exterior elevations (Plates 5, 6, 9, 66, 67).

Parentalia tells us that his original conception, of a re-creation of the ancient Theatre of Marcellus in Rome, could not be realized within the limits of Sheldon's purse; when the Archbishop found himself the sole contributor to his own appeal fund he accepted the challenge and paid for the whole.[85] *Parentalia* suggests too that the final design is much less like an ancient theatre, but the discussion has persistently been confused by the misidentification with Wren's design of a Hawksmoor drawing for St George, Bloomsbury: even some writers free from that error imply that something is known about the first design.[86] It is, however, impossible to say how Wren had initially intended to adapt and reduce for his purpose a prototype basically unsuitable in size, plan and cross-section. Unlike a Roman theatre, Sheldon's needed a permanent roof but since it is an academic and not a dramatic theatre, no stage. Wren recognized that for a building whose primary function was to be the setting for graduation ceremonies, the basic need was for a convenient auditorium in which the focal point would be the Vice-Chancellor's chair. The U-rather than D-shaped plan on which he settled, with tiered seats and galleries, is closer to the kind of theatre that was new in the seventeenth century although it is now called 'traditional'. Even so, he turned the auditorium, so to speak, back to front, seating the Vice-Chancellor in the middle of the semicircle and putting the main processional entrance at the flat end where we should expect the proscenium arch. In the Baroque theatre and its descendants the proscenium frames a deep stage on which perspective and illusionism are employed to give the appearance of reality to a world of fantasy. In the Sheldonian on the other hand the spectacle is real and takes place in the auditorium itself; moreover, it is as convenient and appropriate for the ceremony there to be conducted in the clear reasonable light of day as it is for the fantasies of the proscenium theatre to be lit artificially in a room without windows. The windows were therefore indeed to be an important component of the interior and thus also of the exterior elevations. We may recall Dean Wren's remark that old Christ Church in London was lit like a stage (p. 4). One of the large south windows is now blocked by the organ; the first organ, installed in 1671, was probably an after-thought as no place was designed for it.[87]

Wren's solution to the problems of seating and lighting – and consequently the basis of his elevation – was to provide two ranges of windows, each above a stepped tier of seats. In this way each tier is illuminated by the windows immediately above it, and the centre of the interior receives light from all the windows. The lower tier rises from the floor; the upper is carried between the outer walls at the back and a series of pillars at the front; since these pillars are small in diameter they do not much incommode the sight from the seats behind, and the view from the upper tier is quite clear. This was made possible by the provision of a roof structure carried entirely on the walls without internal supports.[88]

The Sheldonian roof was not only structurally ingenious but also visually elegant, appealing at once to seventeenth-century tastes for Antiquity, allegory and illusionism. Roman theatres were open to the sky, but could be covered temporarily with a *velarium*, a cloth awning carried on ropes, and it is in the fictive reconstruction of this device that the Sheldonian's resemblance to its ancient prototype chiefly survives. Robert Streeter's illusionist panels, painted in his London studio, show the awning turned back to reveal the sky in which an allegory is enacted of the triumph of religion, virtues, arts and sciences; the ropes are simulated by a network of turned wooden rods which form the frames for the paintings suspended from the roof trusses above.

Contemporaries were impressed by the great span of the interior, almost 70 feet across, in relation to the height of the roof space. *Parentalia* quotes from Plot's *Oxfordshire* (1672) the description of a 'geometrical flat floor' based on a diagram in Serlio and designed by Wren's Oxford colleague Dr John Wallis, in which every beam interlocked with and supported the others.[89] Important work was done in this period on beam theory, and while Wren designed a wooden roof truss, built up with diagonal braces much like a modern steel girder bridge, the main beams were indeed fairly remarkable, being composite in both length and thickness (Fig. 1). A combination of iron plates and bolts and locking scarf joints was used to build up the required length from shorter sections; moreover the whole length of the beam consisted of upper and lower members so designed that the upper pieces locked the lower ones and *vice versa*, the stresses in the lower part of the beam counteracting those in the upper. In 1801–2 the whole roof was replaced by the present one, simpler in construction and using the larger timber spans that had become available; until 1759, moreover, Wren's roof had borne an additional load. The utility of the Sheldonian had originally been increased by doubling its function as

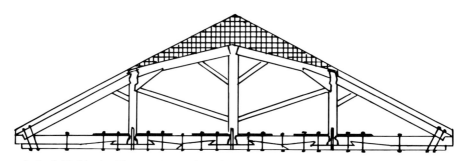

1 Oxford, Sheldonian Theatre. Original roof construction and gable end.

premises for the University Printer, who even before the opening moved his presses into the basement, installed the compositors in the passages under the lower seats, and subsequently stored the unsold stocks of learned books in the roof.[90] This method of all-year usage for a superficially occasional building appealed to the economic sense of administrators and the ingenuity of the architect, but it was far from ideal for those who had to work there. When Hawksmoor's Clarendon Building was constructed on the neighbouring site in 1712–13 the printers moved out leaving only the warehouse in the roof, although books continued to be described as 'Printed at the Theater'. It must have been for ease in identifying and moving stock that Wren provided the seventeen large oval dormer windows (Plate 6) which until 1800 surmounted the stone parapet of the Theatre; the omission of this third tier of windows from the reconstructed roof has substantially altered the elevation.

At the inauguration in July 1669, an event recorded in detail by Evelyn, the University Orator Dr South managed in the same speech to attack the new science of the Royal Society and praise the architect. Since Wren had originally shown his designs to the Society, the conjunction of censure and praise may have been more than incidental, although perhaps South failed to understand the experimental character of the building.[91]

An Antique prototype gave a measure of respectability to any Renaissance design; Wren, however, having abandoned the Theatre of Marcellus, was limited in possible Antique references. In any case, there was no precedent for a building for the conferment of degrees, and the references Wren managed to make are entirely decorative or conceptual: the ceiling, the rounded end of the building and such Classical details as the *fasces* (bundles of rods with axe-heads, carried by Roman *lictores*) placed in front of the Proctors' boxes as emblems of the authority vested in them (Plate 66). It is neither the discovery nor the prerogative of modern architecture that a building's purpose so far affects its appearance that form and function may be inseparable throughout the design process; yet for Wren the need to work from the interior outwards was far greater in the complex and novel brief of the Sheldonian than with his uncle's chapel. The essence of the Oxford brief was an enclosed auditorium in which a large assembly could all see, hear and feel themselves part of the congregation, and an exterior of fitting dignity for the venerable society to which it belonged. If this sounds remarkably like the brief for one of Wren's parish churches, substituting 'church' for 'university', the significant factor is that the Sheldonian was designed well before the question of churches arose. Apart from the ceiling the decoration also has the sober richness of a Wren church (Plate 65). The gallery fronts and columns are painted to imitate marble and the other woodwork is picked out in gold on painted wood graining of the reddish brown hue in fashion at the time and known correctly as 'cedar-colour'.[92]

For the Theatre, then, the exterior design was almost certainly conditioned first of all by where the windows and the supports – for both seating and roof – had to be located; secondly by the need for a principal front which would proclaim in architectural detail the status and in Roman lettering the date and origin of the building (the frieze gives 1668 and Sheldon's function of Chancellor at the time) and afford a ceremonial entrance to the auditorium (Plates 9, 17). In this context there is significance in the pseudo-Gothic doorway opened in the north wall of the Divinity School directly facing the main door of the Theatre and carved by William Bird: it is dated 1669 and crested by the monogram *CWA* (Plate 8), presumably for Christopher Wren Architect.[93]

Successive restorations have left little, if any, of the original external surface of the Sheldonian, although there is no reason to suppose that what we see today is not a faithful record of what was originally placed there. The only serious exceptions to this are in the loss of the dormers already mentioned and the rebuilding of the lantern by Edward Blore in 1838 to his own design and considerably larger than the original: this is now the main light source in the roof space, whereas Wren's cupola, which resembled the one at Emmanuel College, Cambridge, while affording a fine view, was probably for ventilation.

The Sheldonian exterior has received the adverse criticism to which an early work may be prone, not only because it has often been misunderstood but also because it comprises two different and almost unrelated elevations. The unity evident in all aspects of Trinity Library in the mid 1670s is not very common in Wren's architecture; if he cared deeply about it it can have been only for a limited period, that of the Library, the Great Model and the 1675 'Definitive' design for St Paul's, and the Mausoleum for Charles I. Certainly he had not arrived at such a conception of architecture in the previous decade, and the Sheldonian's diverse elevations have little in common beyond their dependence on the arrangement of the interior.

The south front appears to be the more conventional since it is articulated with superimposed orders and blind arcades, the latter perhaps the last vestige of the open arched loggias of the Roman theatre. In spirit the front is nearer the permanent stage set inside the Roman theatre. But the distance of this façade from Antique and Renaissance examples can be measured by the difficulty students have always found in explaining it in terms of sources and prototypes. The circular frames inset into semicircular window heads can be found in Serlio; they are also, like the two-light rectangular windows of the upper storey and the oval dormers on the other sides of the roof, characteristic of French architecture. They therefore raise unanswerable questions of Wren's knowledge of France before he went there – since most of the design seems to have been irrevocably committed before his return. The 'metaphysical sages' (as Robert Bridges called them) round the north end, which are really herms (Antique boundary posts) resemble those in the base court at Vaux-le-Vicomte (Plate 6). There are also several generic rather than specific references in the south front to a long line of Italian and French two-storey church fronts. Modern scholars too have frequently tried to link the way in which the centre bays of the upper storey break into the gable-end with the church façades of Palladio in which two pedimented temple fronts are combined, although it has never been clear how Wren could have known about these since they do not appear in Palladio's *Quattro Libri*. Probably none of the ecclesiastical examples is directly relevant; indeed, closer examination of the Sheldonian front suggests that it is not designed in at all the same way.

The window pattern is dictated by the interior; thus in the outermost bays there are panels and niches instead of windows, even in the basement, because the space within is not part of the auditorium but contains staircases lit from the side elevations. Similarly the lunettes over the three central upper windows are filled in to leave a uniform range of rectangular windows all round the interior. Above this range of windows rises a gable-end; in the Classical language of architecture gable-end and pediment are often synonymous, but functionally and historically they are distinct, and it is clear that we are looking at the end wall of a roofed building rather than at a simplified temple-front, since the triangle rises not above the entablature of an order but above a half-storey or attic which has no order. Into, or out of, this arrangement breaks a proper temple-front in the centre of the upper storey; its combination of arches and pilasters links it thematically to the lower storey, but it projects slightly from the surrounding wall and above the end of the roof, which is of lower pitch in the centre. Moreover, in a motif which Hawksmoor repeated on the front of St George-in-the-East, the mouldings in the flanking parts of the pseudo-pediment thus seem to have been coiled up as a result of the break. Wren was rather fond of inserting a temple-front like a kind of quotation as part of a façade; he did so in a design of 1664 for Whitehall, in the Custom House (1669), in some of the City churches in the 1670s, and as late as 1689 at Hampton Court (Plates 2, 22, 33, 34, 147, Fig. 2). Indeed the use of a three-bay portico above a similar but wider bay-system recurs with striking effect in the west front of St Paul's well into the 1690s (Plate 138).

It is customary to look for prototypes for this façade because both the evolutionary view of art-history and the monographic view of the history of artists are greatly concerned with sources and prototypes. The failure of the exercise in this case, as in many others of Wren's designs, may help to support the view already proposed in general, that Wren's mind did not work this way to the extent that others' did. His architecture was indeed much closer to the aspiration of many more recent figures, in going back beyond received authority to first principles. The architectural vocabulary of his day he accepted, to be learned, assimilated and manipulated; but the phrases and sentences of other men did not interest him unduly. Even on specific and documented occasions of borrowing, such as the Basilica of Maxentius for St Mary-le-Bow (p. 63), or the Mausoleum of Halicarnassus in a theoretical reconstruction (p. 41), his treatment of the original was so cavalier as to alter it totally, somewhat as the Theatre of Marcellus is forgotten rather than remembered in that of Sheldon. Wren did not even start from such concepts as a Temple of Learning.

When we leave the front of the building we find a continuous elevation which extends the rest of the way round the outside, uniform except where doorways

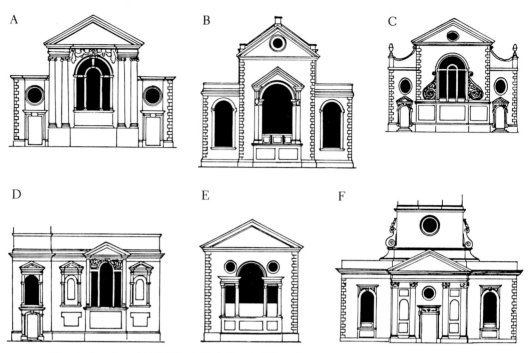

2 Church elevations. (A) St Dionis Backchurch. (B) St Bride. (C) St Mary Aldermanbury. (D) St Mildred, Poultry. (E) St Olave, Old Jewry. (F) St Magnus.

interrupt the window arrangement (Plate 5). The windows and the moulding levels are continuous with the façade; everything else is different. Summerson has convincingly explained this elevation by showing the Renaissance norm from which it is not so much a derivation as a departure. The archetypal Classical elevation has first a basement, usually rusticated and with small windows so that its supporting function for what rises above it is visually expressed. Then comes a main storey, either with, or with the implication of, an order; this is the *piano nobile* or gracious living floor of Italian great houses although ultimately deriving from the days when one retreated under attack to the upper floor leaving only the livestock below. Above this comes the attic, a half-storey which in a great house usually contains little rooms for private living and sleeping, and which in a grand elevation serves rather like a hat or a lid on the main storey. North of the Alps architects tended to continue the tradition of high pitched roofs, as much from aesthetic preference and ease and cheapness of construction as for climatic reasons. Northern Classical elevations therefore often include dormers, placed vertically above other windows and surmounted by pediments or other Classical devices so as to incorporate the roof in the elevation; the round or oval dormer window was common in Renaissance France.

The continuous elevation of the Sheldonian has all these features except the main

38

storey.[94] That such an omission had never been made before by an architect who understood the Classical language was no deterrent to a committed experimenter in the early Royal Society: to Wren, starting at the beginning, the question of precedent was irrelevant. The objection that it could not be done was answered in the doing of it, for the laws thereby broken were not of nature but only of taste. The result gave Wren what he needed, and if it bore some resemblance to the side either of a factory or of a theatre – types of building that often seem only to have a front – that was entirely appropriate, since it was both of these. The Sheldonian is a unique building, often misunderstood, but it is very much of its time – the early Restoration – and some of the experiment embodied in it would bear fruit in subsequent decades.

But there is more to be said. In his view of mathematics as both the framework and the key to knowledge Wren was following Descartes rather than Bacon. We know of no event in his intellectual life comparable to Descartes's dream or Newton's apple; nevertheless the sort of realization that such accidents symbolize must have come to him, and it must have come before he began to design the Sheldonian. Essentially the inspiration of genius is a capacity for greater and more sustained insight than is given to ordinary men. For Wren, the realization was first of all how in architecture he might go back to first principles as Descartes had done in philosophy. More than once he would have to make such a return in the evolution of St Paul's (p. 78), but the Sheldonian, his first major work, was not only the first but also the clearest illustration of what the journey entailed. Thereafter, however, the parallel does not continue: Wren found no satisfaction in the abstractions of philosophy and not enough in the plotting of graphs. Descartes's journey was described and made public in words and in print. Wren's remained private, not because it could not be described but because he chose not to describe it. Nevertheless it may be asked, and to some extent answered, what the principles were upon which he based his newly adopted art, where they can be found and how they are to be identified.

V   PRINCIPLES

Great artists are not usually remembered for the unequivocal clarity or comprehensiveness of their theoretical remarks, nor famous theoreticians for their practical work. We know that Wren did not like fussy decoration such as he saw in the apartments at Versailles, 'crouded with little Curiosities of Ornaments', preferring to their feminine atmosphere the 'masculine Furniture' of the Palais Mazarin.[95] This view of architectural gender is confirmed at the end of his life in the argument over the roof-line of St Paul's. He had designed a simple plinth above the cornice, but the Commissioners insisted on adding a balustrade like that on the Banqueting House: 'Ladies', he wrote, 'think nothing well without an Edging.'[96] In *Tract I* he stated that elevations ought to be higher in the middle than at the ends and convex rather than concave, 'because the Middle is the Place of greatest Dignity, and first arrests the Eye.' He wrote further that oblique lines were discordant unless symmetrical as in the sides of a pediment; that while 'for a Portico the longer the more beautiful *in infinitum*' other façades should be related between height and breadth by a proportion of not more than 3 to 1.[97] These observations are certainly fairly comprehensive; moreover, unlike either the usual Renaissance prescriptions about proportions and the orders, or his own remarks about geometry, they are qualitative statements about shape. Even so, lecture-like notes, analogous to the aphorisms of Leonardo da Vinci or Cézanne, do not serve as more than pointers towards the artist's particular theoretical basis. He expresses disapproval of 'pinnacles' other than statues, adding that 'Pyramids are Gothick; Pots are modern French'.[98] Yet he used them on occasion, and many of his buildings run counter to his stated disapproval of visible roofs.

Yet we have nothing from Wren remotely like Camille Pissarro's letters to Lucien or even Hawksmoor's to Henry Joynes or to Lord Carlisle or Vanbrugh's to Lord Manchester, giving practical reasons for seeing and doing things in particular ways. Modern studies of Palladio received enormous impetus from Rudolf Wittkower's articles on *Principles of Palladio's Architecture* (1944–5) but we should remember, not only that those principles were extrapolated by an art-historian from brief and sometimes peripheral remarks in Palladio's writings, but also that those subsequent studies have shown how far the range of Palladio's own buildings exceeded even the latitude of his published advice to which, for example, neither the printed nor the actual proportions of the Villa Rotonda conform. The period of Wren and his school, like that of Bernini, Borromini and Cortona in Rome, was one of doing in architecture, not of writing, and it is moreover evident in his scientific career that Wren was interested in practical problems and bored alike by theoretical ones and by routine solutions. It is as doubtful that he ever set out to write a theoretical basis for his architecture as it is probable that such a basis developed and changed in his mind: it is the mark of the true expert that he is able swiftly to bring his accumulated knowledge, belief and wisdom to bear on the individual problem when it is presented to him. Except as a purely academic exercise the *Principles of Wren's Architecture* are best understood not in isolation but through the buildings: the great artists of the figurative tradition understood the human skeleton, but they expressed their understanding in figures of flesh that live and move. The observations that follow are therefore perhaps of a kind that Wren would have recognized and even formulated, and they apply with reasonable constancy to his whole career, but they cannot be much further extended.

First something should be said about Wren's attitude to proportional systems. It might be thought that the high value he placed on geometry would have combined with the recommendations of Renaissance theorists to make numerical proportions more than usually important for his architecture. Attempts have indeed been made to show that some of his plans and elevations are based on a system of triangles; such a system might well have attracted Wren by its neatness and its rather specious logic, just as in reconstructing the Halicarnassus Mausoleum he developed a 'Platonic' proportional system based, with total disregard for the dimensions given by Pliny, on the numbers 8, 4, 2 and 1, and then congratulated himself that 'the Ordinance of the whole falls out so wonderfully'.[99] But in actual cases Wren is likely to have mistrusted such received systems as much as any others; in the City churches for example he often allowed plans to be far from rectangular. Moreover, if he made any drawings on this kind of basis none survive. His statements about the beauty of squares and circles are qualitative and hypothetical; he says nothing about their appearance in actual examples. Geometry was for him the end, not the beginning: not an absolute starting point on which to base a design but rather an empirical aim to be achieved through the realization of the design.

In the early sixteenth century Raphael formulated and Serlio first exemplified in print a way of looking at and recording buildings which has since become part of architecture itself: the separation of plan, elevations, sections and details is a convenient way of reducing information about a three-dimensional whole to what can properly be conveyed in two-dimensional drawings. Sir Roger Pratt, writing in 1660, similarly divides the constituents of architectural design.[100] Indeed, the 'feel' of architecture, what it is like to be in spaces or in front of masses, can be conveyed only imperfectly in photographs or perspective drawings, and in words only by suggestion, metaphor, analogy and comparison with other experiences. A hall may be cube-shaped, dark, vast, ornate, vaulted; it may further be of marble, Roman, and like or unlike another known example. Wren brought to architecture a geometrician's feeling for shapes and an observant young man's memories of individual buildings. When he turned, as he certainly did, to the books of Serlio and

Palladio, he found there architecture codified in plans, elevations and sections. It is significant that Pembroke Chapel appears to us as a number of distinct elevations which add up to a whole, for the same is true of the Sheldonian (Plates 14, 66). The separateness of the front from the rest of the exterior there is all too clear, and the interior which unites them does not seem, when we stand within it, to be so much a space as a number of walls folded up like the sides of a cardboard box, with the ceiling as its lid. Part of the box so constructed is occupied by a framework of benches, galleries and columns, and since we find it more intelligible to look at objects than at spaces, this framework makes the dominant impression.

Wren's early architecture at least, then, is one of plans, elevations and sections which fit together with the clarity and precision of a construction kit. Some of the parts are opaque, being walls and screens; others are transparent, being frameworks of pillars and beams or piers and arches. The opaque surfaces include windows, which from the outside show dark areas of pattern rather than views of the interior, and from the inside by their positioning and the quality of glass used show light areas of pattern rather than views of the outside world. Little of the surface other than windows is left bare and plain: exterior walls in particular are broken up by niches, recessed panels, carvings and other relief devices. Very broadly speaking, such a preference for surface relief, as if the wall were a kind of decorative skin on the outside of a building, is characteristic of French rather than Italian Renaissance and post-Renaissance architecture, but here the effect of Wren's travels should not be overestimated. Coming when they did, his experiences abroad must have confirmed in reality what he had already worked hard to discover in illustration. In a scientist's language travel verified what was until then hypothetical; in a layman's terms it strengthened certain tastes and preferences which were either natural to him or already acquired. For already in the front of Pembroke Chapel, above and below the windows, and below the central window, the wall is cut back into shallow recesses, and another device appears there which although not Wren's invention becomes habitual in his use of the Corinthian and Composite orders: a moulding across the top of the pilaster shafts which has the effect of making the zone of the capitals into a continuous false frieze (Plates 11, 33, 79, 139). Since free-standing columns obviously could not be joined in this way the device is strictly speaking incorrect between pilasters, and the proper place for a frieze is in the middle zone of the entablature; however, it has the sanction of both Palladio (in the Palazzo Thiene) and Serlio (in triumphal arches and inside the Tivoli portico).[101] It is as if no wall area must be left quite blank and unfilled; positive features like pilasters and windows are not sufficient in themselves to define the intervening surfaces, which must thus be circumscribed by relief lines. This conception of a wall, as if like a sheet of paper it needs to be parcelled out geometrically, is to be found also in the fifteenth-century architecture of Florence, Rome, Milan and Venice. Wren can have known little of such architecture, but he seems to have followed a similar process of re-invention to that taken in Holland earlier in the seventeenth century by Hendrik de Keyser, some of whose buildings he could well have known from de Bray's *Architectura Moderna* (1631).

We have already encountered the other characteristics of Wren's early architecture that are so consistent as to be considered as principles: a disregard for the Renaissance hierarchy of prototypes and precedents, and the grid framework. The latter dominates the Sheldonian interior visually as well as structurally, but it also underlies very clearly the south front. It appears, too, especially baldly in the design made in not fully explained circumstances for Whitehall Palace in 1664.[102] The original drawing is only one half of an elevation (which may be doubled photographically) for a portico-fronted building to contain staircases and link the Banqueting House to an exact repetition of itself (Plate 2). A wooden model was made of this design, showing only the façades, and the bill in the Whitehall accounts dates its fabrication to the spring of 1665. The only project known to be of this particular period is the one that Charles II sketched privately and personally for Evelyn, as the diarist recorded, on 28 October 1664. Apparently none of the senior officers of the Works, Denham, May and Webb, was party to this scheme; evidently Wren, though he was not yet in the king's service, was involved.

The linking portions of the elevation show a profusion and variety of relieving details; the central portico however is both structurally and visually a grid framework. It is put together not unlike the two-storey church façades of the Val-de-Grâce and the Sorbonne, and the set-backs in the clustered pillars at the corners are similar; in 1664 Wren knew these façades, if at all, only from prints. But his use of a screen of full columns in front of a true portico produces a façade more nearly concave than the progressively projecting surfaces of the Parisian examples. Moreover, the grid-like nature of his design is emphasized by the unbroken line of the lower entablature and the extension of the openings down to the ground so that the lower columns rest on detached and stilted pedestals.

All projects for Whitehall except Inigo Jones's first, of *c.* 1638, centre on either the Banqueting House or a portico with that building doubled, and it would later be Wren's task under James II to build south of the Banqueting House the only grand approach staircase it has ever had. Already in the 1664 drawing the need for adequate stairs to the building and its pendant – the floor level being that of the first order – may have suggested the full space-enclosing portico. Wren moreover seems to have been aware of the importance of levels, or horizontal definitions, in architecture: he makes us aware of them in the Sheldonian, and again in another specially designed building (Plate 22), the new Custom House in Thames Street, his first commission as Surveyor of Works (1669–71). On his appointment he found a design already made, but he reworked it to such an extent that the building was begun in the summer of 1669 to his 'Modell'.[103]

Wren's knowledge of Dutch architecture was appreciable, though not so great as to afford convincing evidence that he had visited Holland: his visual curiosity was always fed and usually satisfied by what he could find 'in paper' and what others could tell him. He may thus have known something of the Dutch market weigh-houses at Leiden, Gouda and elsewhere, which have a pedimented and pilastered upper storey above the room containing the beam scale for weighing the commodities. On the other hand, market halls above open loggias were already characteristic in English towns, and Hendrik de Keyser's arcaded Beurs (Exchange) in Amsterdam was actually modelled on its London counterpart, Gresham's Royal Exchange (1566–71), the grandest example of commercial architecture in England until the Great Fire. Wren may equally well have started from the requirements of the building to arrive at a regular Classical façade with a regular floor plan, for offices above and covered storage and loading bays below. Even the doubling of the columns (Ionic above Tuscan) at the corners of the projecting end pavilions was not only a grammatical but also a structural device, though in general the narrowest supports consistent with stability were desirable, not for visibility as in the Sheldonian but for convenience in the movement of the bulky and often heavy wholesale consignments passing through the port of London. Wren's liking for steeply sloping pediments is again evident, and he used small segmental pediments to break up the cornice line in the intermediate bays as he had done in the Whitehall design.

The Custom House has been discussed out of turn: Wren's pre-Parisian *oeuvre* however includes at least one other college building, at Trinity College, Oxford. For the President, his friend from Wadham days Dr Ralph Bathurst, he designed a range in the college garden in June 1665, just before his departure for France. Bathurst wanted only a single range, but Wren told him that benefactors would be more impressed by a quadrangle, even 'a lame one, somewhat like a three-legged table'.[104] Wren's north range was built in 1665–8, and subsequently a west and a south one were added; Wren's building survives, but with its hipped roof replaced by an extra storey built in 1802. But both what remains and the original drawings show that it was a simple building of domestic character, very like one of the service wings of a great house of the 1660s and undecorated except for the niche in the centre bay (Plate 10, Fig. 3).

3   Oxford, Trinity College. Original appearance of Wren's block.

It is possible that the range containing the Chapel and Master's Gallery of Emmanuel College, Cambridge, was commissioned at the same date, since it was originally planned in 1663 by the Master then, William Sancroft, who in December 1664 became Dean of St Paul's.[105] Building was not begun until 1668, but Sancroft gave considerable funds for the work and kept in touch with his successors at Cambridge about its progress. In the course of 1667 a wooden model was made and delivered to Cambridge, but this would have left time for a design conceived two years earlier to be totally recast in the light of Wren's foreign experiences. Changes were made from the one surviving drawing, which shows the side pavilions of brick with stone dressings (like the Custom House) instead of all ashlar.[106] The central arch, at first semicircular, was widened to a half oval in 1677 a few months before the consecration (Plates 12, 13, 15, 18).

The pediment broken by the clock compartment, the forward break in the entablature beneath it, the use of half-columns instead of pilasters for the central pair and the false frieze of swags and garlands are elements which differ in detail but not in kind from the Pembroke and Sheldonian façades; Wren's problem here was to combine a temple-like chapel front with a clock and belfry and with the gallery that runs across the first floor and indeed lies in front of the chapel proper. Moreover the central bay forms a kind of tower that carries the belfry more organically and presumably for Wren more satisfactorily than was the case at Pembroke. But the breaking of the roof-line into separate pavilions is very French, and the impost arcades with their egg-and-dart moulded architraves and the assured use of a giant order spanning both storeys suggest a wider first-hand experience of monumental architecture than could have been gained from the works of Jones and Webb. The Chapel range at Emmanuel is one of those buildings which seem jewel-like or model-like because their vocabulary is larger in scale than their actual dimensions, and it is this quality which combines with the unorthodoxy of Wren's solutions to strike the casual observer as quaint or picturesque.

VI   EXPERIMENT II

Two experiments conceived in the summer after Wren's return from France remained untried: one for St Paul's and one for the City. Concern with the problems of St Paul's goes back to late 1661 (p. 6), but Wren was not a member of the Commission of 18 April 1663 and seems not to have been officially involved for the next three years. An undated report by Webb, Denham (a Commissioner) and Edward Marshall the mason had recommended taking down and rebuilding the crossing and tower, which had lost its leaded timber spire after a lightning strike in 1561; it was practical enough to request a supply of 3000 tons of stone a year to keep work going smoothly.[107] In fact some money was donated and spent in 1663–5 on patching, demolishing houses abutting on the cathedral and buying materials.[108] There also survives a careful and detailed prescription by Sir Roger Pratt for a piecemeal repair; it is full of good advice about economy in moving scaffolds but essentially it looked at the blisters and not the disease.[109] About 1660 Pratt had written that

> no man deserves the name of Architect, who has not been very well versed both in those old [buildings] of Rome, as likewise the more modern of Italy and France &c, because that with us, having nothing remarkable but the banquetting house at Whitehall and the portico at St Paul's, it is no ways probable that any one should be sufficiently furnished with the variety of invention, and of excellent ideas, which upon several occasions it will be necessary for him to have, who has had but so great a scarcity wherein to employ his judgment.[110]

Now Wren, newly back from France, and invited by Dean Sancroft, spoke out with authority and confidence as both geometrician and architect, offering in the light of his travels a radical and strikingly new solution. *Parentalia* dates his report[111] to the Commissioners 1 May 1666, but 7 May, the date of what seems to be a covering letter to Sancroft, is more probable. In this he wrote, 'Mr Prat's way will be plausible because it will seem to aim at great thrift, which will take with those that . . . are not Judges of Designe'.[112] Certainly the report was prepared in the light of Pratt's paper. For us it is elaborated by drawings to which it refers obliquely and which are almost certainly those Wren had 'with a great deal of paines finished' on 5 August, and those which survive at All Souls.[113]

Wren was careful neither to 'aim at too great Magnificence, which neither the Disposition nor Extent of this Age will probably bring to a period', nor by 'covering all faults with a coat of plaster' to leave it 'still to the next Posterity as a further object of Charity'; mindful that this was 'a pile as much for ornament as use', his middle way would 'neglect nothing that may answer to a decent uniform Beauty or durable firmness . . . suitable to the Expense already laid out on the outside'.

He would 'not propose any thing of meer Beauty to be added but where there is necessity of rebuilding and when it will be neer the same thing to perform it well as ill'. But where the vaults had pushed the piers outwards for lack of abutment they could be rebuilt 'after a good Roman Manner' as easily as in the 'rudeness' of the Gothic style: this judgement would be shared alike by 'an Architect taking his measures from the precept and example of the Ancients' and by a geometrician. The crossing was the most defective part, for the subsidence of one pier had given the tower a list, and the subsequently added interior bracing arches had blocked both space and view 'where it had been more graceful to have been rather wider than the rest'. The 'excessive length' of many Gothic buildings also was 'no other commendable but that it yeilds a pleasing perspective by the continued opticall Diminution of the Collums'.

Wren proposed therefore to replace the whole crossing area by 'a spacious Dome or rotunda with a Cupolo or Hemispherical Roof' carried by four massive new arches (Plates 20, 21); he pointed out that new stone might as well be used for a new structure as for investing an old one, and lead as well to cover a cupola as a spire. He would moreover use the old tower as a support, building the new structure round it before clearing it away, 'partly because the expectations of persons is to be kept up (for many unbelievers would bewail the loss of the old Paul's Steeple and despond if they did not see a hopefull successor rise in its stead) and chiefly', an evident and brilliant answer to Pratt's pedestrian measures, 'because it will save a world of Scaffolding poles'.[114]

Beyond tracing the colonnade and rectangular windows of the exterior drum to Serlio's illustrations of Bramante's design for St Peter's in Rome, and the double-shell dome to Lemercier's Sorbonne church in Paris, few writers have taken this design very seriously – perhaps, it is tempting to suggest, because not much else in it can be traced to obvious sources. It is probable, as has indeed been observed before, that the opening out of the crossing to the full width of the side aisles, over 80 feet, was inspired by the fourteenth-century crossing at Ely, which Wren must have known as the cathedral church of his uncle Matthew; this probability is strengthened by the appearance in the St Paul's design of windows high up in the main piers, adding illumination on the diagonal axes as extra windows do in the Ely octagon. It is certain that the domes Wren saw in Paris impressed him profoundly and fired his imagination for the rest of his life. At St Paul's the drawings show a re-casing of the inside of the nave and transepts, as Jones had done for the outside, in Classical dress, and the form Wren chose of semicircular arcades with a high gallery of depressed arches above, is closely based on the Jesuit church in Paris (p. 9). Certainly too he took from the Sorbonne not only the combination of an inner masonry dome with a taller outer timber one covered with lead but also the device of completely enclosing the inner lantern within the outer dome. But most of the other features of Wren's design seem to be without precedent. For a start, his outer lantern is entirely of wood and its weight is carried entirely by the timbers of the outer dome down to the masonry drum. This, like the tall open metal-work pineapple above the lantern, was intended to reduce weight and allow a thinner masonry shell for the inner dome.

Secondly both inner and outer domes are half-melon shaped, not semicircular, being formed by the rotation of an arc of less than a quarter-circle. This also reduced the amount of abutment needed to support the crossing piers; on the other hand the resulting tall 'gothic' shape is disguised from view by a distraction of the eye. Both, inside and outside, begin with concave fluting, but towards the top the flutes are filled with convex fillets; those on the outside terminate downwards in little oval windows admitting light into the space between the domes and into the inner lantern. In its interior form this reversible fluting occurs in some Renaissance shell-niches – and large scallop shells are to be found in the false frieze round the outside colonnade – but its translation to the exterior seems to stem from an attempt to suggest a continuity, manifestly non-existent, between inside and outside.

Wren was already concerned that the inner dome should not appear too tall while the outer one should rise high over the City; in fact the oculus of the inner dome and the top of the outer finial are within a few feet of the same heights as their counterparts in his final solution built forty years later (Fig. 4). Light, and lightness, concerned him. Apart from the extra diagonal windows in the piers, the drum gave as much light as was structurally possible, and the interior of drum, dome and lantern was as airy and as delicately decorated as he could contrive. The exterior, however, was sterner and simpler, although here again above the colonnade, as in the bases of his giant pilasters inside the cathedral, he used drops and garlands to add relief enrichment.

'For the Incouragement and Satisfaction of Benefactors that comprehend not Designs and Draughts on paper' Wren proposed the making of 'a good and careful large model', as well as for 'the inferior Artificers clearer intelligence of their Business' and in the event of long delay or interruption to ensure the continuance of the same design. He wanted to begin with the crossing 'as being an absolute piece of itself', and as 'an Ornament to His Majestie's most excellent Reign, to the Church of England, and to the great Citie, which it is pitie in the opinion of Neighbours should longer continue the most unadorned of her bigness in the World'.[115]

After some discussion with Wren and May, Pratt wrote a second paper, claiming inability to see a number of the faults Wren found in the old structure, disputing the need for a model – Inigo Jones for example had done very well without one – as unnecessary expense, and exclaiming, 'What pillars, and arches, to be pulled down! What new ones to be erected! What Scaffold, and Engines' to lay the foundation of an endless and incalculable future expenditure.[116] On 27 August at a meeting on site Evelyn, who had been in Rome with Pratt in 1644–5, sided against him and

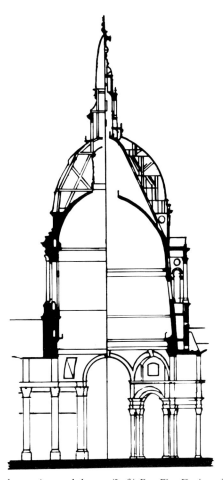

4   St Paul's. Section through crossing and dome. (Left) Pre-Fire Design. (Right) As built.

with Wren, and recorded that of those present, who included May, the Bishop and Dean, other Commissioners and principal workmen, the majority finally agreed in favour of a design and estimate for a cupola. A week later the Great Fire relegated the drawings Wren had already made to the plan chest, as the stones flew like grenades and the lead ran in rivers down the streets.[117] But it is worth comparing that design directly with the final new St Paul's to see how much of its spirit lingers there.

At the same time, it should be remembered that at this stage Wren was not designing a new cathedral, but only attempting to reconcile the vision France had given him of a new architecture with the practical need for worthy repairs to the centrepiece of London. At this time a cathedral meant to him a nave or hall, a domed space and, for London, a portico. That which Jones had added to the old building in the 1630s had the practical function of sheltering the many forms of entirely secular business which traditionally were carried on 'at Paul's'; just as Sheldon had made possible the exclusion of the disedifying rhetoric and buffoonery of Oxford ceremonial from St Mary's Church, his predecessor Archbishop Laud had desired the removal of horse-trading and baser transactions from the cathedral nave. The three components, portico, nave and dome, appear in outline on the other unfulfilled design of 1666, the plan for a new London after the Fire (Fig. 5).

The City plan[118] was based on the acceptance of certain fixed points: the old entrances to the City on the west, north and east, the only road from the south across London Bridge, and the two most important landmarks of St Paul's and the Royal Exchange. These two buildings marked the acute angles of a Z-shaped skeleton of three avenues crossing the City from east to west. The old pattern of streets and alleys was to be replaced by rectangular blocks between these avenues in the western part, and in the eastern part by groups of streets radiating from – and connecting – the Exchange, the end of London Bridge, the Custom House and two open places. Another radial system was planned west of the Fleet River, a minor stream whose flow varied greatly and directly with both the rainfall over Hampstead Heath and the tide in the Thames, into which it ran at Blackfriars. It had earlier been navigable as far as Holborn, but by Wren's time it had become a choked and stinking sewer. His proposed treatment of it derived from the broad canals and basins flanked by quays that were already a well-known feature of Dutch towns, combining land drainage, door-to-door freight carriage and urban spaciousness. The Fleet quays were to have the same 90-foot width as the three principal avenues; moreover, with the precedent of the Seine fresh in his mind, he planned to continue the quays along the Thames all the way from the Temple on the west to the Tower. The Fleet canal and the Thames quay, which appear also on Evelyn's plan for London, were incorporated in the provisions of the 1667 and 1670 London

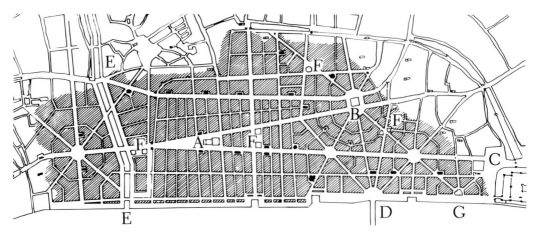

5 Wren's plan for London in 1666. (A) St Paul's. (B) Exchange. (C) Tower of London. (D) London Bridge. (E) Fleet River. (F) Markets. (G) Custom House. Churches are solid black.

Building Acts. The Fleet scheme was indeed carried out, to reduced dimensions, but the canal was roofed over during the eighteenth century to make what are now Farringdon Street and New Bridge Street. The line of the Thames quay was protected, but the alternation of public inertia and private interest gradually eroded both the concept and the location until it became impracticable.

Wren's plan has sometimes been unjustly criticized as lacking the very qualities it shows of naturalness and variety. The block system, familiar today from its wholesale adoption by the settlers of the New World, has an ancestry in Europe dating back to the Romans. English medieval towns, however, tended to irregular growth around a nucleus, like urban villages, and the ideal of the Georgian square and its prototype, Jones's Covent Garden, bringing the country into the town, reversed the relative disposition of buildings and spaces in a city. Wren accepted the block system, but without the rigidity of a chequerboard plan; he varied the widths of blocks, and placed churches at arbitrary intervals on major streets in such a way that they could be seen to advantage but would not restrict traffic. He made gentle, and apparently natural, transitions from the old trunk roads to the new streets. Then he cut through the mass of buildings with broad avenues and radial streets aligned to give vistas towards major buildings or major intersections which would presumably have been marked by monuments. The radial city was a favourite of Renaissance theorists; Wren's system on the other hand is closer to that of Sixtus V's planning in Rome in the 1580s, known to him from printed sources and the accounts of travellers. A similar system of avenues and *ronds-points* underlay the French formal gardens of the seventeenth century, of which his impressions, based on the still young trees, would have been assisted by drawn plans prefiguring the effect in maturity.

Since the City plan remained on paper, Wren's chief concern with rebuilding, as one of the surveyors, was administrative. The end of the 1660s, however, saw him as architect in earnest, not only responsible to the Crown for the Office of Works but also to Royal Commissions for a new cathedral and new parish churches. The priorities and limitations in these two assignments were distinct. The need for churches was the more pressing, since although temporary 'tabernacles' were constructed the parish church was the centre, visual as well as social, of a neighbourhood; it was seen to serve both for public worship and as the only legal place for the registration of baptisms (and therefore births), marriages and burials. But the building, and therefore the designing, of about fifty churches was a piecemeal operation and not a concerted one, and it had no financial basis until the passing of the second Building Act in 1670. Construction would take some fifteen or twenty years, because of the number of sites involved, the resources of the building trade and the limits of the annual income from the coal tax raised by the Act. The pace of the cathedral would also be set partly by income although this was augmented by donations, but the major factor there would, once it had been determined, be the scale of the undertaking. The new St Paul's was not begun until 1675, by which time the first churches were complete, but the establishment of a design had by then concerned Wren, intermittently at first and then constantly, for nine years. The designing of the First Model, constructed in the winter of 1669–70, must have preceded in his mind that of the churches and should be examined before them.

Wren's pre-Fire proposals had aimed at a proper balance between Commodity, Firmness and Delight. The justness of that balance is one of the architect's chief responsibilities, but others are first to establish – if necessary by leading his client in dialogue – the true nature of the building to be designed, and secondly to adjust the ideal to the realities of what can be paid for. For St Paul's the balance altered in several ways between 1666 and 1675, as both the architect and the Commission arrived at a clearer understanding of the work; in this process of review Wren needed, and usually managed, to anticipate the Commission at each stage.

The first need was to restore the choir services, and Wren conceded that the least unsafe part of the ruins was the western half of the nave. He did so with reluctance, from his estimation of the state of the masonry, but with the further hope after such temporary work of being able to 'at least produce some neate fabrick, which shall recompence in Art and beauty what it wants in bulke': the financial future was still very uncertain.[119] And in the first year after the Fire survival itself was the need, in the face of a hard winter, universal ruin and disruption of every kind, and the Dutch naval assault on the Medway towns in the early summer. Early in 1668, however, work began on a temporary choir,[120] but a fall of masonry vindicated Wren's doubts. 'What you whispered in my Ear . . . is now come to pass' wrote Sancroft on 25 April, adding his expectation that Wren in Oxford would bring again 'those excellent Draughts and Designes you formerly favour'd us with'.[121] Speculation is possible about which drawings these were, but that they were the Pre-Fire crossing designs is clear from Wren's reply, which begged the Dean nevertheless to think of 'a new fabrick upon new foundations, artificiall durable and beautifull, but less massive' than the old.[122] He agreed to bring the old designs in a few days, but his mind had changed. A new start would have been extravagant before the fire; now it was necessary. On 24 May he reported more fully on the masonry: the fall was no surprise, and moreover the tower was dangerous.[123] In July the order went out for its demolition,[124] and now Sancroft asked for a design for at least a new choir to propose to and discuss with the King; he made moreover the crucial admission that the scope of the project should not be limited by the amount of money that could then be predicted.[125]

By the autumn of 1669 Wren had worked over in detail and in depth the idea sketched into the City plan – portico, auditorium and dome – and had again reached a novel solution (Fig. 6). Our evidence of the First Model design is limited to the half of the model that survives together with one partial drawing and an adverse criticism written by Pratt in July 1673 when, unknown to him, the design had already been superseded.[126] The surviving half consists of the ten-bay nave without roof, ends or cupola, but from the other evidence we know that the interior, 132 feet long with a central nave 34 feet wide, was to be barrel-vaulted and lay towards

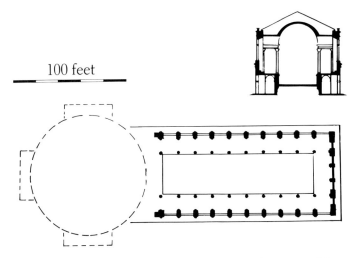

6 St Paul's. First Model. Section across auditorium, and plan with conjectural form of vestibule.

the east, with a domed vestibule on the west at least 60 feet in diameter. Pratt described, and thought unnecessary, the '3 several Porticos all of the same fashion' which probably provided north, west and south entrances to the vestibule. The columns 'two thick' round the drum of the dome were probably coupled rather than two deep, as Pratt considered that they crowded the windows. He also tells us that the cupola itself was without windows. This part of the design gave Wren the dome he wanted both as a geometrical demonstration and as a London landmark, and provided assembly space for processions on great occasions.

The 'auditory' was *more* unusual: the nave had no aisles at floor level, and the galleries above on the inside were thus built over arcaded loggias opening outwards to the churchyard to shelter the traditional secular business 'at Paul's'. What is difficult to decide is whether the loggias continued round under the east window, but it seems more probable that they ended in open arches in the east wall. As was later the case at Trinity Library, Cambridge (Fig. 13), interior levels did not correspond to the exterior but were arranged to give the best use of the space. The nave floor was considerably higher than the base, and the gallery lower than the cornice, of the loggia, and the big windows above the loggia thus gave the interior uninterrupted illumination. The galleries were roofed by series of transverse barrel vaults, and the interior was thus similar in appearance as well as in scale and proportions to St James, Piccadilly, but twice as many bays in length (Fig. 7F, Plates 64, 65). Later in life Wren specified St James as one of his most successful auditories, not least as good value for money, and this resemblance clarifies his conception of a cathedral in 1669–70. In essence it is two distinct but connected buildings, a domed space for beauty and the honour of the City, and an enlargement and adaptation of a parish church for use. However, if the First Model anticipates St James (begun 1676) and practically all the churches, in turn it derives from the Sheldonian.

But the First Model also marks identifiably a development in Wren's conception of space. The imagining of the London plan, and the contemplation of old St Paul's and its problems no doubt contributed to this development as well as the gradual working in his mind of some of his experiences in Paris. The First Model is still composed of disparate parts, inside and outside, but its interior would have been consciously spatial. In the domed vestibule this quality was inherent in its three-dimensional geometry. That the auditory was something more cohesive than the folded-up, galleried box of the Theatre resulted, with greater complexity but no less clarity, from a new understanding of the way space is shaped by solids and defined by axial lines. Auditorium and vestibule, though distinct, were linked by a common axis, and the vestibule though circular could be said to have a major axis, shared with the nave, and a minor transverse one from north to south. Within the auditorium the transverse barrel vaults were naturally readable at right angles to the main axis. Thus, with the height which, for vertical man, is the most readily perceptible dimension in buildings, the other two dimensions were co-ordinated throughout the interior. This order could be demonstrated geometrically in a diagram; in architecture itself it would be a geometrical demonstration.

In the light of this development it is proper to speak of the preceding works and designs as representing Wren's early period. Hopes rose that the 1670s would be a happier decade and that, in the architect's words, when 'a few years will rid away much of the private work of the town . . . handes and materialls will be cheaper', meanwhile a good design might 'encline benefactors'.[127]

VII   RESULTS

Of all the categories of Wren's architecture, the parish churches are the most elusive and least understood, though they receive the most lip-service as treasures of Britain's historical and picturesque heritage. In our time scarcity has enhanced their value, for of the original fifty or so less than half survive in any form and less than a quarter have not been more or less rebuilt. Successively the decline of the City as a place to live, the rise in the commercial value of sites, and the damage of the Second World War have destroyed in turn the need, the economy, and the very fabric of many churches; for several of the remainder transformation has been the price of survival. The least altered are now period pieces with an atmosphere that suggests the London of Dickens, with dark woodwork, mysterious corners and Victorian stained glass in place of Wren's 'stone-coloured' walls, whitewashed ceilings and vaults and clear glass windows (Plates 88, 107).

At the other extreme are the churches whose walls survived the bombing but whose interiors are more or less complete reconstructions. In some it was possible to reproduce accurately, from photographs and fragments, the original plasterwork and mouldings, but in even the most scholarly reconstructions changes have inevitably occurred in seating, lighting and the design of fittings (Plates 65, 68). Aisles have been widened and nowhere do the old high box-pews survive which originally formed, shoulder-high, the visitor's foreground. In some cases modern tidiness is a doubtful substitute for the rather 'hand-made' neatness of the seventeenth century, while the balance of tones in the finishing of surfaces and details is perhaps the most difficult quality of all to reconstruct since it can only be based, after three hundred years, on intuition and taste. In some cases detail has been simplified because it could not be re-created (Plate 92), while the urge to improve on the original with coloured windows, pastiche furniture and imaginative electric light fittings, although natural in a living rather than a dead institution, has not always been in Wren's best interests (Plate 102). Today therefore we are seldom looking at more than a partial survival of a Wren church, and the truth sometimes lies between what we see and the few really good photographs taken during the nineteenth century (Plates 28, 71, 96, 101).

It is possible to understand and indeed to love some of the Wren churches through the veils of time and reconstruction, but while corporately they are an achievement of genius not all were, or are, individual masterpieces. This leads to one of the two further difficulties in studying them as part of Wren's architecture:

the question how far they are all his personal creation in the way that St Paul's or the Sheldonian are. Our general knowledge of his activities in the 1670s and 1680s and the magnitude of the church-building programme would lead us to conclude that he relied heavily on the assistance not only of surveyors and draughtsmen but also of designers. On the evidence of drawings and Hooke's diary we can be more positive and identify Hooke as Wren's collaborator in the programme. Their approach to architecture was similar: Hooke had learned to paint as a boy before going, like Wren, to Westminster School, and at Oxford he came into the same scientific circle. In the period covered by the diary (1672–80) they were on intimate terms amounting to a partnership. But much went unrecorded either in Hooke's terse entries or elsewhere, and Hooke's presence may often be felt rather than proved. Wren also had the technical and administrative help of Edward Woodroffe (*c.* 1622–75) and of John Oliver, a glazier who practised as a surveyor (*c.* 1616–1701).

The final difficulty is that the churches have been insufficiently studied. Building accounts and other documents survive for most of them, and have been read and abstracted by scholars, but much of the information they contain requires interpretation if it is to provide more than the individual dots of a mosaic picture of the whole programme.[128] It is possible to say – though the published literature gives a surprising range of alternative dates – when a given church was begun, finished and consecrated; it is often difficult to say how far work had gone at a particular date, and impossible to say when the church was designed. As a general principle each one is likely to have been worked out as and when its construction had been agreed between Wren and the Vestry, because designs made in advance and laid aside have a way of going out of date both in style and in practicalities. On the other hand, a period of two years or so was not excessive or unusual between the start and finish of the preliminaries, and both Wren's mind and his office must have been full of ideas in various stages of development. Starting dates thus give only a rough guide to the chronology of design.

Statistics too are often more impressive than useful. Even in the true number of churches, about fifty, precision is difficult – and meaningless – since the number depends on whether we include buildings like St Mary Woolnoth, which was only repaired after the Fire (and subsequently rebuilt fifty years later by Hawksmoor), St Michael, Cornhill, St Dunstan-in-the-East and St Sepulchre, Holborn, which were largely rebuilt before the 1670 Act, and for which Wren may have designed little of the first two and only, later, the towers of the last two. Again there are St James, Piccadilly and St Clement Danes, remote from the Fire altogether but two of his finest designs (Plates 65, 68). The often repeated statement that sixteen churches were begun in 1670, the year of the Act, is also inaccurate, and less precise figures give a better idea of what happened.

In the first two seasons, 1670–1, accounts were begun for fifteen new churches, that is buildings whose structures were for the most part new although often foundations and sometimes whole towers and parts of outside walls were reused. St

Vedast was re-roofed at this time, but in the 1690s had become so decrepit as to need total rebuilding by Wren. Four more churches were begun in 1672–3; then there was a pause due partly to the temporary saturation of the building trade and partly, no doubt, to Wren's own increasing concern with St Paul's. Then up to 1680 another dozen were started as the earlier buildings came to completion, and new foundations continued in ones and twos until 1686 when there seems to have been a final group of six. By the early 1690s the Commission had completed its main task, and in 1693 Hawksmoor was paid for transcribing and engrossing the accounts for the Exchequer. However, not all the churches were then finished, and most of the grander steeples were added after 1700 (p. 117).

The order in which the churches were started depended largely on the initiative of individual parish vestries in arranging for demolition and clearance of ruins and subsequently going to Wren – or even inviting him to dinner – 'to put him in mind of building the church'; vestry records mention many such encounters. Wren's remuneration came, like that of the rest of his team, from the Commission, but there are also records of the giving of small tokens of gratitude to the architect on completion. He or his assistants also gave help to vestries in the matter of furniture and fittings, which the parishes had to pay for through subscriptions and donations since they were not part of the fabric under the Act. Wren's capacity here was thus merely advisory, and the design of woodwork was not his responsibility.

In an age of seasoned timber and good craft traditions the standard of finish was high; aesthetic excellence was more variable according to the talent of the craftsman and the taste of the Vestry. Such variations must also be taken into account when identifying the concept of a 'Wren church'; it is also observable that skills in plasterworking and stone- and wood-carving developed considerably during the last third of the century. Undercutting became first possible, then common and finally ambitious as both skill and vision changed from acceptance to defiance of the limitations of the medium (Plates 85, 99). These changes are also evident in the decoration, under Wren's control, of St Paul's (Plates 81, 82, 140, 146, p. 85).

Wren's ideals in the churches, once formulated, remained fairly constant, and the diversity to be found among them owes less to differences in date than to the variety and limitations of sites, the size of parishes, the choice of craftsmen and the architect's desire not to repeat himself. However, he seems not to have been unduly concerned with the basic geometry of the plans.[129] Nearly half have at least one corner departing from rectangularity, and this proportion is not confined to the earlier ones (Fig. 7). His knowledge of structures was sufficient for him to devise new buildings that weighed no more heavily on the foundations than the old; in many cases weight was saved by making the external roof and internal wood and plaster vaulting as a single integral construction (Plates 87, 88). In some cases the medieval builders had already had to work on restricted and irregular sites, and they were tolerant of irregularities even on open ones; centuries later Wren's site surveyors found very odd shapes in both the limits of churchyards and the plans of

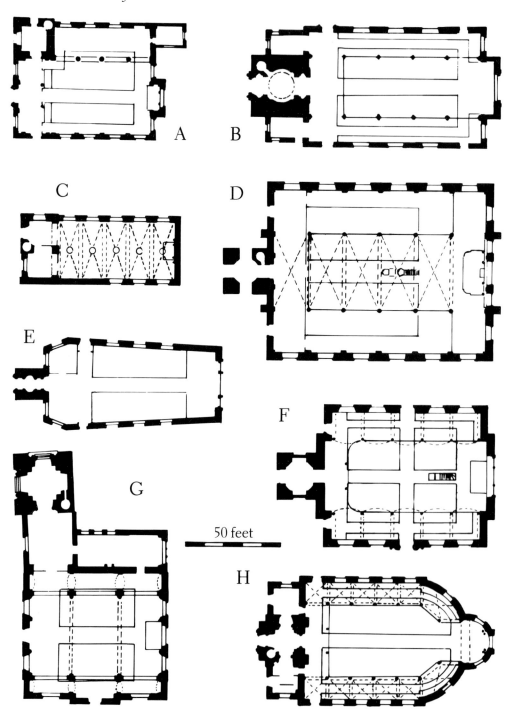

7   Church plans. (A) St Margaret Pattens. (B) St Bride. (C) St Benet, Gracechurch Street. (D) Christ Church, Newgate Street. (E) St Olave, Old Jewry. (F) St James, Piccadilly. (G) St Mary-le-Bow.

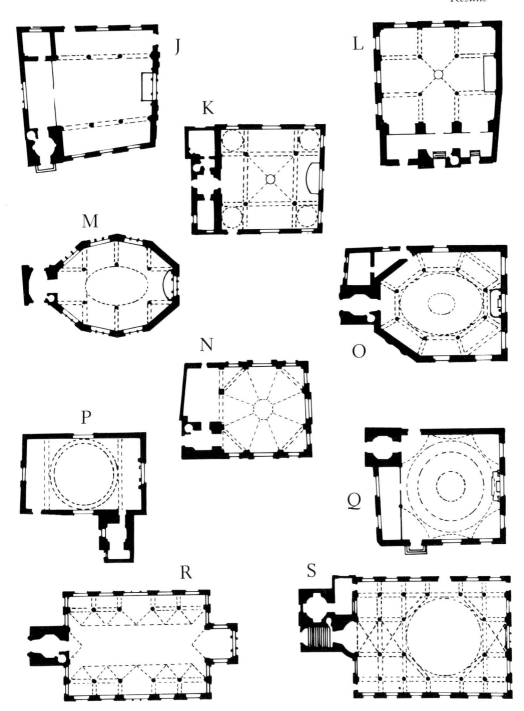

(H) St Clement Danes. (J) St Dionis Backchurch. (K) St Anne and St Agnes. (L) St Martin Ludgate. (M) St Benet Fink. (N) St Swithin. (O) St Antholin. (P) St Mildred, Bread Street. (Q) St Mary Abchurch. (R) St James Garlickhythe. (S) St Stephen Walbrook.

ruined churches, and where significant savings in time and masonry could be made by using old foundations he accepted the irregularity (Fig. 7E, J, M). In some, however, he compromised; at St Martin, Ludgate (L) he was able to restrict the discrepancy to one corner, and at St Lawrence Jewry, where the interior east wall is perpendicular to the main axis but the grand exterior elevation is obliquely set, the difference is only appreciable by comparing the thickness of the windows on either side (Plate 32).

There had been no comparable programme of church building since before the Reformation, and the requirements of the seventeenth-century Church of England were different from those of either the medieval or the contemporary Church of Rome. The importance in Catholic doctrine of the saints as intercessors, combined with the practice of endowing chaplains to pray for the release to paradise of souls presumed to be in purgatory, and the tradition of directing some of one's worldly gains to the decoration of churches produced in the Catholic countries that wealth of side chapels, mausoleums and carved or painted altarpieces which is still one of the mainstays of both cultural tourism and western art-historical study. Moreover from the late sixteenth century onwards the Roman Church's renewed insistence – because its rejection had been fundamental to the Protestant Reformers – on the doctrine of the Real Presence of Christ bodily in the Eucharist, led to an increasingly theatrical emphasis on the main altar of a church by architectural and decorative means.

When in 1711 Wren wrote[130] that 'it is enough if they [Roman Catholics] hear the Murmur of the Mass, and see the Elevation of the Host, but ours are to be fitted for Auditories' he perhaps underrated the desire for clear hearing and sight in the Catholic churches of his time as well as the new emphasis placed on preaching in the Catholic clergy's response to both the criticism and the example of the Reformers.

Many Protestant writers had discussed the form of churches, and some had recommended on acoustical or symbolic (of unity and perfection) grounds the round or centralized plan also favoured, for both symbolic and aesthetic reasons, by Italian Renaissance theorists. In practice it was more convenient to separate the clergy and their entrance, at one end of the church, from the congregation and their entrances. Moreover the Catholic Counter-Reformers stressed the alternative symbolism of the long naved Latin cross as the basic sign of Christianity; the nave of the Gesù in Rome, the archetypal Counter-Reformation church, is as much an auditory as Wren's First Model. Its short chancel approximates to a proscenium stage, and the rhetoric that boomed from the big sounding board over its nave pulpit was no less insistent than that of the Protestant North. Wren's larger churches, too, are basilican auditories (Plates 38, 65, 68, 70); like the seventeenth-century Italians he reserved centralizing experiment for the smaller ones.

In the tradition of Archbishop Laud, and in reaction against Puritanism, the Anglican clergy for whom Wren was working placed considerable emphasis on the dignity of the services in the Book of Common Prayer, and on a suitable setting for them. The altar (or properly the communion table) was emphasized by its correct placing at the east, by a rail in front of it and by a decorative reredos behind it carved in wood, inscribed with the Lord's Prayer and the Commandments and sometimes with painted figures of Moses and Aaron. In a few churches (St James Garlickhythe, St Edmund, St Bride (Fig. 8) and altogether more dramatically St Clement Danes, outside the City) the altar was further distinguished by being placed in a small chancel-like recess (Plates 68, 103, Fig. 7B, H, R). But there was nothing theatrical in its setting: the altar was not to be, as it is in the Catholic churches of the time, the focus of attention as the visitor enters the church; the six candlesticks and carved *Crucifixion* in St Magnus are modern insertions (Plate 42). As the pulpit and the baptismal font were of almost equal liturgical importance, the ritual organization of Wren's churches was separate from, and less definite than, their formal organization, and usually took precedence over it.

This vagueness of order, which those who enjoy identifying national characteristics may find a particularly English compromise, is equally far from the solutions of Calvinist Holland, where the pulpit was the main focus, often followed by the organ with whose voice the singing in hymns and psalms formed a dialogue, the congregation turning to face the instrument. Moreover the Dutch, extreme in religion and self-consciously new as a nation formed by emancipation from Catholic Spain, had little use for tradition. They adapted the big Gothic churches

8   St Bride. Interior before 1822.

brutally, screening the nave to form an auditory, and as likely as not replacing the high altar in the abandoned chancel by the tomb of an admiral. In new foundations they were inventive, with light, bare, regular and quite often centralized churches, either circular, polygonal or Greek crosses (with equal arms).

At the beginning of his diary Hooke was learning Dutch[131] (many a traveller has taken up a language after, not before, his journey) and his drawings include a careful elevation of the Nieuwe Kerk in The Hague which does not seem to have been made from an engraving.[132] Certainly he cultivated Dutch scientific contacts, and some of his independent works such as Bedlam Hospital (1674–6) show considerable Dutch influence; it cannot however be proved that his knowledge was at first hand rather than 'in paper'. Some of the smaller City churches, in particular those based on a Greek cross within a square, are too close to Dutch patterns to be fortuitous, and here Hooke's association with Wren was significant (Fig. 7K, L, O, p. 59). More generally, their discussions are likely to have contributed to the fact that in the first building campaign of 1670–1 Wren had already evolved the whole range of types he subsequently employed.

In both the initial group and the whole programme the most numerous were single-cell buildings, of the same type as Wren's Cambridge chapels (Plates 14, 15) or Inigo Jones's St Paul, Covent Garden. In number these were followed by basilican, nave-and-aisles, interiors, which account for almost all the larger examples. There were also half a dozen hybrids in which, to exploit an awkward site, an aisle was opened on only one side; the largest of these, St Lawrence Jewry, has a flat fretted ceiling with a main span of 47 feet which gives it great spaciousness in proportion to its height (Plate 32).

The two-aisled churches had either cross-vaulted or barrel-vaulted naves. At St Bride, Fleet Street, the impressive barrel vault is supported by unusual pillars composed of two three-quarter columns fused together – a device found in Holland (Plates 37, 38). Whether Wren designed these with galleries in mind is impossible to say. During 1675, when the church was virtually completed, the Vestry consulted with him about the construction of side galleries, and inspected galleries elsewhere before approving a design; they also debated whether to have the fronts finished in grained wainscot or white-painted deal.[133] The galleries effectively made dead space of the aisles, totally subordinate to the nave which, though only 28 feet in span, is one of his major achievements of the 1670s.

Galleries were a feature of many Early Christian churches, being reserved for women. In the seventeenth century they were provided in a number of Jesuit churches, but their function there was to segregate the novices from the lay congregation. Many of Wren's churches originally had a single gallery either at the west or on one side. The Protestant emphasis on preaching rather than ritual encouraged the accommodation of people in tiers, and Wren must have known the French Protestant church (or *Temple*) built by Salomon de Brosse at Charenton near Paris, which had galleries on two levels all the way round the rectangular interior. The extent to which a medieval church can be crammed with eighteenth-century galleries can still be seen at Whitby in Yorkshire; that Wren's method of stacking people was already spatially more sensitive is evident in the Sheldonian, whose formula he came near to repeating in the very large and steep galleries of Christ Church, Newgate Street (destroyed) which were used by the boys of Christ's Hospital School (Plates 70, 71, Fig. 7D). The loss of Christ Church, one of Wren's most lucid and rational spaces, is greatly to be regretted. St Bride survives, though drastically altered, since in the virtual rebuilding of 1957 the galleries were not replaced and the aisles were cut off altogether by collegiate-style inward facing stalls.

At St Bride Wren designed symmetrical side elevations (Plate 36) with entrances in the end bays, west and east; the eastern ones were subsequently closed up, and indeed with the introduction of the galleries they ceased to affect the appearance of the interior. In other churches the implication thus made of a transverse axis was more pronounced. At St Mary Aldermanbury (destroyed) and St James Garlickhythe this was done by variations in the ceiling pattern (Plates 41, 103, 116, Fig. 7R, p. 59). At St Mary-le-Bow Wren designed, instead of aisles, three wide vaulted bays on either side (Fig. 7G). It is characteristic of Wren's oblique use of Antique sources that, without the statement in *Parentalia*[134] that this was in imitation of the Basilica of Maxentius in Rome, we should be unlikely to recognize the borrowing which gave this interior its individual spatial feeling even when, as originally, the side bays housed the galleries.

Wren also knew of the barrel-vaulted basilica at Fano[135] designed and recorded by Vitruvius, and a Vitruvian precedent is again available for his Greek cross churches, of which the earliest, begun in 1670 but largely rebuilt and redecorated after a fire in the 1840s, was St Mary-at-Hill. The four supporting columns of Vitruvius's *cavum tetrastylum*[136] have some connection with Wren's Greek cross within a square, in which both axes have equal emphasis. Nevertheless, as has already been suggested, the immediate source for this type was in Holland, in the Nieuwe Kerk in Haarlem designed some thirty years earlier by Jacob van Campen. Wren only built two other churches of this type, St Anne and St Agnes, Gresham Street, and St Martin Ludgate (Plates 92, 98, Fig. 7K, L); St George, Botolph Lane (destroyed) looks superficially similar on paper but had the tower in one corner and a barrel vault establishing one axis. The form continued, however, to interest architects, and was the basis of several churches designed by Hawksmoor and Thomas Archer for the Fifty New Churches Commission of 1711.

There is also a small group of domed churches, of which St Benet Fink (destroyed) belonged to the earliest campaign (Plate 55, Fig. 7M, p. 59). In response to an awkward corner site Wren devised a decagonal plan with an oval dome carried on six internal columns. The dome was lit by a lantern and the body of the church by large bright windows on the seven sides that were not abutted by the tower or other buildings. Italian architects had developed the oval form in the later sixteenth century as a means of introducing both a feeling of movement and an emphasis on the door-altar axis into a static and unpractically symmetrical circular plan of Renaissance theory. Wren's plan shows his familiarity with Continental developments; it also reveals his characteristic tendency to reduce curves to straight lines and, in doing so, to produce a quieter and more static feeling than that of an Italian oval interior.

St Bride stands in the middle of a small churchyard but none of the fronts is visible from a main street; consequently all are articulated but very simply (Plate 36). Some of the churches were so hemmed in by buildings that their exteriors could not be coherently seen or described; indeed the majority were designed with one 'show' façade towards the street or churchyard, usually either on the east or the west (Plates 33, 34, 73, 87, 93, 94, 97, 110). In these fronts Wren experimented continually with the disposition and shape of windows, mindful always of the need to let all possible light into the building as well as to proclaim the identity and the dignity of the church. Some are derived, like the Oxford and Cambridge façades, from pedimented temple fronts, but many have a predominant sense of geometrical abstraction in which lines are based on grids in the same way that the internal lines of the Sheldonian can be reduced to a kind of scaffolding grid (Plates 25, 27, 31, 39, 111, Fig. 2, p. 38).

Only one church appears to have been begun in 1672, St Stephen Walbrook (Plates 43, 44, 129, Fig. 7S, p. 59). Since the building of the Mansion House in the 1730s it has acquired distinction as the Lord Mayor's church, but other factors gave it anecdotal fame in Europe during the eighteenth century. It is probable that its unique character of coherence, complexity and logic is connected more with the time of its commencement than with its location immediately south of the Stocks, one of the City's chief market places, which was embellished in 1672 by a marble equestrian statue of Charles II.[137] On the exterior the outline can still be seen of the north doorway Wren built to face the market; moreover, in 1679 when the fabric was complete he made new sketches for a portico outside this doorway. But other churches had equally important sites: St Lawrence Jewry for example, next to the Guildhall (Plates 32, 33). To understand St Stephen it is necessary to return from the churches to St Paul's, the First Model for which was brought back from Whitehall to the Cathedral Convocation House in or before June 1672. It had probably been lying unheeded at Whitehall for some time, for it required some repairs.[138] It was also out of date, for in the first quarter of 1672 Wren was paid for 'Directions in the Works, Design & Drawing several draughts of the Church and attendance several times upon His Majesty'.[139] The sum, £100, was considerable (he had received 100 guineas for the drawings for the First Model) and the designs must have been new (Figs 9, 10A, p. 70). *Parentalia* tells us that while there had been some criticism of the First Model as too unlike 'the old Gothick Form of Cathedral Churches' others 'observed that it was not stately enough'.[140]

'After this, in order to find what might satisfy the World, the Surveyor drew several Sketches merely for Discourse-sake, and observing the Generality were for Grandeur, he endeavour'd to gratify the Taste of the Connoisseurs and Criticks, conformable to the best Stile of the Greek and Roman architecture'. In historical

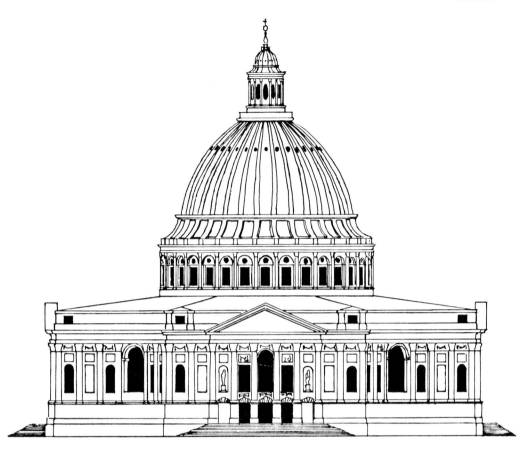

9 St Paul's. Greek Cross Design. Elevation.

sequence the design for discussion must have been that for a large Greek Cross, which exists in a set of meticulous drawings.[141] As probably occurred in the three-porticoed vestibule of the First Model, steps on three sides led up to temple fronts applied to the wall; the fourth (east) side was identical except that as it contained the choir there were no steps or entrance. These four identical cardinal fronts were linked on the diagonals by concave quadrants; inside was a ring of alternately domed and cross-vaulted spaces round the central eight piers which formed four cardinal and four smaller diagonal arches and supported a double-shell masonry dome. This design, as Wren's son was well aware, invites comparison with 'any Church in Europe', and in particular with the designs of Bramante and Michelangelo for St Peter's, and most recently with Mansart's and Bernini's proposals, under discussion when Wren was in Paris, for a huge domed Bourbon chapel to be added to the east end of Saint-Denis.

The Greek Cross design was no doubt made in response to criticisms that the First Model was too modest, but for Wren it also represented a new understanding of

65

what a cathedral could be: a building all of a piece, large in scale, unified in style and form and encompassing all the functions required of it. It represents a European building as no previous design of Wren's had done; it shows an increase in his artistic stature and marks the beginning of what might be called his High Renaissance period, in which the lessons of Antique and modern architecture, which he had so consistently and sceptically scrutinized and tested, were now assimilated and re-combined with his own basic principles of architecture.

By this time, too, he had had to think both of the spatial setting of objects and of the associations of Antiquity, in designing the Monument to the Great Fire, which was built in 1671–6 near the place where it started (Plate 83). There are drawings by both Hooke and Edward Woodroffe, the chief draughtsman for the Greek Cross and Great Model designs at St Paul's.[142] Probably Wren and Hooke were jointly responsible for the final design of a fluted Doric column. Preliminary designs included an obelisk surmounted by a phoenix, the mythical bird that rises from the ashes of its predecessor, and a pillar sprouting gilt metal flames. The choice of the top ornament was left until the column was completed, and Wren decided against a phoenix because 'it will be costly not easily understood at that highth, and worse understood at a distance and lastly dangerous by reason of the sayle the spread winges will carry in the winde'. He would have liked a large statue like those on Roman imperial columns but reported the King's choice of an object that 'would give an Ornament to the towne at a great distance' – a hollow gilt copper ball or an urn emitting gold flames. This suggestion was adopted; it gives a hint of controlled rather than raging flame but rather resembles a gigantic shaving brush.[143]

After the success of the Greek Cross design, Wren complied with the wishes of 'Persons of Distinction, Skill'd in Antiquity and Architecture', *Parentalia* continues, 'as well as his own, and made a very curious [i.e. careful] large Model in Wood'; he 'always seem'd to set a higher Value on this Design than any he had made before or since'.[144] The Great Model (Plate 46) was made over the winter of 1673–4, having been designed the previous spring and summer as a thorough reworking of the Greek Cross with the addition of those features the latter had lacked, a portico and an assembly vestibule. Both designs represent experiments in the process of creating St Paul's, but meanwhile the domed interior of St Stephen Walbrook was not so much a small-scale rehearsal for them as a symptom of Wren's developing artistic sensibility (Plates 43, 44).

The parish church's structural patterns were quite different, its dome being basically a piece of carpentry. Wren could thus design it with small supports, giving an unparalleled feeling of lightness of weight and brightness of illumination. He was able to make the eight arches equal and to introduce light all through them. Moreover, the geometry of St Stephen is perfectly regular. But what makes this church so remarkable is neither the delicacy of the plasterwork nor the accuracy of the angles, but the subtlety of the space which its geometry defines.

From the entrance we pass into a short nave of only two bays with double aisles, to face a chancel of only one bay on the far side of the dome; the main focus of the interior is thus immediately clear. But the space can be read in other ways (Fig. 7S, p. 59). We seem to be inside a set of pillars arranged on a regular grid plan, except that four have been omitted from the centre under the dome. Or again we may see a perfectly regular domed church, with four triplets of columns at the corners of the central space, but extended westwards into a sort of ante-chapel from which we can look into the central symmetrical space. The dome seems to rest on the points between eight arches and the columns below them; in fact there are walls and window arches behind these points, which share with the columns the function of support. These window arches are now the principal light sources, but originally much additional light came from the east windows and from the oval side windows which later buildings have obscured.

Even thus imperfectly, the flooding light and the interior it defines, clear yet capable of alternative readings, have an effect which increases in intensity with contemplation. The decorative enrichment gives softness and substance to the abstraction of lines in the most conventional of symbols: roses, laurels and palms. In this building especially, the geometry that Wren considered to be the basis of the whole world and the manifestation of its Creator, and the light that not only made visible the geometry but also itself represented the gift of Reason – light which was the first thing created by God – all fit into place like a mathematical solution. It is the strongest possible assertion of the true order of the universe.

VIII SPRING

On 2 November 1672 Hooke 'saw model of St Paul's approved by the king': this was the drawings of the Greek Cross design (p. 65), for on 8 February 1673 he noted, 'at Dr. Wrens, told me the Designe of burying vaults under Paules and the Addition of Library Body and portico on the west'. A year later, on 21 February 1674, Hooke was 'At Paules with Sir ch. Wren. Saw module and walkd through it': these two entries refer to the genesis of the Great Model design and the model itself.[145] The model then already stood on its high hollow base so that its interior could be inspected, although it was not entirely finished; the bills had not yet come in for carving and gilding, or for painting the inside and outside to represent stone and the lead covering of the dome. This colouring originally added to the realism of the model, which now depends mostly on its great size.[146]

The documentary evidence of this period (which is tabulated on p. 129) seems confusing until one understands that Wren was acting on several fronts at the same time. Thus only a month after Pratt's belated trip from Norfolk to criticize the First Model it was known at Whitehall that a new Royal Commission had been decided upon, not like its predecessor of 1663 to repair St Paul's but to rebuild it.[147] On 12 November 1673 the warrant for the Commission was issued; among various designs considered, the King mentioned one of which 'We do more especially approve, and have commanded a model thereof to be made after so large and exact a manner, that it may remain as a perpetual and unchangeable rule and direction for the conduct of the whole Work'.[148] Earlier, in mid-September, Wren and Edward Woodroffe were reported to be 'in the Convocation house, drawing the lines of the Design of the church . . . for making of the new Modell'.[149] But since Woodroffe had for the previous six months been drawing designs of the model it is certain that in the Convocation House that week he and Wren were scaling up for the joiner a design that was already settled.[150] Indeed, the accounts for the summer of 1673 included payment for scaffolding and a standard to set out the centre 'of a new dome'.[151] Subsequent site work up to June 1675 included not only the dome area but the digging of foundations for the east end.[152] But meanwhile Wren had been asked to think again: according to *Parentalia* 'the Chapter, and some others of the Clergy thought the Model not enough of a Cathedral-fashion'. Wren therefore 'turn'd his Thoughts to a Cathedral-form (as they call'd it) but so rectified, as to reconcile, as near as possible, the Gothick to a better Manner of Architecture'.[153] Moreover his attitude to consultation changed: he 'resolved to make no more

Models, or publickly expose his Drawings, which (as he had found by Experience) did but lose Time, and subjected his Business many Times, to incompetent Judges'.[154]

Both the clergy's objections and Wren's reaction were understandable. The Great Model was not only too European but too Popish, too close specifically to St Peter's, for some tastes; for others it was merely too far from tradition, while others again had particular reason for preserving the Latin cross plan. To do so emphasized the continuity of tradition and helped to identify the Church of England in the seventeenth century with the Church in England before the Reformation. From an opposite standpoint in the Rhineland the Jesuits built Gothic churches to indicate the continuity of Catholicism there. The Great Model had another potential disadvantage whose significance is stressed antithetically by the Royal Warrant for the design which superseded it: when work finally started in July 1675 it was on the choir of a building 'so ordered that it might be built and finished by Parts'.[155] This was impossible with the Great Model, which was essentially two concentric rings of massive piers and thus committed the builders to completing the whole or nothing.

Like St Peter's, the Great Model is on a superhuman scale: the first moulding under the pilaster bases would be twice as high as eye-level inside the church and twenty feet above the street (Plates 45–51, Fig. 10B). Everything else is of a similar scale, and as the shapes were kept simple and large and the detail unusually restrained the building would have looked its size. A scale which is constant within a building but unrelated to the human figure is a function of Classical buildings from the Parthenon to St Peter's and beyond, and it is significant that the Great Model is Wren's most Classical design in the sense of the word that denotes the balance, restraint, rationality, linguistic orthodoxy and ordered inevitability of the High Renaissance. It is significant too, therefore, that in subsequent designs for large buildings Wren looked towards more humane solutions to the problem of scale.

In dimensions the height of the main arches is about the same as in the present cathedral, and the total area of the church is somewhat greater than now (Fig. 11). Thus although the Model has no identifiable nave, choir or transepts, the four equal arms with the addition of the western vestibule could serve the same functions as the parts of the present building, even if all but the vestibule are read naturally as a ring of connected spaces surrounding the central domed area. Even parts like piers and doorways accord with the large scale already described, and each of the saucer-domed spaces is considerably bigger than an individual bay, except the westernmost one, of the present building.

All these interior spaces are connected, and each of the subsidiary spaces looks across the central area to its opposite counterpart. On the other hand these spaces are shaped, by the piers and the arches joining them, in such a way that each seems to be a more or less complete room, though not a closed one. Each can thus be called static, and their combinations can be called co-ordinated; this static detachment, Classical in feeling, gives little sense of the interior space as a fluid which can move

A

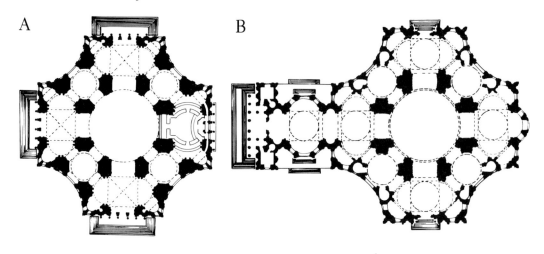

B

C

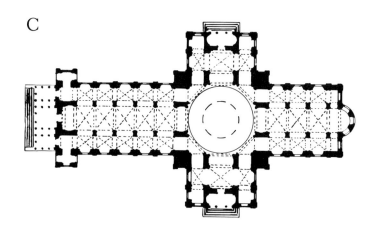

D

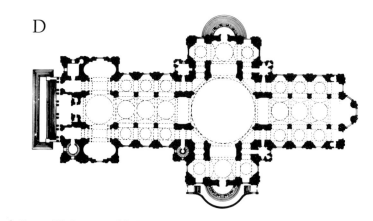

100 feet

10   St Paul's. Plans. (A) Greek Cross. (B) Great Model. (C) Warrant. (D) Executed.

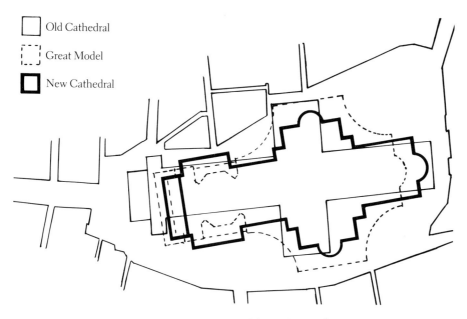

Old Cathedral

Great Model

New Cathedral

11 St Paul's. Wren's site plan, with the Great Model superimposed.

from one compartment to another. The eight piers forming the main arches (the cardinal ones larger than the diagonal) are so shaped, and so large in size, that they restrict views away from the axis shared by adjoining spaces, and make it difficult for any windows except the nearest ones to be seen. The piers in fact dominate any interior view of the crossing, which reads as a columnar rather than an arched system and comes to an end at the base of the drum above the entablature. Vertically as well as in the plan the spaces are linked rather than continuous: the drum forms a horizontal ring, and the hemispherical inner dome above it is divided regularly into coffer panels.

The exterior is also clearly divided into zones, but the outer dome is melon-shaped like that of the Pre-Fire design; in this case its shape was at least partly conditioned by statical requirements to counterbalance the gravity thrust of the two shells. In the main elevations Wren evolved, from his experiments in temple-front façades, a rhythmical system of larger and smaller round-headed windows which is applicable to both the flat ends and the quadrants linking them, and even in a variant to the western vestibule.

The Great Model remains as a 'perpetual and unchangeable' reproach for what might have been. But since it would have cost about the same amount as the present building it would have taken roughly the same time, thirty-five years, to complete. It is unlikely that Wren's resolve to keep his ideas to himself thereafter represents a new attitude to the process of design; he had not previously had the time for revision that a building taking so long offered. The 'perpetual and unchangeable rule' of the Model, which he had already recommended in principle before the Fire, would surely have become an embarrassment to him as he saw the slowly rising building with the ever-changing gaze of a fertile imagination. As a design the Model has a freshness and unity, a perfection which are partly real and derive from the same process of assimilation as St Stephen Walbrook. But those qualities are also in part illusory, because the Model was invented and built in a couple of years whereas the St Paul's we know took a third of a century.

The Classicism of the Great Model was not appropriate either to the designs that succeeded it or to all Wren's other work of the mid-1670s. It suited, however, two buildings related to aspects of the First Model but more sophisticated: both St James, Piccadilly, and Trinity College Library, Cambridge, were begun in 1676. St James's was designed to serve the new residential area of which St James's Square, developed by Lord St Albans, was the centre; the parish became a fashionable one and was able to afford a reredos by the brilliant though not yet famous carver Grinling Gibbons.[156] Originally the church had a doorway in the middle of the south side, facing a street leading into the square, and a corresponding north door towards Piccadilly. A cross aisle through the pews between these doorways marked the north-south axis, but in other respects the interior was, as it is now, a simple aisled nave (Plates 64, 65, Fig. 7F, p. 59). This is the church which in 1711 Wren recommended to the Fifty New Churches commission as convenient and economical and capable of holding 2000 people (which he considered the maximum for a parish church) though such a number presupposed the galleries filled and a good deal of standing room below.[157] On that occasion he was concerned to give practical advice, but the success of the design in his mind must have included its aesthetic quality. The barrel-vaulted nave with transverse vaults over each aisle bay repeats the formula of the First Model auditory. Hooke was apparently present when the foundation stone was laid, and one of the preliminary drawings is probably in his hand;[158] nevertheless the West End church's fine proportions must be due to Wren. The abundant fenestration and (since the post-war reconstruction) the gilded detail and whitened surfaces of the interior reveal as actuality what in the earlier project can only be imagined. The geometry is less obviously pervasive than in St Stephen Walbrook, far less obtrusive than in the Sheldonian, but the calm and order, the sense of immutability and rightness, become more insistent with longer acquaintance.

At Trinity College, Cambridge, the link between the Library and First Model is on the outside.[159] Again the proportions are refined, the detail is simplified and the design of the court front has a lightness that disguises the fact that it is a big building. The story may be apocryphal – although anyone who has sat on a faculty committee will find it characteristic – of how the Master of Trinity, Dr Isaac Barrow, set out the lines of the library: he had tried to persuade the University of Cambridge to build a counterpart to Oxford's Sheldonian, and when the project was 'wholly laid aside' he 'declared that he would go straight to his college, and lay out the foundations of a building to enlarge his back court, and close it with a stately library, which should be more magnificent and costly than what he had proposed to

Spring

them'.[160] Barrow was a friend and admirer of Wren: in 1675–6, as Vice-Chancellor of Cambridge, he was certainly scheming for a Senate House and library, for which some drawings by Wren survive.[161]

Wren's first idea for Trinity Library was characteristically novel – a free-standing circular domed building on a square base (Fig. 12). There was no tradition of round libraries, and the design seems to have been suggested by Wren's enthusiasm for domes combined with the image in Palladio's *Quattro Libri* of the Villa Rotonda, although in common with some other derivations from the Rotonda the library would have had one portico and not four.[162] There is also a Palladian feeling about the bare outside walls and the absence of surrounding architraves to the windows, though this might have been modified in execution. However, the design was not fully worked out and indeed suggests the ascendancy of a somewhat geometrical Fancy over Judgement. The bookcases were to be placed in a continuous ring starting above the door and ending under the lunette windows of the dome, but no means of access is shown in the section drawing of the circular reading room. If alternatively the books were meant to be reached from the passages round the outside the windows provided would have been quite inadequate to see them. Insofar as this design led anywhere it was to the project for a mausoleum for Charles I (1678) and, by way of Hawksmoor's projects, to Gibbs's Radcliffe Camera Library in Oxford sixty years later.

The final design for Trinity Library is the long upstairs hall of medieval monasteries and colleges, entered at the ends; only the north staircase and entrance were built (Plates 19, 60–3). We know a good deal about the design because we have what amounts to a set of specification drawings in Wren's own hand, including a

12 Cambridge, Trinity College Library. First design.

sheet with the principal details, capitals and mouldings, as well as a letter of explanation.[163] Wren asked for his original drawings to be sent back because 'in the handes of the workmen they will soon be defaced'; he is only known to have made one visit to the site, but the mason and later the joiner were sent to London several times for discussion and instructions, and there is no reason to suppose that Wren was not responsible for the minor differences between drawings and building.

As is often the case in Wren's architecture we have a first design that is quite different from the final one, but for neither have we any preliminary working sketches to help us discover how he arrived at the design. For the final one the process can to some extent be deduced, however, from our knowledge of the site and from remarks in Wren's letter. Grandeur was of the essence of Barrow's scheme, and the two-storey façade of the library, 55 feet to the parapet, stands well above the three-storey sides of Nevile's Court, whose original elevations were prolonged by eight bays to adjoin the ends of the library. Wren's letter mentions that the library floor is level with the second storey of the older buildings, but this continuity is only one of several reasons he gives for the ingenious disposition of façade and interior. Moreover on the outside to the court the continuity is actually denied so that the library seems to be of a quite different order, scale and entity from the rest of the court. This distinctness is emphasized when we look obliquely up at the side ranges and see over them the ends of the library walls and roof and the big single arched windows that light its end bays.

Wren expressly rejected the possibility of using a 'single' or giant order of which the most famous example was then in Michelangelo's side palaces on the Capitol in Rome. He did so on grounds of expense and proportion, but it was also a matter of his taste at this time. For a building in everyday use and the completion of a pleasant complex for scholars to live and work in, the superhuman scale of a St Paul's was not appropriate. The superimposed arcades of the Theatre of Marcellus as well as those of Sansovino's Library of San Marco in Venice have been seen as the inspiration of Wren's design, but once again he seems to have started not with a prototype to be imitated but with the task of matching his general conception of grave but pleasant geometrical architecture to the individual requirements he either was told of by the Master or saw for himself. His visually simple façade composition is only the basis for another that is both visual and rhetorical, both more complex and less conventional.

Classical aesthetics would require the inner bones to be expressed on the outside and the library floor thus to be at or near the cornice over the lower columns. Wren filled in the lower arches to make rectangular 'porches', a device of which he had 'seen the effect abroad in good building': French domestic architects in the middle of the seventeenth century sometimes inserted a mezzanine floor above the ground storey with its windows in the lunettes thus formed in the arcades. This infilling also enabled Wren to imply such a correspondence between skin and skeleton, and at the same time to bring the floor of the library down immediately over the openings. The ground storey he consciously modelled on the Greek *stoa* with a central row of columns 'according to the manner of the ancients who made double walkes (with three rows of pillars, or two rowes and a wall), about the forum'; he used 'two rows and a wall' so as to close the loggia at the back, that is the side facing the river and away from the court (Plate 155). Above this, the internal height of the library is not half but almost three quarters of the total, and the rows of book stacks on either side of the central aisle are continued at the same height along the walls under the windows; these are very large, 16 feet high or over half the height of the interior (Fig. 13).

The arrangements on successive levels of columns, bookcases and windows correspond one with another; the flat grids of which the Sheldonian seemed to be constructed here become fully three-dimensional, and this co-ordination of lines and dimensions is carried right through the building. In the original construction the ceiling was for some reason finished as a single plane surface; in 1850–1 the present fret pattern was put in as a not wholly accurate attempt to realize the original intentions shown in Wren's drawings. Even the back façade, which differs from that to the court, shares in the same bay-system of piers and windows. The court front is uniform except for the four roof-line statues marking the centre bays and the figurative relief in the tympanum of the middle arch. The end sections, as already mentioned, can only be seen over the side ranges of the court (which indeed are cut away behind their façades to admit light to the big windows): these sections were conceived by Wren as 'two squarer places' with '4 lesser Celles not to study in, but to be shut up with some neat lattice dores for archives'.

At the back of the library the divisions and the end bays are unobscured by other buildings. This elevation appeals more to modern taste because it is plainer and

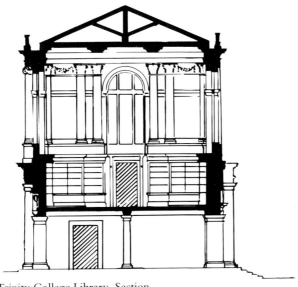

13   Cambridge, Trinity College Library. Section.

bolder, with single bands of stone between the windows instead of an order, and a large expanse of bare masonry around the lower openings (which are unglazed). The detail, nevertheless, is as close in feeling to High Renaissance models as that of the court front, and the method of distinguishing the centre and ends is as understated and subtle: the doorway form of the end bays, below the 'squarer places', is repeated exactly in the middle bay.

Yet if Trinity Library's exceptional economy and co-ordination of design embody to perfection Wren's High Renaissance phase he was nevertheless not a High-Renaissance architect; in European chronology he belongs to a late-Baroque generation bounded by Guarino Guarini (1624–81) and Carlo Fontana (1638–1714). Trinity Library has other qualities which, while a broader view of cultural history may identify them with the Baroque age, are in themselves not so much Baroque in style as characteristic of Wren's empirical attitude to invention and of that alternative to geometrical perfection which finds a place in his aesthetic: the effect on the eye. The marked difference between the elevations is one of those qualities. It is less brutal than in the extreme case of the Sheldonian, where the function of the interior framework is the only common link between the parts of the exterior; because it is less brutal we make a connection with Wren's greater experience and maturity in the 1670s. There is a common basis of design, visual as well as structural, between all the parts of the library; but it is far from the metaphysical ideal of unity of the High Renaissance. Each front at Trinity is right for the way it is seen; the court front is framed by side buildings and the beholder's interest is naturally concentrated between them; the river front stands on its own and needs strong horizontals to give it coherence and the appearance of strength, with the massive features of the end bays to support it like a pair of book-ends on a mantel shelf. The second quality, epitomized by the filled arches towards the court, is the degree to which the design depends on the illusion that the inside is like the outside: the geometrical demonstration is overlaid by the imaginative discovery.

Wren's long letter of explanation says much about practical details, like the use of marble to deaden footsteps in the centre floor and wood for warmth in the reading bays, and the design of windows to be rain- and even snow-proof; it does not mention, because he had probably not yet devised it then, the ingenious supporting system of tie-bars concealed within, and floor arches below, the book stacks. Although when this was discovered during repairs in 1923 it was considered to be still effective, in the opinion of the architect in charge of the building's recent comprehensive renovation it can never have been of much use.[164] The letter says little about decoration and less about beauty or grandeur. That in itself is not strange, for the drawings speak more clearly than words. It is far more curious, if it is true, that having devised, described and set up the experiment, Wren perhaps never travelled to Cambridge to see for himself the result. But that too would be characteristic of his confidence.

The library took fifteen years to complete, but its design, once settled, was not significantly altered. At St Paul's Wren continued to exploit to the utmost the latitude which, according to *Parentalia*, the King allowed him after the approval of the Warrant Design in May 1675 'to make some Variations, rather ornamental than essential, as from Time to Time he should see proper'.[165] We should now therefore return to the story of St Paul's in the light of Trinity Library.

It has been suggested that after the rejection of the Great Model Wren, in a mood of despair and cynicism, resurrected drawings made much earlier, perhaps before the First Model. But the drawings he brought 'again' to Sancroft in May 1668 were most probably the Pre-Fire design, and there is moreover good reason to suppose that the stated date of the Warrant design is the true one. The reasons for the difficulty have for long been first that it seems so complete a reversion to a Gothic cathedral in Classical dress, secondly that it seems to rely heavily on Jones's St Paul's – in the form of the portico,[166] the gable-ends and the nave and aisle windows, and thirdly that the Warrant is unattractive even without comparison between it and the Great Model (Plates 56, 57, Fig. 10C, p. 70).

But a reversion to a Gothic cathedral was exactly what Wren was asked to offer, and there was no good cause to forget either the architecture of Jones or the piety of Laud which inspired it. The brevity of the manuscript Warrant itself, which is in strong contrast to the long formal document approving the Great Model design, might indeed be taken to imply that it was considered, like the Greek Cross drawings, 'for Discourse-sake' rather than with the force of law.[167] By 14 May 1675, the date of the Warrant, that design must indeed have become no more than a discussion document, and it is perhaps significant that the drawings, with the Warrant stitched to them, were returned to take their place in Wren's own collection of drawings.[168]

We are left then with the observation that we do not like the appearance of the Warrant design with its tall pagoda-like spire rising from a domed cylinder which in turn opens out of a larger dome looming over the basilican outline of the church below; to imagine our distaste shared by the author of the design is easy, but hardly justifiable. Certainly the design satisfied all the requirements that had become evident in the previous seven years: a plan traditional in both shape and the way it could be used, an elevation that combined the 'cathedral form' with a vocabulary indebted to Jones and equally identifiable as un-European and un-Catholic. Its relative austerity was a Protestant virtue, but it had grandeur and scale and provided an identifying landmark for the City. Moreover it was capable of being built and finished 'by parts'. As has already been suggested, the revival of features of Jones's St Paul's could be seen as desirable. And if the design has a sparseness in comparison with either the Great Model or the present building the same may be said of the Cambridge Senate House and the round Trinity Library designs in the light of the building that followed them. While in the case of the Great Model we can only predict hypothetically that Wren would have made changes, the Warrant design's currency as an accepted project was a matter of only a few weeks. But it is possible to consider the Warrant design more positively. The crossing would have had a grandeur quite different from any other design. Of its eight *equal* arches, the cardinal ones opened into the vaults, the diagonals were closed by large coffered semi-domes. The dome above would have been modelled by the light from the eight big windows in the drum over it, and contrasted with the smaller hemispherical blind dome over the windows. Various surviving sketches, which it is impossible to place precisely in the sequence of designs, show nevertheless that the Warrant's reminiscences of Roman baths and the Pantheon are not accidental or illusory. It is thus unlikely that Wren made or presented the design with his tongue in his cheek.

The Warrant design takes its place logically in the development of St Paul's, for it was the last of a succession of returns to first principles, or instructive experiments, each of which increased Wren's understanding of the task ahead of him. The schematic sketch in the City plan (p. 50) shows the first fresh start with the basic elements of dome, nave and portico on a razed site. The First Model is if anything more unconventional, to such an extent that it has not always been accepted that Wren put the dome at the west end; this design, however, is (or was in the model) worked out in terms of the desirable and the feasible. The Greek Cross was a very similar exercise but as it started from quite different premises the results are equally different. From this the Great Model is a logical development, or rather a re-thinking, since all the pier shapes and most other details were worked out afresh. Up to this point the scope of Wren's brief had been expanding; with the rejection of the Great Model it was narrowed but also clarified by the specification, which could not have been envisaged back in 1668 by either architect or clergy, both of what it should be and of what it should not.

The process which followed was one of re-working similar to that between the Greek Cross and the Great Model. The conviction with which Wren must have presented the Warrant design soon gave way to a belief that he could do better architecturally – visually – within the latitude privately allowed him by the King. Soon the design had passed through the stage identified from sketches (by Summerson in a classic article)[169] as the Penultimate, and on to what might be called the 'Definitive' one – though designs given that appellation rarely remain so – on which building and a new series of accounts began in July 1675.[170] Wren found most room for improvement firstly in the dome and secondly in the relationship between this, the part about which he had always cared most, and the rest of the building (Plates 58, 59). The geometry and chiaroscuro inside the Warrant dome and its timber spire outside were no substitutes for a broad and lofty masonry cupola; on the other hand such a cupola needed massive support structurally and also visually. To secure the structure meant re-designing the piers, making the diagonal arches smaller than the cardinal ones, and in general altering the thickness of walls and the proportions of aisles. To provide a visually adequate base for a dome that is really too large for the building, Wren abandoned the basilican outline of the Warrant, or rather concealed it behind the screen walls that give St Paul's its all-round, two-storey elevation (Fig. 14). Moreover, a method occurred to him by which the physical length of the nave could be disguised, with more feeling of

14 St Paul's. Section through nave. (Left) Bay-centre. (Right) Pier-centre.

centrality and less of length (Fig. 10D). Inside the cathedral he did this by replacing the two western bays of the nave by a single longer and wider bay, so that as in the Great Model the nave and choir are of equal length with a vestibule or introductory space at the west end (Plate 135). On the outside also choir and nave appear almost equal in extent, since the Morning and Evening Chapels are built out wider than the nave and have a different pattern of wall articulation from the rest (Plate 75).

Consideration of both visual and structural requirements leads to the conclusion that all these changes must have been made during those midsummer weeks of 1675; moreover, the Definitive design can be exactly identified with a fine south elevation showing western towers based on Bramante's Tempietto and a cupola based on Michelangelo's St Peter's. The dating of this drawing has caused much scholarly controversy, in which irrelevant arguments have entirely overlaid the proper evidence: briefly, while the elevation, which is in Wren's own hand, is not itself dateable, another version exists of the dome only, in the hand of Woodroffe and therefore before his death in October 1675.[171]

The Warrant design certainly seems very imperfect in the light of the Definitive; the latter would in the ensuing thirty years undergo a process of change. As the building gradually rose, so did the level above which alteration remained possible and below which everything was fixed. In retrospect the design was thus not definitive: nevertheless from the foundations upwards it marks Wren's recognition of certain limits within which he would have to work. Most important of all were the statical limitations in the design of a dome that would not be finalized till the end of those three decades; as idea succeeded idea in sketches so did the rising masonry narrow the range of possibilities. The screen walls would play an important part in this process. Besides their massive appearance and the concealment they gave to the 'Gothic' flying buttresses of the main vaults, they had at least a temporary statical function (Plate 143). Ultimately the dome would have to be a balanced statical system, but domes can be highly unstable during construction and the lateral bracing of the screen walls was probably essential while the structure was unfinished.[172]

If the Warrant design is a characteristically novel Wrenian response to complex circumstances, the Definitive design is in many respects a Renaissance cathedral. It is the closest, in style as well as date, to Trinity Library. The long horizontals and punctuating buttress-strips of the Warrant elevations are replaced, in the two-storey elevation afforded by the screen walls, by a co-ordinated system of horizontals and verticals, in which the coupling of the pilasters and the resulting reduction in width of the bays between them emphasize the verticality of the building. The inevitable length is made up of many upright units, and the extent of the nave is broken by the projections of the western portion (Plates 80, 144). There, and in the transept ends and the corner bastions of the crossing, different window forms appear from those used in the side bays of nave, choir and transepts, although all belong to a common family. Moreover, as in Trinity Library, things are not what they seem to be. The bays of the screen walls are treated in a quite novel way, since the only function there for windows is to light the galleries over the aisles (which do not communicate with the interior of the church). Those windows are accordingly tucked in between the lower entablature and what expectation leads us to read as windows although they are in fact niches framed by aedicules (Plate 81). Behind them are unroofed spaces open to the sky. Here, because it suited his purpose, Wren used an Antique source, deriving the aedicule with a broken base from Serlio's reconstruction of the upper walls of the Pantheon. In Serlio such displacement of the proper order of elements could be described as Mannerist; in Wren, who was still making his own rules, necessity seems to have preceded invention as it did in the elevations of the Sheldonian.

The drawings of the Definitive design, of which several survive, do not show the rustication with which all the plain sections of wall were finished (Plate 58). It is not unknown in this period for rustication to be omitted from a drawing for economy in draughtsmanship,[173] but since the drawings are otherwise very highly finished it is more probable that the rustication was introduced in the first of a number of changes designed to soften the lines of the elevation: in particular it mutes the impost moulding that runs from the apse windows at the east through the aedicule niches and across all the bays of the upper storey. This change must have been made very rapidly, since rustication is specified in the masons' contract of 17 August 1675,[174] but on occasion Wren worked extremely fast.

A rare engraving, which is now the only record of a lost autograph drawing, implies that the interior design was also settled up to the vaulting (Plate 59). It clarifies moreover the interior of the dome, which was to have had three shells altogether. The outer dome was to consist of two shells close together, of slightly different curvature, and the third internal shell was to be hemispherical and considerably lower, with a large central oculus. Below that again, and above the rectangular windows of the dome, was to be a rim concealing from the church floor the ring of oval windows lighting the inner dome.

In the Penultimate design Wren lowered and narrowed the diagonal arches under the dome and made them segmental instead of semicircular, but he also inscribed larger arches above them to give the illusion, to be seen in the actual building, that the dome is supported like that of St Stephen Walbrook on eight equidistant points. He introduced large windows between the upper and lower diagonal arches, reviving the system of lighting he had proposed in the pre-Fire crossing project. But the invention of the much larger and heavier dome and the screen walls meant heightening also the corner bastions of the crossing, on which the screen walls abut; the diagonal windows then disappeared into the quarter galleries within the bastions (Plate 52). The geometry of these structures is easily misunderstood, to such an extent that the quarter galleries are sometimes wrongly said to be unlit. Window-cleaning must always have been a problem, but each quarter gallery should derive light by two windows from the open areas that lie behind the screen walls. As galleries they have never been very useful except for the accommodation of floodlights and remote organ pipes. The illusion of equal arches, and the contrast of semicircular and segmental shapes, have been much criticized, but Wren's care in introducing these features and his persistence in retaining them suggest that he found them visually acceptable. Not only are they part of the engineering of the building; they also have a visual function in dividing the crossing into a vertical system of distinct horizontal rings or zones analogous to the division of the external elevations in both walls and dome.

The exterior dome is again shaped by the rotation of an arc of less than 90 degrees, but the upwards sweep of its rather pointed outline terminates in an unbroken horizontal ring at the base of the lantern (Plate 58). The effect of this balance would have been a dome full of majesty and movement, seeming to float almost without weight above the body of the church; its reminiscence of Michelangelo's St Peter's would have shown all the grace of the latter but none of its tensions. In the end Wren chose otherwise, but to regret that he did so is the easier because the smaller version of this dome he designed three years later was never realized either (Plate 74). In 1678 Parliament voted £70,000 for a mausoleum for Charles I to stand east of St George's Chapel at Windsor, but the money was never raised. Wren made a design and estimate, for a circular building indebted to both Michelangelo's dome and the Tempietto, an apt prototype for a martyr's shrine. The mausoleum was to be set in a shallow moat and to be embellished with allegorical figures; the inner face of the double-shell dome was to be painted, and according to *Parentalia* the walls were to be lined in black, white and coloured marble with gilt bronze capitals.[175]

One soaring structure was both designed and built in this period and still brightens the London sky: the steeple of St Mary-le-Bow (Plates 39, 126). The spire as a form was one of the Gothic period's greatest contributions to architecture, which ever since has symbolized human aspiration for the divine, the heavenly and the infinite. When in the middle of the fifteenth century Alberti wrote his book on architecture to remedy the deficiencies of Vitruvius, he was faced with the problem of reconciling the verticalism of a form unknown to the Romans with Classical architecture to remedy the deficiencies of Vitruvius, he was faced with the problem the spire or steeple as a stack of little temples.[176] Wren first designed for St Mary-le-Bow a domed 'pepper-pot' above the belfry,[177] but the steeple built in 1676–80, after the church was finished, is a far more elegant realization of Alberti's formula. The corner pinnacles above the tower, composed of four scrolls leaning together, recall the medieval tower in which a little lantern was carried on four flying buttresses, the Bows of the church; the accounts use the same name for the scrolls higher up in Wren's steeple between the circular stage and the square one above it. If those were Wren's inspiration, what he made of them was so successful because he understood that a sequence of distinct storeys can be made seemingly to flow, by continuity of line, both in the profile of the spire against the sky and in the placing of the elements – columns, scrolls and corners – which make that profile.

In the conduct of the work at St Paul's Wren also set out limitations of an altogether different kind. *Parentalia* reminds us that the cathedral was designed by one architect and built in his lifetime,[178] and the way in which building proceeded can only be explained by Wren's distrust of the Warrant's phrase 'so ordered that it might be built and finished by parts'. The choir – which by tradition was always built first – might be finished alone and further building left for another day, another architect, perhaps for ever. The best insurance against this event was to start building as soon as possible over the widest possible area. Thus as early as March 1676 contracts were made for the western piers of the dome, and during 1677 work began on the transept ends and in the following year on the nave. Foundations were laid for a west front in 1684 though its design was still uncertain. Yet the choir was not opened until 1697; by then the abandonment of any part of the cathedral would have appeared a reproach to the nation and a mockery to the world, although still not an impossibility.

IX SUMMER

The success of Wren's resolve not to exhibit his ideas after the rejection of the Great Model is shown by the failure of contemporary prints to show – as they claimed to do – what the cathedral was going to look like. Seventeenth-century scaffolding, like that still used in some parts of the world, consisted of wooden poles covered with wattle screens; it effectively wrapped up the growing building from view, and the printmakers in search of 'exclusive' news were reduced to trying to relate what they could recover from the Great Model to what they could glimpse through chinks in the screens.[179] The developments discussed in the preceding pages were indeed known to few, if any, outside Wren's intimate circle; to the rest of the world the changes were a matter of curiosity, not of right to knowledge, and in Wren's behaviour there was no deceit. It is appropriate to turn for the moment from the cathedral inside its chrysalis to other works contemporary with its first fifteen years of growth.

The accidents of opportunity rather than personal choice account for the diversity of style and scale in Wren's work in the 1680s: in style it ranges from Classical through the vernacular to Gothic revival, and in scale from the domestic almost to the imperial. In a society in which superfluity of churches was the norm, Wren's achievement as a religious architect was unique and the result of unforeseen disaster. In the context of the chronic financial difficulties of the Stuart dynasty the large scale of the secular works entrusted to him by three successive sovereigns is only a little less remarkable; on the other hand those works all bear the marks of economy in either their materials or their execution.

Chelsea Hospital was founded in 1682 by Charles II, and there is no substance in the story connecting Nell Gwyn with the project. Charles's decision to keep a regular army – even against the will of Parliament – gave him some obligation to provide for pensioners; in meeting this obligation his motives included not only a desire to keep his army's goodwill but also the particular concern of Sir Stephen Fox, former Paymaster to the army, whose philanthropic interest went so far as buying the site himself for the purpose from the Royal Society.[180] Moreover the King was spurred by example in both France and Ireland. In 1680 the Duke of Ormonde, Viceroy of Ireland, founded Kilmainham Hospital near Dublin, designed by Wren's Irish counterpart William Robinson. Both Kilmainham and Chelsea, however, are based in concept on the Invalides founded in 1670 by Louis XIV, and when the Duke of Monmouth wrote to the French minister Louvois in

1677 asking for drawings of that building – which were sent[181] the following year – the prospects of both Kilmainham and a similar building near London were under discussion. But whereas Libéral Bruant's Invalides is all of stone, Chelsea is of brick except for the frontispieces; it is also smaller and consisted in the original plan of a single three-sided court 300 by 230 feet which has come to be known as Figure Court from Grinling Gibbons's statue of the founder which stands in its centre (Plates 114, 115, 154). The brickwork was completed by 1685, and the following year James II authorized the addition of open courts to the west and east (Plate 113). Although a set of drawings of the Invalides remained in Wren's possession the resemblance between Chelsea and the sequence of courts that make up the Parisian building lies not architecturally, in either elevations or plan, but in the intention behind the buildings and the basic form of large blocks with wards on several floors. Wren also had the close example of Hooke's Bedlam Hospital (1674–6) whose single long line of two-storey blocks punctuated by taller pavilions set new standards for the admission of light and fresh air into institutional buildings.

The warm brickwork, creamy frontispieces and large windows (originally casements, not sashes) soften and brighten the effect of what is basically a large barrack-like building of three storeys with attic accommodation in the high-pitched roof. The elevations in the main resemble the domestic street architecture of post-Fire London. Brick was cheaper, quicker and less pretentious than stone, and the roofs contravene Wren's own opinion in *Tract I* that public buildings should have flat roofs or domes.

Nevertheless neither the size nor the scale of Chelsea is domestic, and both are new in Wren's work and in English architecture. Hatton's *New View of London* (1708) comments that the Royal Hospital 'would be taken by strangers rather for the Palace of a Prince than a habitation for Pensioners'.[182] While individual windows in Figure Court are of human scale their thirty-bay repetition along the sides demands another scale altogether, which Wren attempted to provide in the Portland stone frontispieces, appropriately Doric for a soldierly building (p. 88). These essentially decorative elements are related to the scale of the whole, rather than to the parts, or to the human occupants, and they also serve to unite the three-storey side elevations with the two-storey system of the centre block which contains the hall and chapel. Their giant pilasters and columns, their colour and their strong and compact shapes allow the eye to read them as units and therefore to read the brick elevations also as large units rather than as accretions of many single bays. At Trinity College Wren had expressly rejected the giant order (p. 74); at Chelsea it was the only possible means of reconciling the architectural to the human scale. Its selective use, only in the centre of each internal and external elevation, is similar to Webb's solution twenty years earlier at Greenwich; Webb's projected complete palace there would, like Chelsea, have been a three-sided court open to the Thames, with a central portico leading to a vestibule (Fig. 18, p. 107). Another of Webb's projects, made for Whitehall in the 1660s and with some features in common with Wren's 1664 project (p. 43), probably suggested the placing of hall and chapel on either side of the vestibule.[183] Instead of a dome, Wren had hoped at Chelsea to re-erect one of Jones's west towers from St Paul's (Fig. 21A, p. 115), but whereas in Wren's mind respect for a work of his predecessor would have preserved it, in the view of the clergy respect for a consecrated structure apparently required its demolition rather than secular re-use.[184]

In design and application the giant frontispieces of Chelsea are no less pragmatical than the elements of the Sheldonian. As in that building things are *made* to work; as in Wren's reconstruction of the Mausoleum (p. 41) 'the Ordinance falls out wonderfully'. The north and south porticos between hall and chapel are generally admired, but critics have found the pilastered side frontispieces embarrassing to explain. Into these features, flat towards the court but projecting on the outer elevations to contain the lavatories, Wren incorporated the general window pattern in such a way as to conflict with the logical visual structure of a Classical portico. In the side bays the third-storey windows are so crowded under the entablature that they are exceptionally short, whereas in the middle bay the entablature is broken to allow the window at its full height. At the same time a balustrade immediately above the door echoes those in similar positions at the extremities of the elevation. In a Doric portico each member fulfils a visual function and expresses what was originally a structural one: thus a pilaster expresses the load-bearing function of a column but carries little weight, being only a thickening of the wall. Wren on the whole made the domestic pattern of the windows subordinate to the expressive stately pattern of the temple-front; in the middle bay, however, both the windows and the Doric order are subordinate to a larger, more abstract, pattern in which the whole wall except the top of the pediment breaks back to make a vertical accent as high as the roof-top. The dominance of geometrical abstraction over Vitruvian rules is also evident in the lantern, where the lower windows are inserted into the plinth under the upper ones, in the same way that windows were earlier inserted under the niches in the screen-wall aedicules at St Paul's (p. 80).

The larger-scale running together of Classical elements too has a contemporary parallel at St Paul's in the decoration of the transept ends, which was being carried out by 1683. In the 'Definitive' drawing (p. 79) the pilasters in the upper storey are clearly defined against the wall surface, and the areas of relief decoration are distinctly framed. In the building, however, Wren's favourite device of a false frieze between the capitals has become so rich that the capitals almost fuse into a single horizontal band of relief; moreover the effect of fusion is increased by the extension of carved enrichment through the shafts of the pilasters on either side of the central window (Plate 79). The eye therefore reads the whole upper part of the transept end as a single unit and does not without conscious effort distinguish the parts of the decoration. The floral panels in the imposts of the nave arcades, too, show a change from the choir (Plate 134), where they look like festoons, to the nave (Plate 139) where they are more freely composed.

At Chelsea the grandest of the interiors are the vestibule, with its smaller Doric pilaster order wrapped round the walls and an octagonal brick cone supporting the lantern, and the chapel to the east (Plates 167, 69). The hall with its flat ceiling is a plain room with the primary function of a dining room. The chapel's plaster barrel-vault comes down to arches over the windows – a single row of round-headed ones on either side, as in the hall – and is very like the nave without the aisles of St Clement Danes (p. 90) which is contemporary with it. The apsidal east end contains a simple wooden reredos and panelling; early in the eighteenth century its semi-dome was painted with the *Resurrection* by Sebastiano Ricci.

The ward blocks show Wren's practical side. They run the length of each floor on either side of a central wall, and each ward is divided into cubicles by wooden partitions and curtains, with gates opening into a corridor on the window side. Thus each pensioner had both ample light and freedom from draughts, both the feeling of community to which the professional soldier is used and the opportunity for a measure of privacy when he desired it (Plate 112).

While work proceeded at Chelsea, at Winchester Charles II's new palace was begun early in 1683 (Plate 160). The King was anxious for work to be as rapid as possible, and when he died on 6 February 1685 the main block was roofed and the plasterer's contract signed. The domed vestibule and hexastyle portico, however, were scarcely begun, and the six marble columns given by the Duke of Tuscany cannot have been intended for the portico.[185] The latter is now known to have been designed as an upward but not an outward extension of a one-storey colonnade similar to that fronting the hall and chapel at Chelsea. That is to say, the portico was to be applied to the front of the upper floor, which was to rest on the colonnade. The palace was virtually abandoned on Charles's death, although succeeding monarchs considered completing it; it was later finished as a barracks, and burned down in 1894. A model had been made but seems to have soon been lost, and surviving prints and drawings of the building are unreliable and contradictory.

However it is possible to say that in plan Winchester looked back not only to Webb's designs for Whitehall and Greenwich and across to Chelsea, with which it shared the medium of brick with stone dressings, an intermittent giant order and a central vestibule, but also as far away as the Versailles of Louis XIV, in the way in which its court widened in a series of setbacks leading to the base court facing the city. But whereas the central upper room at Versailles was the king's bedroom, in which every day of his reign officially began, the central room of Winchester was to comprise the staircase hall. A preliminary list of rooms shows that Wren intended to provide apartments for the King and Queen and the Duke and Duchess of York, and that the King's Side was to incorporate council rooms; attempts to establish a final disposition of rooms have been unsuccessful, but an interesting feature of the ground floor plan – therefore beneath the state rooms – was the continuation of the colonnade to form an internal corridor the whole width of the palace.

Chelsea is less 'modern' than Winchester according to Wren's own theoretical norm, because it rises to a pitched roof whereas Winchester had a horizontal parapet with a dome which was almost certainly to be a square-plan 'Mansard' one of the French type. But there were strong reasons of both economy and status for this difference, which is one between the palace of a ruler and the home of his retired subjects: Charles could not afford, either financially or politically, the range of architectural advertisement of monarchy at the disposal of his cousin in France. Nevertheless Winchester, which can now only be imagined by reference to Chelsea, was large in scale as well as dimensions, and the experience of its design was to be of service to Wren when Hampton Court was commissioned from him (p. 95). Chelsea on the other hand was succeeded by the rebuilding, for James II in 1685–7, of the Privy Gallery range which was by then probably the most irregular part of Whitehall Palace.[187] Apart from the Tudor hall and chapel and Jones's Banqueting House, Whitehall appeared to consist on the outside mostly of single and terrace houses of varying degrees of modernity in finish from timber-framing and tile-hanging to brick with dormered roofs. The new range was in the last category (Plate 161). Its life was short, since it was totally destroyed in the fire of 1698, but architecturally – even politically – its significance was considerable. Besides a new gallery and council room it contained James's Catholic Chapel and a staircase; the Chapel will be described later (p. 92). The stairs rose round the walls of a square cage lit by a glazed wooden roof lantern and not only led to the main floor of the new range and the chapel gallery but also, for the only time in its history, gave an adequate entrance to the Banqueting House through a door pierced behind the original (and present) position of the throne. It seems that the panels of Rubens's ceiling were turned round, after their first restoration in 1686–8, to read from this doorway; after the 1698 fire, in which the Banqueting House was saved, the door was sealed up and in 1973 the ceiling was finally restored to its original arrangement.[188]

Wren was probably responsible for the insertion of sash windows in the Banqueting House after the fire. Sashes were increasingly used from the early 1670s, although their cost and complexity made them a sign of status as well as modernity. It is tempting to suppose that they were among the inventions for the improvement of building that came from the early Royal Society, but if their inventor wrote a specification it has not survived. Besides allowing greater control of air circulation in rooms than casements, sashes made it possible to dispense with mullions and transoms and thus to provide the large rectangular windows that characterize eighteenth-century Georgian house fronts in distinction to seventeenth-century ones. The Banqueting House sashes are first mentioned in November 1703 when several were blown out in a hurricane.[189] The process by which Jones's building was modernized also occurred elsewhere – in Wren's Chelsea in the 1770s by Robert Adam – just as in the nineteenth century many Georgian buildings acquired a Victorian look when their small individual panes and glazing bars were replaced by the new large sheets of plate glass.

Wren's early buildings, and his pre-Fire project for St Paul's, had made no concessions to their neighbours; later on circumstances led him and experience equipped him to make sensitive compromises. Indeed, his sceptical (a Royal Society word) attitude to received artistic rules must have helped him to extend and widen the Renaissance concept of *mode*. Most cultures in history have reserved certain decorative or formal characteristics for particular classes of building. It is, for example, a defensible thesis that Gothic was primarily a religious style in the Middle Ages, and in addition medieval architects inherited from Antiquity a well-developed typology of buildings. In the Renaissance Serlio, developing Vitruvius's identification of the Doric order as masculine and the Corinthian as feminine, recommended such distinctive uses as the Doric for churches dedicated to martyrs like St Peter and St Paul – consistently disregarded by Wren in the designs for his cathedral – and the Corinthian for virgins, especially the Virgin Mary. Sixteenth-century developments in the concept of style, in architectural illustration and in the design of backgrounds for historical paintings and stage performances took place in parallel with the scholarly process of codifying Classical architectural language and the artistic one of enriching it through complexity and metaphor. By the last quarter of the seventeenth century it was possible for an architect anywhere in western Europe to be both knowledgeably eclectic and historically minded; Wren, like his pupil Hawksmoor and the Austrian Fischer von Erlach (1656–1723), was both.

Particular considerations of association underlie the style of several of Wren's mature works; the first is the Royal Observatory at Greenwich, which was built in 1675–6 for the use of the first Astronomer Royal, John Flamsteed (Plates 53, 54). The choice of its elevated site in preference to such alternatives as Chelsea and Hyde Park seems to have been Wren's: Greenwich Mean Time should thus indirectly be numbered among his inventions. Moreover, although the building was carried out and paid for by the Ordnance, not the Works, the royal warrant for its construction specified Wren as the designer.[190] Astronomy had formerly been, in his own word, his 'Trade', and he is unlikely to have taken less than a normal interest in the design of the Observatory, which he described in 1681 in a letter to Bishop Fell, the Dean of Christ Church, Oxford.[191] The site he chose was that of a disused fort on Greenwich Hill: if it occurred to him in 1675 that the fort was off the axis of the Queen's House and Webb's unfinished palace, the advantages of a ready-made solid and steady foundation must have outweighed the discrepancy. As a building, as a word and indeed as a concept *observatory* was new and no more specific than a place for observing the heavens: the mechanical dome with a steerable tracking telescope familiar to us was still far in the future. Wren explained to Bishop Fell that the Greenwich telescopes were used out on the terrace; 'the roome keepes the Clocks and the Instruments that are layd by'. The building 'was for the Observators habitation and a little for pompe'. Contemporary prints show instruments being used within the octagonal room, but its tall casement windows were certainly in part for observing with the naked eye and partly also, in the same way as those of St Stephen Walbrook, symbolic of the light of reason. The geometrical regularity of the central room, too, was appropriate, but the frankly archaic Jacobean turrets and scrolls above and around it require another explanation. There was as yet no image or imagery for a scientific age; Wren seems to have thought in terms of the summer-house, the philosopher's study and the fortified look-out, and the novelty of the science was perhaps better expressed by reference to Wadham (p. 29) than to Athens.[192]

The correspondence with Dean Fell in 1681 occurred because the latter had commissioned Wren to complete the late Gothic gate tower of Christ Church college, and Wren referred to Greenwich because he wanted to dissuade Fell from setting up an observatory in the tower. Apart from the look of it, for which Wren would 'for lesse charge than a pidgeon house provide all the housing necessary', vibrations made a belfry unsuitable for a telescope housing.[193] Tom Tower (named after the great tenor bell) was therefore completed as a belfry in 1682 (Plate 120). Wren more than once in his writings opposed Gothic to a 'better' (that is Classical) style, but his attitude remained flexible towards a style whose name was still synonymous more with barbarism than with pointed arches and ogees. He told Fell that the tower 'ought to be Gothick to agree with the Founders worke', but added, 'I have not continued soe busy as he began'.[194] His solution to the problem of finishing a half-built medieval edifice was original and successful. Whereas later Gothic Revivalists tried to find Gothic equivalents for the Classical orders or the statical system of posts, beams and arches which they embody, Wren started from the solid geometry suggested by Wolsey's massive bastions, and produced a bold simple shape, square at the base and rising to a buttressed regular octagon. There is very little of the 'busyness' of Tudor Gothic, and few of his buildings are such clear demonstrations of his feeling for simple geometrical forms. The fact that they are nearer to geometrical than to customary beauty seems the more remarkable when we consider that most styles of revival depend to a large extent on association either of ideas or of forms. His tracery patterns and mouldings are conventional, and Oxford masons, trained in the continuous process of recutting which Oxford stone engendered, were well equipped to realize them. But most of Tom Tower is composed from two motifs from medieval geometry: the octagonal plan of the bastions and the ogee arch which appears in miniature in their tracery panels. Wren uses the ogee both two-dimensionally, to complete the big window below the clock and to form the cresting over the belfry apertures, and three-dimensionally to cap the bastions, the corners of the clock stage, and as a leaded dome over the belfry. That Tom Tower is not 'like' any medieval building is part of its undoubted success; its geometrical origins are to be found in the 'pepper-pot' steeple he envisaged for St Mary-le-Bow but had discarded well before 1680.

Thirty years later, reporting on the state of Westminster Abbey, Wren told the Dean of Westminster that 'I have among the parochial Churches of London given some few Examples (where I was oblig'd to deviate from a better Style) which appears not ungraceful, but ornamental, to the East part of the City' – meaning London as opposed to Westminster.[195] At that time (1713) there were three of his Gothic towers in the City: St Alban, Wood Street (a paraphrase of Magdalen College, Oxford, added to a Gothic rebuilding), St Dunstan-in-the-East and St Mary Aldermary (Plates 119, 121, 123). The last was rebuilt at the same time as Tom

Tower in a Gothic style, supposedly as a condition of the gift of the necessary money by a private donor. The accounts were kept separate, but the work was in the charge of Oliver (p. 56), and Wren was surely responsible for the chief interior feature, the pretty plaster fan-vaults (Plate 118) in nave and aisles.[196] These are however not of the same form as the one he inserted into Wolsey's gateway; that of the nave is much closer to an earlier piece of seventeenth-century Gothic, the Convocation House under the Bodleian Library (1634–7) to which Wren had provided a new doorway (p. 36). In the nineteenth century the removal or alteration of fittings and addition of stained glass gave an increased but partly spurious Gothic character to the interior of St Mary Aldermary. The old tower was re-cased in 1701–03, with four massive corner buttresses and extended ogee pinnacles, possibly Hawksmoor's last design in the office (p. 118). The pinnacles were originally enriched with floreated ornament like those surviving on the east gable of the church, and the quatrefoil parapets there and on the tower originally ran all round the building. Wren's third Gothic church tower, St Dunstan-in-the-East (1695–8), has a spire based on the pre-Fire steeple of St Mary-le-Bow (p. 82); at St Dunstan the evident appeal of such a piece of engineering to Wren gave rise to several legends about his doubts or confidence in its stability. The Gothic tower of St Michael, Cornhill, was added by Hawksmoor in 1718–24. When Wren wrote in 1713 two other towers were being repaired with new windows and pinnacles: St Christopher-le-Stocks (destroyed) and St Sepulchre, Holborn. These were probably by Dickinson, Oliver's successor in the churches office and, through his work at Westminster Abbey, something of a Gothic expert.

One of the marks of a great architect is his ability to respond to the challenge of differing circumstances; nowhere did Wren do so better than at St Clement Danes, outside the City (Plates 68, 77, Fig. 7H, p. 58). His replacement for the decaying medieval church was built in 1680–2; the termination of the east end in an apse, a feature unique among his parish churches, was primarily a response to the site. The old church had a rectangular chancel, with a south aisle cut short on the east by the line of the Strand; in the new church Wren truncated both south and north aisles symmetrically, and by curving their ends and extending the altar recess as far as the old chancel he made the maximum use of the space available.

The interior is both elegant – Evelyn[19] called it 'prettly built, and contrived' – and geometrical: the convergence to the east in plan is very similar to that upwards in section in the Warrant design for St Paul's (Plate 57). The apse is semicircular with a semi-dome decorated, like the niches in the aisle walls at St Paul's (Plate 134), with a Roman type of lozenge coffering also to be found in Philibert de l'Orme's chapel at Anet. The plaster ceiling is decorated with flowers, leaves and cherub-heads, with a large royal coat of arms; with the apse it suggests richness confined within strictly defined limits, but much of the effect of the interior is due to its overriding geometry. The apse is framed by the broader curved east end of nave and aisles; this is perceptibly less than a semicircle in plan, and the last, narrowing, bay is distinguished from the nave by an angular change of surface in both walls and ceiling. We are thus made very precisely aware of the interior shape. As in two basilican churches of the late 1670s (Piccadilly and Newgate Street, Plates 64, 70) the interior elevation at St Clement is divided like the archetypal Palladian *exterior* (p. 38) with a main storey containing the order and a supporting basement half-storey consisting of square masonry piers clad in wainscot; the gallery fronts thus become an integral part of the elevation. The same system appears in two further basilican churches begun about 1685, St Andrew, Holborn, and St Andrew-by-the-Wardrobe (Plate 106), but its exceptional logic evidently did not appeal to later architects, the majority of whom continued through the eighteenth century to treat side galleries as interpolations between the pillars of the nave.

Since the aisles at St Clement are cross-vaulted the spatial effect is quite different from St James, Piccadilly, with an emphasis on the east end which is more theatre-like than in any other Wren church. Nevertheless apart from the eastern bays the church is basically similar in plan to St James. The difference can be interpreted as a dramatic narrowing of the structure of galleries, pillars and vaults common to both churches, and it is significant that the pair of columns that stand in front of the apse are related not to the curves of the vaults above but to the rectangles of nave and aisles. This is clear from the diagonal arches they carry; the arches appear to be canted, because they are oblique sections of a single half-cylinder, exactly as each of the other north-south pairs of arches consists of perpendicular sections of a half-cylinder.

St Clement Danes survived little altered until 1941 when it was gutted in an air raid; painstaking reconstruction, completed in 1958, has restored most of its original character, although the seating has been reduced to suit the uses of the Royal Air Force Central church and the woodwork is surely darker in tone than Wren intended. One other feature of St Clement is in later imitation of Wren: the pretty steeple was added to his re-casing of the medieval tower by Gibbs in 1719–20.

St Paul's was always in Wren's mind, but the small domed churches of the late 1670s and the 1680s were independent geometrical experiments in the form that so fascinated him, rather than rehearsals, as St Stephen Walbrook had been, for the cathedral. In St Swithin, Cannon Street (1677–81, gutted 1941, demolished 1960) a north aisle with a gallery was annexed to a square church with an octagonal dome and triangular corner ceilings (Fig. 7N). The dome was shallow, richly decorated with plaster relief, and lit by bull's-eye windows in the diagonal faces (Plate 93). The west, south and east sides of the church had large round-headed windows which originally must have given the interior the same brilliant clarity as St Stephen Walbrook. The north aisle and gallery, which were intended to make the fullest use of the site, were lit almost entirely from the main space; in comparison with it they were rather dark and patently subordinate. Wren by this time knew that light could be used negatively as well as positively in interiors; St Swithin's purity was damaged in 1869 by re-orientation and the insertion of window tracery and neo-Byzantine painted decoration, and the missed opportunity of restoring its pristine state after the War is the more regrettable.

Wren also used dormers with bull's-eye windows in St Antholin (1678–83, demolished 1875–6) and St Mary Abchurch (1681–7). Like St Swithin, St Antholin (Plates 89, 91, Fig. 7O) had a square tower with an octagonal spire, but of Portland stone instead of St Swithin's leaded timber structure. St Antholin was a revision of the early church of St Benet Fink (p. 63); again it was suited to an irregular site, and instead of a decagon was a stretched octagon with an oval dome. The formula of a dome supported on columns and beams with a continuous aisle around them is similar to the octagonal Marekerk in Leiden of the 1630s, and from Hooke's interest in Dutch architecture and his authorship of the polygonal lecture theatre of the College of Physicians (1672–8)[198] it is tempting to see his hand in St Antholin. On the other hand, the water-colour which is the best record of its appearance emphasizes not only the clarity of illumination but also the force of the network of beams between the tall columns, the walls and the dome. This church and the Sheldonian (Plate 66) seem to have come from the same mind.

St Mary Abchurch (Plates 100, 104, Fig. 7Q) is deceptively simple: a single square cell is surmounted by a circular cornice, to which the transition is made by a series of pendentives, and from which rises a dome with four windows. The surface of the dome in this case is part only of a hemisphere which would only be completed at the level of the corbels under the pendentives; the latter in fact are downward extensions of the same surface as the dome. How far Wren's feeling for geometry could on occasion be intuitive rather than reasoned is shown by the fact that, whereas in the classic example of the Pantheon in Rome the diameter of the dome is equal to the height from floor to summit, making a perfectly spherical interior, in Wren's church the sphere if completed would not fit into the space and its lowest point would come well below the floor level. The fine painting of the dome (probably by William Snow, 1708–9)[199] may not have been part of Wren's intention and to some extent obscures it. The wooden reredos, however, is contemporary with the building and is the only documented work done for a City church by Grinling Gibbons.[200]

St Mildred, Bread Street (1681–7, destroyed 1941) was a small rectangular church distinguished, like St Stephen Walbrook and St Swithin, for the quality of its plasterwork as well as of its organization (Plates 108, 109, Fig. 7P, p. 59). The central part of the cell was covered by a saucer dome on pendentives, the remaining spaces at the west and east ends by sections of barrel vault. Once again Wren made full use of the site and managed to provide a large window in the middle of each wall; that on the west wall was subsequently blocked by the organ.

An oval dome was probably considered for Wren's only experiment in Catholic church architecture, James II's Chapel at Whitehall, although the building seems finally to have been constructed with a depressed half-oval vault. The Chapel was inaugurated on Christmas Eve 1686 (p. 16) and opened to the public five days later, when Evelyn attended Mass there. James had come to the throne committed to returning England to the Roman Catholic Church, and on the second Sunday of his reign (15 February 1685) had heard Mass in his oratory at Whitehall with the doors wide open. Evelyn did not miss the significance of either that gesture or the more formal one embodied in a grandiose chapel next to the Whitehall street:

> I was to heare the Musique of the Italians in the new Chapel, now first of all opned at White-hall publiquely for the Popish Service: Nothing can be finer then the magnificent Marble work and Architecture at the End, where are 4 statues . . . in white marble, the works of Mr Gibbons, with all the carving & Pillars of exquisite art & greate cost: The history or Altar piece is the Salutation. The Volto, in *fresca*, the Assumption of the blessed Virgin according to their Traditions with our B: Saviour, & a world of figures, painted by *Verio*. The Thrones where the K. & Q: sits is very glorious in a Closset above just opposite to the Altar: Here we saw the Bishop in his Miter, & rich Copes, with 6 or 7 Jesuits & others in Rich Copes richly habited, often taking off, & putting on the Bishops Miter, who sate in a Chaire with Armes pontificaly, was adored, & censed by 3 Jesuits in their Copes, then he went to the Altar & made divers Cringes there, censing the Images, & glorious Tabernacle placed upon the Altar, & now & then changing place; The Crozier (which was of silver) put into his hand, with a world of mysterious Ceremony the Musique playing & singing: & so I came away: not believing I should ever have lived to see such things in the K: of Englands palace, after it had pleas'd God to inlighten this nation.

Evelyn's description is the fullest we have, though it can be supplemented by the building accounts.[201] The Chapel was basically rectangular with a west gallery for the royal pew, with an organ loft on the north. Hardly had it been opened than the Chapel was enlarged by the addition of a southern chapel above which in a second gallery was placed the great organ made by Renatus Harris with a case carved by Gibbons. Besides the mural painting by Verrio (in oil on plaster, not fresco) the decoration included altar pictures by Gennari, a wooden pulpit by Gibbons and the huge marble altarpiece by Gibbons and others. This had the life-size allegorical figures mentioned by Evelyn and also angels and reliefs, one of which had silvered figures; a great deal of gold leaf was applied to the details in walls and carvings.

After James's flight from Whitehall in November 1688 the Chapel was never used again. The fittings were dismantled; the case of the great organ, which Queen Mary gave to St James, Piccadilly, survives there, and parts of the altar-piece are at Burnham-on-Sea and Westminster School. The Chapel itself burned down in 1698; it is best reconstructed in the mind's eye, but while the loss of its sumptuous decoration is regrettable, its significance for the study of Wren was less architectural than historical. The same combinations of carved and painted decoration, interior architecture and illusionism, were to be found in May's interiors at Windsor, for which Wren was not responsible, and if May had not died early in 1684 he would have been the obvious person to take charge of the Whitehall chapel. Wren took upon himself May's duties, and while decorative ensembles of this kind were scarcely close to his conception of architecture as eternal and mathematical there is no reason to doubt that he considered – and proved – himself able to supervise them when they were needed. Earlier indeed, in 1676–8 he must have been responsible for the alterations to Charles II's Anglican chapel at Whitehall. These included a new wooden reredos (for which a drawing survives in the Wren Collection at All Souls) and a canopied throne with a cupola and a base supported by three life-size gilded boys.[202] Now, in the state rooms adjoining the Catholic Chapel, and in a new building by the waterside begun in 1688 and finished for Queen Mary (Plate 161), he had charge of the provision of painted ceilings and heraldic and figurative chimneypieces.[203] None of this work survived the Whitehall fire, but the experience of its provision was valuable preparation for the design of Hampton Court in 1689.

X AUTUMN

Hampton Court reflects perfectly the legendary British spirit of compromise. From the main entrance it is still the building of Cardinal Wolsey and Henry VIII with many battlements and pinnacles and spiral chimneys; from the gardens it is the chief architectural monument of the reign and the personality of William III. The King's desire for the grandest effect at both a favourable price and the greatest speed resulted in the construction of half a new palace and the retention of half the old, and the first rooms to fall to the breaker's hammer included those in the additional building at the south-east corner constructed for Charles II in the early 1670s and probably designed by Wren. William of Orange landed at Brixham on 5 November 1688 and on 13 February 1689 assumed the throne of England vacated by the flight of his cousin and father-in-law James II. On his first visit to Hampton Court ten days later he took a liking to the place, and although both he and Queen Mary found it old-fashioned they agreed to make it one of their principal homes. By April repairs and alterations were in hand and Wren was probably at work on ambitious designs for a completely new palace. By midsummer he had arrived, after a succession of different projects, at the final design on which work immediately began, and while from a much earlier date a great new royal building must have been a day-dream in his mind, within the specific terms of this site and this occasion all the extant designs were made within no more than three months.

The grand project, for which plans and elevation sketches survive,[204] would have retained from Henry VIII's palace only the Great Hall, probably refaced, as the centre of a complex of buildings and courts roughly 650 feet square, whose shape and size were determined by the Great Hall, the river and the line of Charles II's canal (Fig. 15). The courts were open-sided as at Winchester and Webb's Greenwich, except the one which was to contain the state rooms. In the final building the north-west half of the Tudor palace was retained, as well as the Great Hall, to face which Wren designed across the court a colonnade screen leading to the new King's Staircase (Plate 148). Two new ranges were built, the King's Side on the south and the Queen's Side on the east, giving the impression of a great block approximately on the site of the closed court in the Grand Project; the angle between these ranges encloses the Fountain Court (Plates 150, 164).

Even in its executed form, and still more in the first project, Hampton Court shows the full assimilation of ideas which had been in Wren's mind for some years. In his secular architecture the richness and variety of texture were new, but the

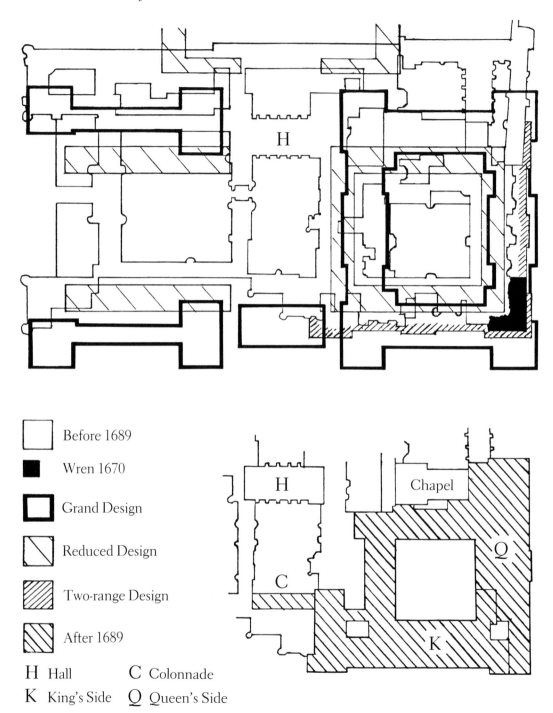

Before 1689

Wren 1670

Grand Design

Reduced Design

Two-range Design

After 1689

H Hall   C Colonnade

K King's Side   Q Queen's Side

15 Hampton Court. (Above) Grand Design (opaque) superimposed on Wren's composite of a survey (outline) and two different projects (hatched). (Below) Wren's executed building in relation to the old Hall and Chapel.

relative plainness of Chelsea and Winchester perhaps depended more on economy than on preference, since the concern with textures he learned in France was already in evidence at St Paul's. The giant order and flat roof-line had already appeared at Winchester, and the elevation of the Grand Project owes a good deal to Webb's Greenwich design. Nevertheless Hampton Court is Wren's first secular building on a scale approaching that of the Louvre, even though the closed court of the Grand Project would have occupied less than a quarter of the Cour Carré of the Louvre, and the executed Fountain Court is even smaller (117 × 110 ft). The south and east ranges form the biggest block, excepting St Paul's, that Wren ever built: 310 × 320 feet. Moreover, the presence of a scale man in one of the sketches for the Grand Project suggests that Wren was now fully aware of the importance of human scale in big buildings.

Wren's final design provided, with the minimum of time and expenditure, not only two sets of state rooms but also the illusion of a complete modern palace both from the river and from the approach through the Home Park from Kingston. We think today of those fronts as facing gardens, but a contemporary drawing shows a coach and retinue arriving at the east side.[205] It is unlikely that either Wren or the sovereigns were unaware of Jules Hardouin Mansart's enlargement of the Palace of Versailles; the Hampton Court façades are very nearly as large, both in dimensions and in number of bays, as those of the main block at Versailles, and rather less monotonous; the English palace, at a similar remove from the capital, must have been intended as the counterpart of the French. Although in the first years of his reign William III was often abroad in campaigns against the alliance of James II with the French, Hampton Court was hurried on under the eye of Queen Mary in preparation for the peace and leisure for which William hoped and worked. In his last two years he did receive embassies there, and though he died at Kensington it was from Hampton Court that he rode out one afternoon in February 1702 only to suffer the fall from his horse which brought on his last illness. William was not the boorish republican he is sometimes imagined to be, and both in form and in decoration Hampton Court bore his personal and regal stamp no less than Versailles does Louis XIV's or Windsor did that of Charles II. Moreover, William's passion for speed and his chesty constitution also affected the design.

Wren evidently concluded that half a palace was not the occasion for dramatic massing of wings and pavilions. Like the walls of St Paul's, the south and east fronts of the palace are essentially screens (Plates 147, 149). They speak of status, and by the differentiation of window size they indicate that the principal floor is upstairs; otherwise they imply little and say nothing of the interior arrangement. Some of the main rooms rise into deeply coved ceilings inside the mezzanine above, behind blind rounded windows. All the blind ones now have glazing bars painted on them, but originally the four nearest the centre of the east front were painted by Louis Laguerre with emblems of the Seasons. Nevertheless the façades of Hampton Court were sited, and their articulation devised, with considerable care, and sash windows were used throughout.

The dimensions and the placing of the exterior fronts were determined by several factors. The centre of the east front could only be on the axis of the canal built through the Home Park by Charles II in the 1660s, while the length of the south front was certainly related to the position of the Great Hall on the north side of the palace. Wren was careful, as he had been at St Paul's, to build his new façades outside old foundations so as to avoid uneven settlement. The main fronts also do not prepare the visitor for the placing or the size of the Fountain Court, neither of whose axes coincides with those of the fronts; in the court twelve bays are crammed into the width of nine of the fronts. The eccentric placing was chosen partly from a desire to demolish less of the old palace, partly in order to align the north arcade of the court with the Tudor gateways to the west; in doing so he may have adopted some of the lines of the old court. The crowded rhythm of the bay design was at least partly a deliberate contrast with the spaciousness of the exterior fronts. Wren had written in *Tract I* that 'In Things that are not seen at once, and have no Respect one to another, great Variety is commendable, provided this Variety transgress not the Rules of Opticks and Geometry'.[206] Recently cleaning of the Fountain Court has removed distracting soot stains and shadows and restored the original balance in tone and colour between brick and stone, so that both frontally and in foreshortening the various decorative forms are distinctly readable even though they are almost all run together: the triangular pediments almost touch each other and quite touch the lions' tails under the roundels, while the brackets below the main windows can be seen to run into the arches of the ground floor. In order to disguise the shift of axis between the court and the east front Wren arranged two apses inside the east arcade on either side of the court axis; one is blind but the other leads into the central vestibule of the east front (Plates 152, 153). He knew, at least from engravings, the common use of shifts of this kind between court and garden in Paris house planning.[207]

Wren's Hampton Court is built of brick with stone dressings; this mixture is sometimes described as an importation from Holland at the wish of William III, but it was already well established in England. The major factors in the choice of materials were speed and, secondarily, economy. As in the enlargement of Kensington House, which William and Mary had bought for a suburban residence soon after their accession (p. 102), a sense of haste was constant, which led to building accidents on both sites before the end of 1689. The contrast of warm orange brick and cool stone colours is nevertheless a beautiful one, although Wren started on most of the south front with a mixture of Headington, Reigate and Beer stone with some Portland, whereas subsequent work was mainly in Portland stone. The resulting asymmetrical variegation of colours on the south front, which has been retained in the renovation of 1970, was probably forced on the architect by the combination of the King's urgency and a shortage of Portland stone. In 1689 the French, at war with England, were masters of the English Channel, cutting off the transport of stone from Portland to Greenwich: at Hampton Court, a new venture, the effect was immediate, whereas at St Paul's work continued for some months on supplies already laid in. Wren was later obliged to use other stone, less noticeably, at St Paul's, but it appears that some of the blocks, delivered after the resumption of normal supplies, had lain for too long washed by high seas on the quay at Portland: the sea salts thus leached into those pieces led to their eventual ruin in the twentieth century.

Parentalia tells us that William and Mary were extremely pleased with their palace, and that moreover the King 'was pleased . . . to excuse his Surveyor, for not raising the Cloysters, under the Apartments, higher; which were executed in that Manner, according to *his* express Orders'.[208] This circumstantial account was almost certainly handed down by the architect to his son, but in John Macky's *Journey through England and Wales* (1722), which was known to the younger Wren, the plausible explanation is added that the King's asthmatic complaint led him to want as few stairs as possible. *Parentalia*'s phrase *not raising the cloisters higher* has been taken to mean that the level of floors and elevation was altered during construction,[209] but this tortuous interpretation is negated by drawings and accounts. The low setting of the principal floor was established at the design stage, and in the Fountain Court it led to the same kind of illusionism as in Trinity Library; at Hampton Court the arches are partly filled in by recessed segments, so that the principal windows are at a normal inside height above the floor. The inconsistency is not immediately noticed between the levels of vaulting, arcades, window-sills and our expectation of where the floor should be (Plate 150).

On the external fronts Wren adopted the Palladian formula of basement, main storey (with mezzanine) and attic, but he altered the proportion of window to wall. Palladian basement windows are normally small so that the supporting function of the solid wall is apparent to the eye. By using large basement windows and reducing the masonry almost to a set of piers Wren reduced the *visual* stability of the elevations: basement, main and attic windows are all of equal width. On the east front the effect is disturbing to modern eyes for two further reasons. First, the geometrical logic of equal windows is broken by the use, which seems to be original, of a different size of glass pane in each storey, with a fourth, extra large, size in the three lights of the central room (Plate 147). Secondly, in the frontispiece to that room the half-columns and pediment make the elevation seem top- and middle-heavy, and the dark voids of the three gateways to the court below leave even less feeling of support than the window bars of the other bays. The three big windows, moreover, were extended in the final drawings down to floor level, increasing the impression of a façade dropped under its own weight. Yet we tend to look at this elevation through Georgian eyes, and it is open to question whether Wren found it unsatisfactory. It is possible, for instance, to read the pedimented temple front as a motif applied *above* the basement, like the one which occurs on the upper storey of the Sheldonian (p. 37). There is a drawing for the Greek Cross design for St Paul's (Fig. 9, p. 65) with a very similar trio of openings between the basement piers of a portico,[210] and the same relationship of voids and solids can be traced back to the 1664 Whitehall portico design (p. 43). Moreover, a similar arrangement of the central seven bays occurred at Winchester (Plate 160) although there the pillars came down to the ground. Hampton Court belongs to the international Baroque of the late seventeenth century, and in common with many monuments of that style it is meant to be looked at in a single sweep of the eye.

Carving not only forms an overall decorative skin to the palace; it also emphasizes the person and the status of the monarch. Although it was central to the Revolution of 1688 that William and Mary were sovereigns of England by invitation and the will of Parliament, their title to the throne was by descent. William would have it remembered that he was a prince, the nephew as well as the son-in-law of James II and, like his Queen and cousin, a grandchild of Charles I. He was not averse to court ceremonial and court art, and within the financial limits set by Parliament he encouraged and enjoyed them. The richness of the Earl of Portland's embassy to Versailles in 1699 dazzled even the French, and Hampton Court was intended to do no less. Like several other seventeenth-century rulers Williams liked to match himself with Hercules, who appears in the east pediment trampling on Superstition, Envy and Fury (Plate 156) and whose lion-skin in Portland stone (Plate 151) frames each of the roundels in the Fountain Court.[211] Those on the south side of the court enclose not windows but the *Labours of Hercules* painted by Laguerre, now indecipherable. Over the gateways in the east front appear, besides the English rose and the Scottish thistly (Plate 159), the two snakes that were strangled by the infant Hercules, a Dutch emblem of liberation. The south front bears the sovereigns' names, and the keystones of the ground floor windows have their joint monogram, so miraculously undercut that birds nest behind them. This is the decorative language of Versailles (Plates 157, 158) and it was continued in carved trophies, garden ornaments (most of which have disappeared) and in painting inside the palace.

William was a soldier, the last English king consistently to lead his army into battle. Mary's taste was more domestic; she taught the ladies of the court to knit and forbade them to swear, and her special preserve at Hampton Court was the Water Gallery, a Tudor building by the Thames which early in the reign was refitted for her with a sequence of rooms, marbled, lacquered, mirrored, Delft-tiled and so on. Probably much of this work, which was demolished in 1700 to improve the view from the King's apartments, was designed by the Huguenot Daniel Marot.

When Mary died from smallpox on 28 December 1694 the structure of the palace was practically complete including the carved decoration of the fronts and court and the colonnade leading to the King's Staircase. Work stopped and was not resumed until after the Peace of Ryswick (September 1697) which gave William at least temporary security in which to think again of his favourite residence. By 1700 the King's Side was fulfilling its intended purpose, but after William's death Hampton Court served succeeding monarchs as a country retreat rather than a state residence. Since the reign of George III much of the palace has been used for 'grace-and-favour' apartments in the gift of the sovereign and the fabric and state rooms have received maintenance and, more recently, restoration. The state apartments are the largest surviving group of the English Baroque period, although they are not as sumptuous as the smaller suites in noblemen's houses such as Chatsworth and Boughton.

An estimate by Wren of April 1699 stated that the decoration of many rooms was 'long since designed'; several overmantel designs by Grinling Gibbons among the Hampton Court drawings in the Soane Museum were certainly made before Queen Mary died since they show symbols appropriate to the joint sovereignty.[212] Some of the plainer marble fireplaces in the palace, although not identifiable, may be those recorded as moved from Charles II's palace at Greenwich when work stopped there. In 1699 Antonio Verrio, the leading decorative painter of the two previous monarchs, returned to the royal service to paint the King's Staircase and two ceilings on the King's Side. The walls of the state rooms were lined with brocades or panelled, the fireplaces were adorned with carved overmantel frames of fruit and foliage to contain looking glasses or pictures. The tall gallery in the south side of the Fountain Court was fitted up with wainscot below and frames above for the Raphael Cartoons of the *Acts of the Apostles*, which, deposited in the Victoria and Albert Museum, still belong to the Royal Collection.

But Wren must largely be both dissociated from the splendours and excused from the deficiencies of the Hampton Court apartments. Gibbons's drawings already mentioned do not correspond to the work carried out in the palace, but at that time it was customary both for the architect to decide the location, extent and character of the detail and for the craftsman to choose figures, objects and patterns. Moreover, Wren's estimate of April 1699 was not accepted, and on 12 May it was announced at the Treasury Board that the King had 'appointed Mr Talman to have the care and overseeing of this work'. Talman was, as Deputy to the Earl of Portland, in charge of the gardens at Hampton Court, and on the basis of this and the appointment of 12 May he is often said to have been particularly favoured by William III. More significantly, he was not only a Comptroller of Works as capable, like May before him, of architectural design as of preventing irregularities; he had also by this time, again like May, a specialist private practice in the design of great houses, for whose interior finishing he aimed to provide a complete team of craftsmen and decorators. Insofar as a single mind guided its finishing, the King's Side at Hampton Court should be placed to Talman's credit.[213]

The carcase in which Talman had to work, however, had been Wren's responsibility, fitting in an enfilade on each side with galleries and private rooms behind them towards the Fountain Court. To the modern visitor the arrangement is inevitably confusing since much of the obligatory tourist route is at variance with palace usage. Even on a floor plan, however, there are confusing features: the south-east corner between the two sides, the less formal layout of the east side undertaken by Wren, not Talman, for Queen Anne, and the arrangement of the rooms at the north-east corner by Vanbrugh early in the reign of George I for the Prince of Wales, who as George II continued to make minor alterations until the death of his Queen in 1737. There is not very much to say about Wren as a planner of interiors at

Hampton Court; the complete palace he first envisaged, however, would have been very different.

The spirit of the Grand Project survives in the grid-like regularity of the elevations we see; here it is significant that the early sketch elevations were worked out on bays of 10 and 15 feet, corresponding in the one remaining plan to a grid scored into the paper with a stylus.[214] Moreover the elevations give enough clues to show how adequately, logically and symmetrically the King's and Queen's Sides would have been accommodated in the closed court. And here the council chamber would have been placed, unlike Winchester, under the dome in the centre of the west range, flanked by the two main staircases. In its regal planning as much as anything else, this Hampton Court would have rivalled Versailles.

Wren's work at Kensington House (later Palace) was far more modest. In June 1689 William and Mary bought the Earl of Nottingham's house to the west of Hyde Park as a home from which it would be possible to go for the day to Whitehall, which William found too damp for his chest. Work immediately began on enlarging and modernizing the house, built early in the seventeenth century, and over the next four years two new courts and additional pavilions were carried out to Wren's designs with economy (in brown-yellow London stock brick) and speed, not to say haste: part of the new building fell down early in November 1689, shortly before the more serious accident at Hampton Court (p. 18). Architecturally the most notable parts of this suburban mansion were the Clock Court (Plate 162) west of the main building (1689–92) and the King's Gallery block south of it (1695–8). The latter is in red brick and considerably more monumental; both in a preliminary design (known from a description) and in execution it bears the marks of Hawksmoor's style, and as he was resident Clerk of Works at Kensington this range would have been suitably, though not by obligation, deputed to him,[215] as were some private commissions of the early 1690s.

A country house practice would have been within Wren's competence, and the drawings in the collection at All Souls include a few house designs of great interest, most of them unidentified. Wren seems, however, to have considered himself a public architect and to have been content to leave May, and later Talman and Vanbrugh, to go their own ways in private architecture, and he was certainly not the inventor of what estate agents and popular histories call the 'Wren house', rectangular, usually brick-built with a hipped roof, and actually invented before the Civil War and brought up to date after the Restoration by May. On a number of occasions Wren must have given advice about the design of houses. The claims of three larger ones to his authorship must be considered: Easton Neston, Northamptonshire, Tring, Hertfordshire, and Winslow, Buckinghamshire. The evidence and the conclusions to be drawn from it differ in each case, and the first one's claim must be rejected.

The monumental stone house at Easton Neston, whose masonry and roof are dated 1702, was later acknowledged by Hawksmoor as one of his 'own children', and there is no good reason to doubt that this building was entirely designed by him

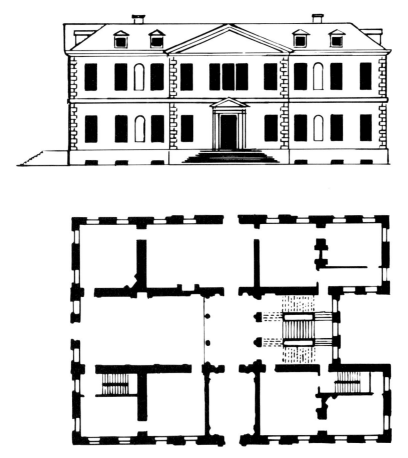

16   Tring Manor. Plan and elevation.

and begun about 1695. But the most specific of several early sources to mention Wren's name states that the latter designed the wings some years earlier than the main house. Easton Neston was built for a kinsman of Wren by marriage, Sir William Fermor, later Baron Leominster, and both architects were in touch with him in 1686–7.[216] The wings, of which one survives, are modest in style, of brick with stone dressings; the major reason against accepting Wren's authorship is that Hawksmoor, who was remarkably loyal, later called them 'good for nothing'.

The question of Tring Manor is no less complicated, though Wren's authorship is attested by his contemporary Roger North who knew the house well. It was built for Henry Guy, Secretary to the Treasury in 1679–88 and 1691–5; it is usually said not to survive, and always dated about 1670 for no better reason than that Guy acquired the estate in 1669. But recently discovered eighteenth-century measured drawings of the building confirm that its structure is embodied in the present apparently late Victorian house (Fig. 16). Features of the interior planning, moreover, resemble Easton Neston and suggest strongly that Tring was designed in the middle of the 1680s; Wren is known to have gone there in 1687[217] and the house must have been habitable in 1690 when William III dined there. Tring and Easton Neston are very similar in overall dimensions. Both were designed with a long two-storey hall to the south and a grand staircase to the north of the passage between the central west and east entrances; both had, in effect, a gallery across the house above this passage. But since similar spatial ingenuity appears in a project by Hawksmoor for another house (Ingestre), dated 1688,[218] the most probable explanation is that Wren designed Tring somewhat earlier and Hawksmoor, with knowledge of it, designed Easton Neston somewhat later.

The long elevations of Tring were so designed that niches on both storeys corresponded to the ends of the cross-walls which contained the chimneys, and this suggests that Wren may have started with a grid plan and worked into it all the desired interior features. But apart from this suggestion of grid-logic the façades of Tring are as much screens, unrevealing of the interior, as those of Hampton Court or Hawksmoor's Easton Neston. The same may be said of the third house, Winslow (Plate 163).

Winslow bears the date 1700 and was built in 1699–1702 for William Lowndes, who succeeded Guy at the Treasury; Wren examined the building accounts and a number of tradesmen were London men well known to him.[219] This established that Lowndes wanted and obtained the best services available; accounts were not always read by the designer of a building, but Winslow's studied simplicity, fine proportions and structural logic suggest that Lowndes's high standards extended to the choice of architect. The rooms on all floors are arranged between end staircases, and south and north rooms are separated by a three-foot thick spine which encloses all the flues and terminates in a single magnificent row of chimneys above the roof.

After the death of William III Wren seems to have undertaken no new designs himself except the final ones for the dome and towers of St Paul's and the London steeples. Although his powers do not seem to have diminished, Wren approaching seventy had reason to accept the natural tendency for his years towards gradual disengagement and greater selectivity of interest. His assistants were capable men: Hawksmoor, Dickinson, the admittedly tiresome Talman and later the energetic Vanbrugh. St Paul's had become part of his life, and its completion was vital to him. Of the two great secular opportunities of the later 1690s Greenwich, being actual, was the more exacting and consequently the more in need of selective delegation; the other, Whitehall, was never more than an elaborate dream, but so wonderful a dream that for some weeks after the fire of 1698, until the King abandoned Whitehall (p. 17), it must have occupied him totally.

In 1951 an additional elevation for Whitehall was discovered, showing the new parliament building and a connecting corridor to the palace that were previously only known from Wren's plan; it seems to be in Talman's hand and thus makes even clearer the fact that he neither designed nor drew the other fourteen Whitehall drawings now at All Souls.[220] Next to St Paul's, this must be the opportunity

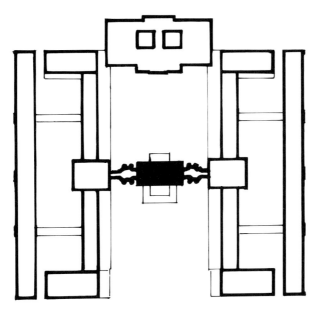

17   Whitehall. Plan for a new palace centred on the Banqueting House. 1698.

which Wren would least willingly have given away, and there are indeed no signs that he did so. Not only the draughtsmanship but also the vocabulary of detail, the general lines and equally some idiomatic features are unmistakably Wren's. The two projects embodied in these drawings are remarkable for their thoroughness, their maturity and their relation to Wren's creativity as we find it expressed in Hampton Court and Greenwich (Plate 165, Fig. 17).

In the larger scheme the Banqueting House is the nucleus, forming the centrepiece of a court open eastwards to the river and also looking westwards into a closed court on the park side; additional ranges formed three subsidiary courts on either side. Wren was particularly concerned during the fire that the Banqueting House should be saved, and saved it was; nevertheless his respect for it was no less practical and pragmatical than his respect for Antiquity. His experience with Chelsea and subsequent large buildings had shown him that the basic problem of incorporating Jones's hall into a new palace would be one of scale. To demolish it was doubly unthinkable since it had survived the fire; to reface it would have destroyed the external identity of a fabric that was both historically significant and very pretty. His solution was to increase its scale by setting and by implication, fronting it between cylindrical staircase towers. He seems in effect, but without any kind of arithmetical exactitude, to have carefully related the whole palace in size and scale to this central building; the big pavilions at the ends of the river and park fronts are very slightly larger than the Banqueting House and the main courts are slightly more than twice its width. Moreover, the pillars that articulate all the main elevations are graded in a hierarchy of three sizes; the smallest, the order of Jones's building, is repeated in the half-columns of the central block on the park side, while the largest appears only in the towers and portico of the central group; the intermediate order is used in the big end pavilions. The elevations are tied together not only by the repeated verticals of the pillars but also by the way in which the orders are related to the division into storeys; this is done with less artifice than in Trinity Library and more smoothly than in the east front of Hampton Court. The floor level of the Banqueting House is used as the base level for the whole hierarchy of orders, but this is half a storey above ground. Wren's evident preference for the ground-based elevation of Chelsea rather than the Palladian formula of Hampton Court means that in the side ranges and the buildings facing the park the pattern of openings and horizontal mouldings cuts across that of the orders; it is as if alternate beats of a single rhythm have a different timbre. The rhythms are varied but their intensity is consistent throughout the palace. The division into blocks and the provision of the stair towers give an impression of height as against sprawling length that is rare in English secular buildings of the seventeenth and eighteenth centuries – Wren's own included. Except in the river elevation the surface enrichment is obtained by strictly architectural means: mouldings, pillars and changes of plane. The large masses, the preference for half- or full columns rather than pilasters, and the use of square piers in the towers, would have made a building of commanding power and romantic grouping that would hold shadow even in the grey moist air of the Thames-side.

The details are those with which Wren had long been familiar, and some are idiomatic to him; the second storey windows crammed under the entablature of the park front recall those in the Chelsea frontispieces, while in the end pavilions of an alternative elevation to the park the big arch windows with vertical strips partly filling them and a heavy beam running below them are very much in the spirit of Trinity Library. The scheme identified ever since *Parentalia*[221] as the second also looks back to the projects of the 1660s for a palace with the Banqueting House doubled on either side of a central portico. The total area of the buildings is smaller and the interrelation of storeys is simpler, but the scale is as monumental as in the first scheme.

Greenwich, unlike Whitehall, could be a reality (Plate 166). The foundation of a hospital for seamen as the counterpart to Chelsea for soldiers appealed both to compassion and to patriotism. The project seems to have been entertained already by James II, but the first practical step was taken in 1692 when Webb's King Charles building, a deserted shell since about 1670, was temporarily employed to house the wounded from the battle of La Hogue. Wren was involved in discussions with the Navy Commissioners the following year, but events moved slowly. The site of Greenwich Palace, including Webb's building, was granted by William and Mary in October 1694,[222] but another eighteen months passed before the issue of a royal warrant for the completion of the original block and the addition of a base block behind it.[223] By the spring of 1698 the present basic layout of the Hospital had been fixed, with a block balancing King Charles's on the east, as Webb had intended (Fig. 18), and two courts farther south containing wards and the hall and chapel,

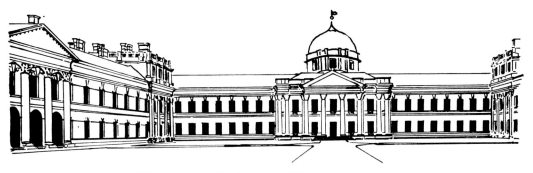

18 Reconstruction of Webb's project for Greenwich Palace.

fronted by colonnades leading towards the Queen's House; these framed the vista between it and the river. Greenwich is thus a building without a middle, and it is desirable to examine not only the implications of this deficiency but also the events that led to it (Fig. 19).

Hawksmoor, whose passion for Greenwich was life-long and whose connection with it almost as long, hoped as late as 1728, the date of his pamphlet (p. 17), to provide a middle in the form of a huge chapel between the Queen's House and the Hospital, and even considered moving the house bodily farther south to make room for such a building. The grandly imaginative schemes recorded in his many drawings were improbable in the sense that almost from its inception the Hospital Committee's income from both royal and other subscriptions and supplementary sources was too restricted to satisfy even more moderate designs; they were impossible because the strip of land 115 ft wide – the extent of the Queen's House – between Wren's two courts remained throughout the period of construction the property of the Crown and therefore could not be built upon. There is little doubt that if administrators had shared Hawksmoor's enthusiasm this land could have been acquired and used. From 1690 the Queen's House was the official residence of the Earl of Dartmouth as Ranger of Greenwich Park. Although Queen Mary is supposed to have been fond of it she never used it, and its venerability as a work of Inigo Jones was constantly in conflict with attempts to make it more useful. Thus, according to Hawksmoor, Mary wished to revive a project of the 1660s for adding corner pavilions to the house, and when about 1710 the Hospital acquired the lease of the house the ground floor windows were lowered, sash frames were installed, and the exterior was thickly stuccoed.

As early as May 1695 a site committee reported the desirability of acquiring for the Hospital the vista land, but although Wren and Samuel Travers, the Surveyor-General of Crown Lands, signed the report,[224] it had no effect; moreover they had apparently committed themselves to a different view. As Surveyor of Works Wren seems to have consented to a crucial restriction of the site, for on 4 October 1694 he and Travers, in sending the Treasury a plan of the proposed area, recorded a joint recommendation 'that in any grant thereof there be a reservation of the way laid out

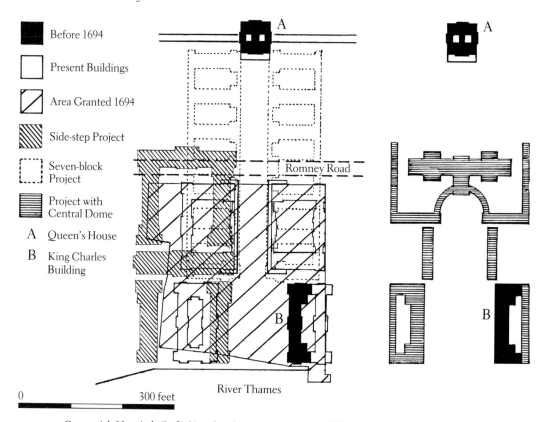

Before 1694

Present Buildings

Area Granted 1694

Side-step Project

Seven-block Project

Project with Central Dome

A Queen's House

B King Charles Building

A

Romney Road

A

B

B

0   300 feet

River Thames

19 Greenwich Hospital. (Left) Site plan showing executed buildings and two early projects. (Right) Alternative early project similar to Fig. 20.

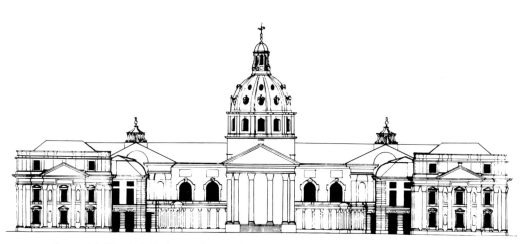

20 Greenwich Hospital. Project with central dome.

in the Map leading from the house there called the Queen's House to the River of Thames'. The grant, drafted two weeks and issued three weeks later, was based on that plan, and it is significant that the site only extended south from the river as far as the line of the present Romney Road, which had not then yet been made. Admittedly the only known copy of the joint memorandum does not bear Wren's signature, but the Treasury had asked his opinion jointly with that of Travers, the plural is used throughout, and it is in his 'Court Orders' book (p. 16).[225] On the other hand he did draw out a very beautiful design (Fig. 20) with a large domed room in the centre, blocking the Queen's House, and this must be earlier than is usually supposed – before October 1694 – since it does not fit within the bounds of the site granted.[226] At this stage he thought of Greenwich in terms of Chelsea, with the same disposition of hall and chapel flanking the domed room, and the same small colonnade in front of them. The sequence of open courts recalls Winchester; the dome and portico suggest a memory of Le Vau's College of the Four Nations. But in accordance with what Hawksmoor's pamphlet calls Queen Mary's 'great Passion for Building' and 'fixt Intention for Magnificence' it was to be larger and more ornate than Chelsea: William and Mary might well wish to outshine Charles II.

Two further designs, both larger but more utilitarian, were very probably made after this scheme but before the definition of the site, which they also exceed. One, which survives as a plan,[227] side-steps the Queen's House problem by placing the whole complex east of the vista and abandoning King Charles's building which (again according to Hawksmoor) was only saved from the hammer by Queen Mary's intervention (Fig. 19). The third project, which was drawn out in some detail, proposed seven ranges (hall or chapel and six ward blocks) on either side of the vista, with arcades linking their inner ends and running up to the Queen's House to form a long closed court.[228] A further plan, with only four pairs of blocks, does fit the site, and introduces a coupled colonnade resembling, but narrower than, the one finally built.[229] But Wren probably now turned to other work until late in 1697. By then he was Surveyor to the Hospital and work had begun on King Charles Block. Moreover the Earl of Romney had bought the Rangership of the park and the lease of the Queen's House and begun to divert the road that ran through the house to what is now Romney Road. This effectively limited the site on the south permanently, even after Sir William Gifford obtained the house in 1710 as both Governor of the Hospital and Ranger, although in Hawksmoor's private mind the new road remained moveable. Early in 1698 Wren produced plans for a hall for the Hospital, and King William Court, of which it forms the north side, was begun. The four pairs of blocks had been spaced out to three; soon afterwards the middle ones were turned round to make the present three-sided courts.

Wren's attitude to Greenwich was more detached – although he took overall responsibility – than in the case of William's palaces. Greenwich was not under the control of the Office of Works and while giving his services for nothing he was architect by appointment, not *ex officio*. From that appointment in 1696 Hawksmoor was his personal assistant, becoming Clerk of Works two years later; in 1705 he was made Deputy Surveyor and attended the Directors' meetings in Wren's stead. Hawksmoor's grand schemes were drawn on his own initiative and not for the Directors, but he had collaborated in drawings with Wren from an early stage. Moreover, the west range of King William Block, begun in 1698, and the base block of Queen Anne Court, begun in 1700, are generally excluded by modern scholars from the canon of Wren's work and accepted as Hawksmoor's. The varied fenestration shapes and patterns and dramatic contrasts of scale of the King William building have too much of Fancy and too little of Reason to be by Wren; nevertheless he must have countenanced them and even, with a generosity that was not misplaced, admired the inventiveness of his younger colleague. In any case, as with the City churches, and as in a present-day architectural partnership, the responsibility of the head of the firm concerned standards more than style.

Until the railway age the fastest approach to Greenwich was by water, and from the river the Hospital is still in appearance the perfect ensemble it never became in fact. In 1711 the river view was enhanced by the decision to double the end pavilions of King Charles Block and its unfinished pendant; Ripley's Palladian completion of Queen Mary Court cannot be seen from the main approach any more than Hawksmoor's King William building. Inigo Jones set, at Greenwich as in Whitehall, a problem for his successors; Wren's greatest achievement at Greenwich was to accept the challenge of the Queen's House and devise a framework in which the problem might be solved. The backs of buildings and the insides of courts concerned him less than the great central tableau in which the domes and colonnades frame not only the small-scale Queen's House but also the landscape and the sky in the same way that trees do in a landscape by Claude Lorrain. The domes, much higher and richer in execution than in the first drawings, make Greenwich one of the most beautiful architectural groups in English architecture; the clusters of columns which form diagonal buttresses give them the same sort of variety of shape and lighting as the towers of St Paul's which followed them in date.

The decoration of the Hall in 1708–27 was to bring fame to the painter James Thornhill, and although we do not know precisely Wren's intentions he must have had a painted ceiling in mind (Plate 169). The vestibule, opening up into the dome, is decorated with illusionist painting as well as with gilded mouldings, royal cyphers and portrait medallions; yet the strongest impression is of its spatial geometry and the engineering which supports and defines its surfaces (Plate 168). Wren's whole architectural career can be interpreted through domes; those of Greenwich may also be seen as a last rehearsal for St Paul's.

XI 'RESURGAM'

When the Surveyor in Person had set out, upon the Place, the Dimensions of the great Dome, and fixed upon the Centre; a common labourer was ordered to bring a flat Stone from the Heaps of Rubbish, (such as should first come to Hand) to be laid for a Mark and Direction to the Masons; the Stone . . . happened to be a Piece of a Grave-stone, with nothing remaining of the Inscription but this single Word in large Capitals, RESURGAM.

This accidental discovery, related in *Parentalia*, was as appropriate to the resurrection of the cathedral as the emblem of the phoenix (p. 66) with which Evelyn specifically symbolized the new building early in 1697.[230] Two years after that, both ideas were combined in Cibber's relief on the south transept (Plate 79).

When the choir of St Paul's was at last opened on 2 December 1697 it looked very different from its appearance today. There were no coloured and gold mosaics, and the colours were restricted to white and stone colour, the light brown of the woodwork, the black and white marble paving, the crimson of cushions and draperies and the gilding of fringes and carved relief, the foliage frieze and the glory of rays in the apse (Plates 132, 133, 134). In the apse stood the communion table, without an altar canopy; the four fluted pilasters of the apse were heightened with blue and veined in gold, and the rest was painted white with marble veining. The floor was not raised by steps from the level of the crossing; the choir stalls stood a whole bay further to the east, and between the arches of the first bay from the crossing stood a screen of wooden columns carrying the organ (Plates 141, 142). In fiction Wren is supposed to have hated the organ, but visually its chief characteristics were the fine case carved by Gibbons and a curious system of rising glass sashes which no doubt were originally intended to keep builders' dust out of the instrument.[231]

While the organ and screen did not block the view they were large enough to give a sense of enclosure within the choir, and on the completion of the whole building they would give a sense of separation to the beholder under the dome. The distribution of lighting and the wall colouring, however, were uniform throughout the interior, which was entirely painted in a light tone.[232] As there were no seats in the crossing the radial pattern of the paving was always visible and contributed to the sensation of standing in the middle of a central space (Plate 142).

A note in *Parentalia* suggests that Wren wanted the dome to be finished in mosaic; if so, it would have been geometrical rather than figurative.[233] The same note seems to be the origin of persisting confused ideas about an altar canopy: there is a model at St Paul's for a reredos to frame the east window, but the extant drawings for a free-standing structure represent not an altar canopy but Hawksmoor's designs for an equestrian monument to William III.[234] The redecoration of Wren's building became an issue as soon as it was opened, and Sir James Thornhill's false perspectives framing the *Life of St Paul* in the dome cannot have pleased the architect since they exaggerate the interior height which he had so carefully calculated. Some of the worst attempts to dress up St Paul's have been thwarted or rectified, and like all large and complex buildings its aspect changes with the sky and the seasons. But three centuries after its commencement the building is inevitably darker, and it may be necessary to employ artificial light now that the balance of the natural cannot be recovered. While many people still come to St Paul's because it is the house of God, many more come because it is a famous building or a surrogate concert hall, and the paraphernalia of tourism and television inevitably continue a process of disruption which began in the 1860s and 1870s with the rearranging and mosaic decoration of the choir, the removal of the screen, the bisection of the organ and the opening of a clear vista from the west door to the east window (Plate 136). But a building of continued usefulness becomes the sum of all the things it has ever been. The still small voice of Wren's clear light and calculated grandeur can still be found, but it must be listened for amid the surface impressions which crowd around the visitor.

Wren's conception of the interior did not change greatly from the 'Definitive' design of 1675 (p. 81). Indeed the chief differences even from the Great Model are the more humane scale of the parts – arches, doorways, mouldings – and the greater profusion of mouldings and carved ornament (Plates 49, 72). As in the Great Model, the interior surfaces are much less patterned than the exterior; relief, however rich, is almost restricted to areas and edges which clarify the shapes and directions of those internal spaces that were to be the supreme geometrical demonstrations of Wren's career. He cannot have intended the emotions to be excited by the interior of St Paul's which has often been called cold. It has also been called Protestant, which is what it was meant to be.

For his son, Wren's great achievement at St Paul's was to have completed it in one lifetime; that in itself amounts to no more than a combination of organization, endurance and practical knowledge. But Wren's achievement was as much an artistic one, in complexity, ambiguity and consistency. The crossing, the heart of the interior, is complex and ambiguous; it has none of the transparent logic of twentieth-century Functionalism, yet the patterns of its arches upon arches derive essentially and visibly from its character as a work of engineering, and the transition from unequal to apparently equal arches at the level of the quarter-galleries arrests visually the gravity and the verticality of the statical structure. The nave and choir are distinguished from the crossing by function and by shape, yet a consistency of design unites them. In this a major part is played by the smaller pilaster order which forms the imposts of the nave arcades and runs throughout the interior, into the corners behind the crossing piers and even into the westernmost bay of the nave where it is developed into full columns (Plates 134, 135, 136, 139).

The combination of a pilaster order with arches resting on imposts is a commonplace of ancient Roman architecture and its derivatives, and Wren used it already in the south front of the Sheldonian. During the sixteenth century Italian architects developed a linguistic complication by making the imposts into pilasters of a smaller order running through the main one (for example, Sansovino's Library of San Marco in Venice and Palladio's Basilica in Vicenza). In Rome Michelangelo on the Capitol and Vignola in the Villa Giulia extended the device by making the small order carry beams instead of arches; in Paris Wren saw both entablatures and arches combined in Le Vau's College of the Four Nations. A similar use of two sizes of pillars and arches is the basis of Palladio's Venetian churches and others derived from them, as it is of St Paul's, and it is tempting to suppose that Wren knew this. However, his small order is Composite, that is richer than the Corinthian of the large arches and therefore in the correct sequence to be placed above, not below, the larger. This reversal characteristically disregards precedent, but it is in conformity with Wren's own statement (p. 28) that things seen near at hand may be more complicated.

Although it is only by the artifice of words and pictures that we can consider the inside of a building before the outside, the transition from either aspect to the other embodies the greatest ambiguity of St Paul's, and one of which Wren, who had come to conceive his designs entirely in three dimensions, must have been fully aware. Not only the dome but the whole building consists of an interior and an exterior which are unrelated, and this illustration of Wren's opinion that things not seen together need not agree (p. 76) was the most momentous consequence of the invention of the screen walls (p. 78). It is here that he shows himself most clearly a child of the Baroque age, not the Renaissance: without clues to the relationship the eye is disposed to accept each aspect separately. It is characteristic of the visual basis of much of Wren's logic that the analysis of what cannot be perceived is relevant only to the critical understanding of his architecture, not to the experience of it.

The exterior of St Paul's has also undergone changes. The first was made in Wren's lifetime, when in 1717 the Commission decided against his wishes to terminate the elevation in a balustrade: his retort about an *edging* (p. 20) was not only justly barbed but also formally precise. For the balustrade between the peristyle and the attic of the dome, which he himself designed, softens the transition from one zone and diameter to another while maintaining the distinction between them; the similar balustrade above the body of the cathedral, on the other hand, softens the hard edge he intended between building and sky (Plates 75, 80, 82, 137). The effect is particularly unfortunate over the eastern apse, where Wren had built a scrolled parapet; only on the west front was the balustrade omitted. The hardness of geometrical edges also appears in certain angles of walls: at the eastern corners of the choir and the corners of the transepts the block-like character of the masonry is shown, as on each face of the building the pilasters are set away from the corner

(Plates 80, 82, 84). The secondary angles, however, in the corner bastions of the dome between the main arms and in the projections north-west and south-west of the nave, are defined negatively, by the indentation between the sides of two pilasters (Plate 144).

Later changes should also be noticed. St Paul's was originally all white except for the lead grey of the dome; even the leaded caps of the west towers were painted and shaded to imitate stone cut into panels.[235] For most of its life, however, the cathedral paid for by coal has been stained by soot from London's hearths, so streaked by rain and wind as to superimpose on the surface relief an arbitrary pattern of black and white. Although in the 1960s the stonework was cleaned and its brilliant whiteness temporarily restored, the damage was more than skin-deep; the grey tone to which much of the building has already turned does, however, leave the surface textures and relief enrichments appreciable. The City has also changed. Since 1940 more ground space has been opened around St Paul's to the benefit of photography, and the heights of surrounding buildings have been limited. Wren seems always to have accepted that his cathedral would be surrounded by other buildings, and around 1710 Hawksmoor drew out a scheme for uniform blocks enclosing it;[236] but until late in the nineteenth century the whole of the screen walls still rose above the rest of London as they appear in Canaletto's view of the City. In the last twenty years tower blocks have destroyed that view.

It was not only in the matter of balustrades that Wren took especial care. The basic form of the elevations was settled in 1675, and he could only make, in the light of experience and changing ideals, minor changes in the style and extent of carved detail (pp. 80, 85). Four problems remained – the design of the west portico, the stability of the dome, its appearance, and the shape of the west towers – all of which were open to reconsideration until building reached the stage where a final decision was imperative.

The design of the portico became important about 1687–8, when Jones's old portico was finally demolished and the new building at the west end, excepting the steps, reached the level of the church floor. One of several studies for a giant single-order portico – although not the one usually reproduced – is in Hawksmoor's hand and embodies a monumental inscription with the names of both William and Mary; it is thus datable 1689–94 and shows that Wren was still uncertain about the design while construction was proceeding on the west front without the columns of the portico.[237] Ultimately, about 1694, he decided on columns of the same orders, size and rhythm as the pilaster articulation surrounding the cathedral (Plates 137, 138). *Parentalia*'s explanation of this decision by the lack of large enough stones at Portland is too simple:[238] Wren could have designed the entablature as a series of flat arches, but it would have projected too far in front of the towers to gain from them the abutment such arches would require. It is important to realize that such a portico would have been far larger than Jones's (Fig. 21): the lower order alone *as it was built* is almost as big as Jones's, and the entablature spans, which Wren did key together from smaller stones, are as wide as all but the middle one of Jones's mono-

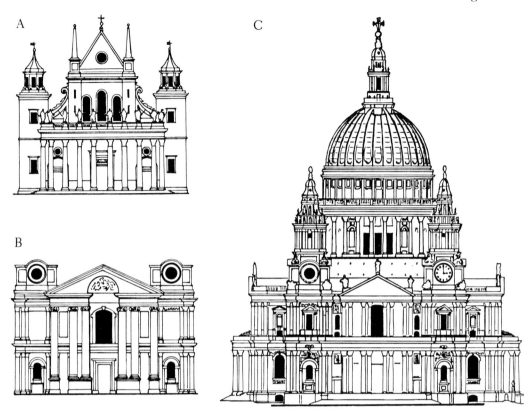

21 St Paul's. West front. (A) Inigo Jones's front. (B) Design for a giant portico. (C) Wren's final design. All to the same scale.

lithic spans.[239] In the 1680s and 1690s Wren was interested in contrasts of scale, but the decision against this gigantic accent was surely aesthetic as well as structural; moreover, the double portico, wider below than above, indicates as no other feature does the cross-section of the interior spaces.

There remained the dome and the towers. By 1698 work over the crossing had reached the Whispering Gallery (whose acoustical properties are an unintended side-effect of shape) above the eight crossing arches; above that level the drum is conical, not cylindrical, and the joint solution to the inseparable problems of structure and appearance evolved as each course of masonry narrowed both the aperture and the range of available options. The building season of 1700, in which the masonry went up from the base of the inside pilaster order to the floor of the outside peristyle, opened the most critical period of the design. It took another three years, to the end of 1703, to add the next 23 feet to the top of the inside pilaster capitals and those of the small order inside the peristyle. At the same time the west towers had reached the cornice around the top of the church; work there came to a virtual stop in 1701, and the towers were only taken up in 1705 after the construction, inside the south-west tower, of the 'geometrical' spiral staircase, the steps of which were let into the already completed masonry shaft. The delay in the towers cannot have been due either to this addition or, since no less than six firms of masons were at work on the cathedral, to the distribution of labour. Nor can the principal cause of delay have been uncertainty about the financial future of the work, although until its resolution in June 1702 this was a contributory factor. Wren was uncertain how to proceed, although in 1702–03 six approved engravings were issued based on his drawings.[240] Five in fact record superseded original drawings from the 'Definitive' stage, including the lost drawing that shows the inside of the Michelangelesque dome (p. 81). The last, a west elevation on two plates by Simon Gribelin, shows the new addition of clock stages to the towers, although not as executed: the towers are still based on the Tempietto, but the dome appears as carried out up to the top of the peristyle. At the same date unauthorized engravings were made, purporting to reveal what Wren still kept to himself: William Emmett produced a pirated plan and west elevation as well as totally fictitious views of the interior of the tall single-shell cone and dome he supposed to be Wren's intention.[241]

A sheet of drawings for the west towers dated February 1704 probably marks the end of the period of indecision in both towers and dome.[242] During 1705 the peristyle was carried upwards and the inner brick structural dome was built; by the end of 1707 the brick cone above it was finished and the timber outer dome was ready for leading. This had been done by October 1708 when the lantern was completed. Structurally, the lantern is a device for securing the dome, while the cone is a device for raising the height and increasing the visual impact of the lantern. Visually the cone has no effect, since it is hidden by the masonry dome from within and the leaded timber from without (Fig. 4, page 49). Thus the idea of a double dome, which Wren had first met in Paris and first drawn out after his return (p. 48), became a reality, and with a total estimated weight of 67,000 tons took its place among the engineering achievements of the world.

In the first years of the new century Wren needed to calculate, crudely by modern standards but to the limits of the knowledge of his day, a geometry at once statical and aesthetic. A cut-away drawing reveals the logic, predictable from theory but imperceptible in experience, which forms the structure like a huge eight-ribbed umbrella. There is a direct continuity of forces from the foundations below the crypt through the eight main piers up to the main roof, and thence up through the eight filled-in buttressing bays which interrupt the uniformity of the peristyle (Plate 145). Higher still, eight of the ribs of the outer dome give visual rather than statical continuity from the peristyle to the columns of the lantern.

Statical needs shaped the inner dome and visual considerations the outer one. For nearly thirty years from 1675 the towers were to be simple geometrical forms of cylinders with hemispherical caps; probably for almost as long Wren retained the 'Definitive' image of a central dome rich in surface relief, ringed with projecting column-buttresses and somewhat pointed in profile. By 1698 the crucial decision had been made to taper the whole drum inwards above the main arches, and from this followed the necessity of setting back the outer dome above the peristyle. But only at the last moment does Wren seem to have produced the complete reversal by which all the main dome's complexity passed to the towers in exchange for the Tempietto image of a hemisphere above concentric cylinders (Plate 138).

Wren's authorship of the dome has never been questioned, but it has been suggested that the exciting complexity of the towers, with their play of convex and concave forms, shows the hand and mind of a younger master – presumably Hawksmoor. This suggestion cannot be sustained, for three reasons. First, the cathedral was above all others Wren's personal building; secondly, the drawing dated February 1704 indubitably reveals his hand; thirdly, the dome and towers seem consistently to have been complementary in shape, and their final reversal is equally consistent. In distant views the lacy elegance of the towers is the perfect foil to the solid geometrical severity of the dome; at closer quarters their varied projections and complex profile make combinations of shape which alter with every change of viewpoint, whereas the dome remains always the same.

During the final years of work on St Paul's the London skyline saw other changes almost as exhilarating. When the main accounts of the Commission for rebuilding the churches were closed in 1693 most of the new buildings had towers, some crowned by pinnacles, turrets or small lead steeples (Plates 24, 30, 33, 40, 73, 86, 87, 89, 94, 97, 100, 105, 109, 122). But only the Portland stone steeple of St Mary-le-Bow (Plates 39, 126) rose to a height remotely approaching the 225 feet which the cathedral towers would eventually reach; the other famous Wren steeples were not unfinished, they had not yet been begun. This group of structures has justly received much comment and much admiration for their author's fertile invention, which seems to have blossomed into forms that were emulated but seldom equalled by later architects; documentation of the big Wren steeples, however, is poor, and the question of how they came to be erected has remained unanswered and indeed scarcely asked, and only rather tentative suggestions can at present be made. Perhaps Wren designed and brought to completion in 1680 the Bow steeple as a specimen of what, in terms of design, he could do and of what, in terms of expenditure, ought to be done elsewhere. In January 1697 the House of Commons discussed the extension of the coal tax, due to expire in 1700. A Bill, primarily to finance the completion of St Paul's, also provided for the many parish churches said to be still unfinished.[243] Gradually, in the light of the Bow example, the new idea of 'complete' began to be seen above the houses and around the cathedral (Plates 105, 124, 125). It is quite probable, therefore, that one consideration in the final simplification of the outer dome and complication of the west towers was their larger relationship to the other new additions to the skyline: thus the simplicity of the City's principal landmark would properly be unique.

The leaded steeple of St Augustine and the equally slender stone needle of St Dunstan-in-the-East in the 1690s (Plates 84, 123) were followed soon after 1700 by major additions above the parapets of towers already completed at St Bride, Christ

Church and St Magnus (Plates 36, 127, 130). The original tower of St Michael, Crooked Lane (destroyed), was damaged in the 1703 hurricane (p. 87) and its three-stage leaded timber steeple, cylindrical with corner buttresses (Plate 131), was constructed after 1708, as were the final group, built by the younger Edward Strong, of St Vedast, St James Garlickhythe, St Michael Royal and St Stephen Walbrook (Plates 116, 117, 128, 129). These were, as far as we know, Wren's very last designs. Since Hawksmoor had left the City churches office in 1701[244] there is no good reason for his involvement with these last works. Moreover, Hawksmoor on the whole builds his towers and lanterns of bare abstract blocks and uses columns or pilasters as accessories, whereas the steeples of the Wren churches after 1700 are, like St Mary-le-Bow earlier (Plate 126), essentially made up from the orders. Hawksmoor, for whom Fancy held no snares but was welcome, could reduce architecture to solid geometry to an extent never tried by Wren. In Hawksmoor's skylines we wonder that cold stone and straight lines can so capture our imagination and even our emotions; in those of Wren the marvel is that Alberti's formula of superimposed temples (p. 82) can take so many forms and yet always retain its identity. This is true even of St Vedast, the steeple closest to the art of Borromini in its mixture of concave and convex surfaces.

'Architecture', Wren had written, 'aims at eternity'. As a young man he had looked into the heavens, first with the naked eye and then through the lens, and had believed that he understood something of both the order and the mystery of what he saw. In his eighties, as he looked up, he must equally have believed, with both pride and humility, that he saw something of the same order and the same mystery in the shapes he himself had raised towards the sky.

NOTES

Year dates are given New Style. Christopher I is the architect's father; Christopher III is the architect's son. Works cited in short form may be found in the Bibliography under the same keywords. BM means British Museum (British Library). PRO means Public Record Office, London.

1 *Parentalia, or Memoirs of the Family of Wrens; viz. of Mathew Bishop of Ely, Christopher Dean of Windsor, &c. But chiefly of Sir Christopher Wren . . . Compiled, by his Son Christopher; Now published by his Grandson, Stephen Wren, Esq; With the Care of Joseph Ames, F.R.S. and Secretary to the Society of Antiquaries* (London, 1750). Christopher III was elected FSA in 1725; Ames was a bibliographer rather than a writer on antiquities (J. Evans, *History of the Society of Antiquaries* (Oxford 1956) 68, 90). The 'Heirloom' copy containing many inserted prints and original manuscript papers was published in facsimile in 1965 by the Gregg Press. Three preparatory manuscripts survive: in chronological order they are BM MS. Add. 25071; All Souls, Oxford, MS.313; Royal Society MS.249. The BM draft, marked on f.2 'collected, and collated, An: 1719', contains bound together several incomplete drafts which do not entirely duplicate either each other or the published text. The manuscripts are discussed, in the context of Wren's *Tract I*, by J. A. Bennett in *Architectural History* XV (1972) 6–7.

2 Christopher III to John Ward, 24 Feb. 1739 (BM MS. Add.6209, f.207).

3 Whinney and Millar, 255. Wren was knighted on 14 Nov. 1673 (at Whitehall at 5 a.m. according to Aubrey (Dick, 51)). Christopher III told Ward in 1742 that the bust 'was the Performance of Edward Pearce, about the Year 1673' (BM MS. Add.

6209, f.220), and there is no reason to doubt this date. Wren wrote from Paris, 'Monsr. Abbé Charles introduc'd me to the Acquaintance of Bernini, who shew'd me his Designs of the Louvre, and of the King's Statue' (*Parentalia*, 261).

4 'Low of stature, and thin' (J. Ward, *Lives of the Professors of Gresham College* (1740) 106). Monconys in 1663 called him 'grand Mathematicien quoy que petit de corps' (R. T. Gunther, *Early Science in Oxford* II (Oxford 1922) 389. See also *Parentalia*, 181, 346.

5 *Parentalia*, 256–60. Of William Prynne, the controversialist, Wren 'sayd once, that he had the countenance of a Witch' (Dick, 314). Since Prynne's views had incurred physical disfigurement there is some understatement in the remark.

6 Summerson, *Wren*, 29, 53, 59, 60; Sprat, 311, 317; *Parentalia*, 199, 207–8, 215, 217–18, 247.

7 24 Feb. 1677; probably at Whitehall, since St James's only became the principal Chapel Royal after the 1698 Whitehall fire. Dr Holder (see n.14) officiated. The register is PRO RG8/110. Wren's children were baptized, and both his wives were buried, at St Martin-in-the-Fields, the parish church of Scotland Yard (Little, 92, 107). His first marriage was in the Temple Church. Jane Fitzwilliam was born sometime between 1639 and 1653. The second marriage may have been somewhat precipitate: Hooke

records it on the day, but not the lady's name, and he did not meet her until 7 April (*Diary*, 275, 284). The daughter Jane was born on 13 Nov. 1677. Jane Fitzwilliam's first cousin on her mother's side was Sir William Fermor, later Lord Leominster (1648–1711), the builder of Easton Neston (see n.216). He was, with Evelyn, a godfather to William Wren (Little, 107).

8 Aubrey, who as an expert on Wiltshire obtained information from the parish register, believed that Wren 'made himself a yeare younger than indeed he is' (Dick, 51). In fact the Christopher baptized in 1631 died immediately. The date of 1631 has recently been revived (*Victoria History of Wiltshire* XI (1980) 95) but Christopher I recorded the correct dates in his copy of Helvicus's *Theatrum Historicum* (1618) now in the National Library of Wales. See Little, 17–18.

9 *Parentalia*, 142. The notes were 'undoubtedly by my Grandfather' (Christopher III to Ward, BM MS. Add.6209, f.209). They are discussed (erroneously as by Sir Christopher) by Weaver, 139–42. Christ Church is clearly the medieval, not the Wren, church. An estimate by Sir Christopher for buildings at Whitehall, 15 May 1685, was printed by Elmes, 10, as of 1635 and consequently attributed to Christopher I; at least one modern author has been misled. For the correct date see *History of the King's Works* V 287, n.5.

10 The roof may have been in the Rectory or in the church, the chancel of which was embellished with plaster reliefs and inscriptions in about 1639. The Puritans objected to these, and according to the testimony of Robert Brockway, plasterer, in 1647, he had done the work about eight years previously at the expense and under the supervision of Dr Wren (J. Waylen, 'Christopher Wren of East Knoyle,D.D.', *Wilts. Archaeol. Mag.* III (1857) 115–19).

11 *Parentalia*, 146.

12 Evelyn, IV, 235. Nearly two years before the most famous comet, Halley's.

13 *Parentalia*, 181–95, and inserts in the Heirloom copy after p. 194.

14 Holder (1616–98) had married

Wren's sister Susan. He was a musician, mathematician, FRS and an early speech therapist. In 1674 he became Sub-Dean of the Chapel Royal.

15 Sir Charles Scarburgh (1616–94) lost his Cambridge fellowship early in the Civil War but received an Oxford MD in 1646; he then went to London and became a member of the College of Physicians in 1648 and Reader to the Barber-Surgeons' Company in 1649.

16 In 1649 or 1650 (R.B. Gardiner, *Registers of Wadham College* I (1889) 178); in the year ending 25 June 1650 according to college records (Little, 25); *Parentalia*, 182, gives 1646.

17 *History of the King's Works*, V, 266.

18 *Parentalia*, 210–12.

19 P. Fréart de Chantelou, *Journal du Voyage du Cavalier Bernin* (Paris 1930) 202.

20 Summerson, *Wren*, 23, 30, 34, 38.

21 *Parentalia*, 198–9. Writing to the Treasurer of Christ's Hospital School in 1694, Wren stressed the desirability, and the rarity in England, of education in drawing (*Wren Soc.* XI, 74).

22 ibid. 260, where the exchange with Matthew is mentioned in the footnote to the text of Sprat's letter.

23 As pointed out by Webb, *Wren*, 45, and again by Little, 39.

24 G. F. Barwick, ed., *Life of Dr John Barwick by his Brother* (London 1903) 168. According to W. Dugdale, *History of St Paul's Cathedral* (2nd ed. 1716) 148–9, the old choir stalls had been totally destroyed after the Civil War and a temporary choir was fitted up at the east end in 1662.

25 *De Paschate*, not on Pascal (died 1662) as usually stated (BM MS. Lansdowne 698, ff.136–45; Heirloom *Parentalia*, after p. 350). The determination of Easter and the navigation of the Ancients were both suitable subjects for an astronomer seeking to promote the social relevance of his discipline.

26 J. Summerson, *The Sheldonian in its Time* (Oxford 1964) 5–6.

27 *Wren Soc.* V, 14; XIII, 40–4; XVIII, 177–80. M. Whinney, 'Sir Christopher Wren's Visit to Paris', *Gazette des Beaux-*

Arts, 6/LI (1958) 229–42. 'Bernini's Design of the Louvre I would have given my Skin for, but the old reserv'd Italian gave me but a few Minutes View . . . I had only Time to copy it in my Fancy and Memory: I shall be able by Discourse and a Crayon to give you a tolerable Account of it' (*Parentalia*, 262).

28   *Wren Soc.* XIX, 119.

29   id. XIII, 40.

30   ibid. 40–1.

31   ibid. 17. Wren had originally intended to leave at Christmas (*Parentalia*, 261). In fact when his return from Paris was reported by Oldenburg to Boyle on 6 March it must have been very recent, since Justel wrote to Oldenburg on 14 March as if he were still there (H. Oldenburg, *Correspondence*, ed. A. R. and M. B. Hall, III (Madison/London 1966) 48, 11).

32   Oldenburg (ibid. 230) saw the plan on 17 September. Evelyn showed his own plan to the King on the 13th (*Diary*, III, 463) and later told Sir Samuel Tuke that 'Dr Wren had got the start of me' (*Diary and Correspondence* (1894) III, 188).

33   *Parentalia*, 269. Hawksmoor, *Remarks* (below, n.44; *Wren Soc.* VI, 18).

34   Wren is often said to have long been Denham's deputy. He is so described in Aubrey's life of Denham (Dick, 184) but without date. According to *Parentalia*, 263–4 (but with the events dated a year too early) the deputation was only made in Denham's last days of life; nothing in Works records suggests otherwise.

35   From No. 79 to No. 49. *Survey of London*, XXII (1950), 58, Pl. 55b. See n.245.

36   *Walpole Soc.* XXXI (1946). Pl. xxa.

37   Vertue's engraving of the Whitehall plan, published in 1747, is reproduced in *Wren Soc.* VII, Pl. VI; although Vertue gave 1680 as the date of the drawing he used, the original can be shown to have been made in 1669–70 by Ralph Greatorex, who was paid £60 in October 1670 (*History of the King's Works*, V, 264–5).

38   *History of the King's Works*, V, 154, also for the refitting of the range (still extant) east of the Chapel for the Duchess of York, 1670–4. The Chapel reredos was built

to Wren's design in 1676 (PRO Works 5/27).

39   C. G. T. Dean, *The Royal Hospital, Chelsea* (1950) 122–3.

40   Evelyn, IV, 341.

41   Wren to Sir William Fermor, 14 May [1687]. The year can be established by the reference to James's policy and the incidence of Whitsun which the letter mentions (M. Whinney in *Archaeol. Jnl.* CX (1953) 210). The text is printed in *Wren Soc.* XII, 23, and Sotheby sale, 6 July 1953 (298).

42   Luttrell II, 12.

43   Printed in *Wren Soc.* XVIII.

44   N. Hawksmoor, *Remarks on the Founding and Carrying on the Buildings of the Royal Hospital at Greenwich* (1728). Partly reprinted in *Wren Soc.* VI, 17–27.

45   Luttrell IV, 328, 343, 351.

46   *Parentalia*, 292 (as 1710). Edward Strong's final bill for the lantern masonry was entered in Dec. 1708 (*Wren Soc.* XV, 172); the accounts do not record a ceremony. The memoir of Edward Strong senior (1652–1724) dated 12 May 1716 and printed by R. Clutterbuck, *History and Antiquities of the Country of Hertford* I (1815) 168, states that he laid the stone on 26 Oct. 1708. This could be a slip for the 20th, Sir Christopher's birthday (Lang, *St Paul's*, 241 n.2); it is reasonable to suppose that the task was shared by the senior mason and the architect's son.

47   D. Green, *Blenheim Palace* (1951) 43, 58, 233, 237.

48   *History of the King's Works*, V, 37; Colen Campbell, *Virtruvius Britannicus* I (1715) 5 gives 'Mr Wren' as the architect.

49   Vanbrugh, *Letters*, 123.

50   Colvin, *Dictionary*, 803. See also *History of the King's Works*, V, 33–4.

51   Treasury meetings 10, 13 Jan. 1690 (*Wren Soc.* IV, 73); *History of the King's Works*, V, 159.

52   Vanbrugh, *Letters*, 11–13; *Calendar of Treasury Books 1705–6*, 21, 133. The bibulous clerk has not been identified.

53   D. Green, *Blenheim Palace* (1951) 106.

54   *Historical MSS. Comm.* Portland X, 145.

55 Lang, *St Paul's*, 250–1.

56 The *Letter Concerning Design*, written from Naples, was circulating in London in 1712. Although according to Shaftesbury's bibliographers it was first published in the 1732 edition of the *Characteristicks* it can be found in copies of the 1714 edition but not the subsequent ones. It is not mentioned in the 1714 title page, and close examination shows the letter to have been separately printed and inserted with some violence to the make-up of the volume. The inference is that the insertion was made later to bring old stock up to date.

57 K. Downes, *Vanbrugh* (1977) 260–61.

58 *Wren Soc.* XVIII, 9–10.

59 See n.1.

60 Colvin, *Dictionary*, 921. A large drawn view of the Monument (Victoria and Albert Museum) made for one of the Hulsbergh engravings (see n.63) and dated 1723 is signed jointly by Hawksmoor and Christopher III.

61 Copy of Wren's letter to the Society, BM MS. Add.25071, f.115. According to *Parentalia*, 247, there were notes on the problem as late as 1720.

62 *Wren Soc.* XVIII, 181–4.

63 id. XIV, xii; *Walpole Soc.* XXII (1934) 136. Draft proposal for a larger work in BM MS. Add.25071, ff.65–6.

64 Whinney, *Wren*, 7.

65 RIBA Prize Essay 1936, 'The Tyranny of Intellect' (*RIBA Jnl.* 3/XLIV (1937) 373–90). Revised as 'The Mind of Wren' in J. Summerson, *Heavenly Mansions* (1949) 51–86.

66 *Parentalia*, 200–01.

67 ibid. 351–3.

68 Sprat, *Royal Society*, 62.

69 Book of Wisdom (Vulgate xi.21: Omnia in mensura, et numero, et pondere disposuisti).

70 *Parentalia*, 261. Cf. *Tract I* (ibid. 351): 'Architecture aims at Eternity; and therefore the only Thing uncapable of Modes and Fashions in its Principals, the Orders'.

71 Italian sketch-book, 20 Jan. 1615; J. A. Gotch, *Inigo Jones* (1928) 81–2, fre-quently quoted thereafter.

72 Pliny, *Nat. Hist.* XXXIV. 65.

73 *Parentalia*, 351.

74 ibid.

75 *Wren Soc.* XI, 21. Whinney, *Wren*, 41–2.

76 *Parentalia*, 352.

77 Willis and Clark I, 146, 155–6; RCHM *Cambridge*, 148, 153–4. An elevation in the College (*Bicentenary Memorial Volume*, f. p. 223) is not in Wren's hand.

78 H. Wotton, *Elements of Architecture* (1903) 51–2; Gunther, *Pratt*, 22; V. Scamozzi, *L'Idea dell' Architettura Universale* (Venice 1615) I, 51, is a common source for both. The separation of exterior, interior and fittings designers individually responsible to the patron had of course been customary in the sixteenth century and earlier.

79 *Wren Soc.* V, Pls XXIII–XXVI.

80 *Architettura* (1619 ed.) III, 64. Wren's capitals (Plate 16) are of an unusual type.

81 *Oxford Hist. Soc.* XCV (1933) 304; LXXXIII (1926) 285–90.

82 T. Birch, *History of the Royal Society* (1756) I, 230.

83 The Vice-Chancellor's accounts include in 1662–3 the payment to Bird and in 1663–4 a gift of plate costing £6. 17s. 6d. to Wren for his 'pains' as designer and 8s. 6d. for the return journey of the model (*Oxford Hist. Soc.* XXX (1895) 71, 72).

84 Bodleian MS. Bodl.898. Some details were printed in *Wren Soc.* XIX, 92–9, where it was not understood that the volume is a fair copy.

85 *Parentalia*, 335; *Oxford Hist. Soc.* XXX (1895) 68; Bodleian MS. Bodl.898.

86 *Wren Soc.* III, Pl. XVI.

87 By [Bernard] 'Smith, a Dutchman' for £120 according to Anthony Wood. A temporary organ was hired for the opening ceremony. *Oxford Hist. Soc.* XXI (1892) 223; XXX (1895) 71. A pretty design (*Wren Soc.* IX, Pl. 41) for a small organ case over a doorway, decorated with the three crowns of the University crest and a bishop's mitre, looks like a suggestion for the Sheldonian.

88 If the analysis given here is correct, Wren must have taken all the major

decisions about the structure before going to Paris, and what he saw there in the recently built Vigarani theatre in the Tuileries Palace can have done no more than confirm his thinking.

89 *Parentalia*, 335–8.

90 H. Carter, *History of the Oxford University Press*, I (1975) 46.

91 J. Summerson, *The Sheldonian in its Time* (Oxford 1964) 4; Evelyn, III, 530–33. Another early ceremony, the reception of the Prince of Orange (later William III) on 9 Dec. 1670, is described by Anthony Wood (*Oxford Hist. Soc.* XXI (1892) 209–10).

92 Bodleian MS. Bodl.898, f.182.

93 H. M. Colvin, *The Sheldonian Theatre and the Divinity School* (Oxford 1974) 21. Bird was paid for 'the new dore' in 1668–9 (Vice-Chancellor's accounts, *Oxford Hist. Soc.* XXX (1895) 70).

94 Summerson, *Sheldonian*, 9–10.

95 *Parentalia*, 261.

96 *Wren Soc.* XVI, 131.

97 *Parentalia*, 352–3.

98 ibid.

99 *Tract IV* (*Parentalia*, 368).

100 Gunther, *Pratt*, 21–30.

101 Palladio, *Quattro Libri* (Venice 1570) II, 14; Serlio, *Architettura* (1619 ed.) III, 64, 99, 104, 108.

102 All Souls II. 73 (*Wren Soc.* VII, Pl. x); K. Downes, 'Wren and Whitehall in 1664', *Burlington Mag.* CXIII (1971) 89–92.

103 *History of the King's Works*, V, 345–8; T. F. Reddaway, 'The London Custom House 1666–1740', *London Topog. Record* XXI (1958) 1–25. A recent attempt by W. Kuyper, *Dutch Classicist Architecture* (Delft 1980) 119 and Pl. 242, to discern the hand of Hugh May in the design, concentrates on its superficial rather than its essential elements.

104 *Wren Soc.* V, 14, Pls IV–V.

105 Willis and Clark II, 703–10; RCHM *Cambridge*, 62–6.

106 *Wren Soc.* V, Pl. XII.

107 *Wren Soc.* XIII, 13–14.

108 W. Dugdale, *History of St Paul's Cathedral* (1716) 149, records expenditure of £3586. 5s. 1¼d. on repairs between August 1663 and August 1666, 'whereof much was

on the Portico'.

109 *Wren Soc.* XIII, 14–15.

110 Gunther, *Pratt*, 23.

111 *Wren Soc.* XIII, 15–17.

112 ibid. 44.

113 Wren to Sancroft, 5 Aug. 1666 (*Wren Soc.* XIII, 45); drawings id. I, Pls v upper, VI–VIII.

114 These three paragraphs are based on the May 1666 report (*Wren Soc.* XIII, 15–17).

115 ibid. 17.

116 ibid. 18.

117 Evelyn, III, 448–9, 454. Pepys's account of the fire is longer and more dramatic.

118 *Wren Soc.* XII, Pl. XXV; *Parentalia*, 267–9. For the rebuilding see T. F. Reddaway, *The Rebuilding of London after the Great Fire* (1940).

119 *Wren Soc.* XIII, 20–2 (before Feb. 1667), 45 (24 Nov. 1666 or 1667).

120 ibid. 22–3.

121 ibid. 46.

122 ibid. 46–7.

123 ibid. 47–8.

124 ibid. 23.

125 ibid. 49.

126 Gunther, *Pratt*, 213–14. *Wren Soc.* XIII, f.p. xiv; N. Lynton, *Burlington Mag.* XCVII (1955) 40–4.

127 *Wren Soc.* XIII, 46–7.

128 Studies have been based on the collected accounts in Bodleian MSS. Rawl. B.386–8, but these only run to *c.* 1694. A fuller set of accounts was transferred in 1980 from St Paul's Cathedral Library to the Guildhall. Extracts from accounts and parish documents were published in *Wren Soc.* IX, X and XIX. On post-war restorations see the pungent criticism of Ian Nairn in *Architects' Jnl.*, 15 Jan. 1959, 99–104. Earlier changes include the blocking of windows such as the main east one at St James, Garlickhythe (Plates 103, 116).

129 John Clayton's measured drawings of 46 churches, originally published in 1848–9, are reprinted in *Wren Soc.* IX.

130 *Parentalia*, 320.

131 11 Dec. 1672.

132 BM MS. Sloane 5238, No. 47

(repr. Hooke, *Diary*, 397).

133 *Wren Soc.* XIX, 11–13. The altar wall of St Bride was remodelled in 1822–3 by John Deykes. The present *trompe-l'oeil* painting is an ambitious pastiche of the original (but not necessarily Wren's) design.

134 *Parentalia*, 314. The statement is often wrongly imputed to Hawksmoor.

135 *De Architectura*, V. i. 6.

136 ibid. VI. iii.

137 S. Perks, *History of the Mansion House* (Cambridge 1922) *passim*. According to J. G. White, *History of the Ward of Walbrook* (1904) 75, 'Sir Christopher Wren is said to have lived at No. 5 [Walbrook]; this may have been during the period that he was rebuilding the Church of St Stephen'. This is not borne out by surviving rate assessments (City of London Record Office) and another reason must be sought for the building's exceptional quality. Drawings for the portico scheme are discussed and illustrated by J. Summerson in *RIBA Jnl.* 3/LIX (1952) 126–8 and in *Architectural History* XIII (1970) 41 and Fig. 26. See n.246.

138 *Wren Soc.* XVI, 199.

139 ibid. 197.

140 *Parentalia*, 282.

141 *Wren Soc.* I, Pls XVI–XVIII.

142 BM MS. Sloane 5238. *Wren Soc.* V, Pls XXXIV–XXXVII. Woodroffe's meticulous penwork appears in Pls XXXV right and XXXVII right.

143 *Wren Soc.* V, 45–51. Another iconographical structure, Temple Bar, marking the western entrance to the City between the Strand and Fleet Street (Plates 23, 76), was built in 1670–2 and was removed in 1878 to Theobalds Park, Cheshunt, Herts. The traditional attribution to Wren is worth considering for the following reasons. (1) The rebuilding of 1670–2 was due not to the fire but to the road-widening Act of 1662. It had peculiar royal ceremonial associations: even today the monarch asks permission 'at Temple Bar' before entering the City. To enforce the Act the gateway was paid for by the Crown, since the City had tried to avoid the work on grounds of expense (T. F. Reddaway, *The Rebuilding of London* (1940) 38, 40–1, 193, 291). It would be reasonable

for Charles's personal interest to extend to the involvement of his new Surveyor. (2) The design is unlike any other city gateway in England or abroad, and the absence of obvious sources is at least suggestive of Wren's authorship at this period. The detail, now much weathered, is consistent in quality with that in the early churches; the masons were Joshua Marshall and Thomas Knight. (3) The windows in the centre of the east and west faces are of an unusual design which next appears in the aisles of St Paul's at the 'Definitive' stage (1675) and in the building (Plate 78). Whinney, *Wren*, 107, saw the St Paul's windows as somewhat French in character'. In both buildings an architrave with ears or lugs is combined with a semicircular head, without the pediment or cornice which would surmount a French or Italian example. In both cases the design seems to relate to the particular problem of inserting a round-headed window into the capital zone of a Corinthian order. At St Paul's the round-headed windows were taken over from the Warrant elevation which had buttress strips and not pilasters. There the solution is typical of Wren; can its anticipation five years earlier have been accidental? (4) Christopher III included Temple Bar in the first draft of *Parentalia* (BM MS. Add.25071, f.64) whereas the Middle Temple gateway of 1684, which is now known to have been by Roger North, does not appear until the second draft (f.113). (5) The new gateway may have formed a more discreet substitute for the 'Triumphal Arch to the Founder of the New City' proposed at Ludgate in the 1666 City plan (ibid. f.51 and *Parentalia*, 268).

144 *Parentalia*, 282.

145 *Diary*, 12, 27, 87.

146 *Wren Soc.* XVI, 202–07.

147 Henry Ball to Sir Joseph Williamson, 15 Aug. 1673 (*Wren Soc.* XIII, xviii).

148 *Wren Soc.* XIII, 26–31.

149 Tillison to Sancroft, 22 Sept. 1673 (ibid. 51).

150 *Wren Soc.* XVI, 201.

151 ibid.

152 ibid. 206.

153 *Parentalia*, 282.

154 ibid. 283.

155 Warrant of 14 May 1675 (*Wren Soc.* I, Pl. ix).

156 *Survey of London* XXIX (1960) 31–51. Building accounts do not survive, but Hooke recorded on 3 April 1676 (*Diary*, 224) 'St Alban's Cornerstone layd'.

157 *Parentalia*, 320.

158 *Wren Soc.* IX, Pl. 17.

159 Willis and Clark II, 531–55; RCHM *Cambridge*, 231–4, 237–41. The old library had been severely damaged by fire in 1665. The college issued an appeal in Jan. 1676 and took the formal decision to build on 22 February, starting work the next day (P. Gaskell and R. Robson, *The Library of Trinity College, Cambridge* (Cambridge 1971) 13–16. The Library of Lincoln Cathedral was built in 1674 'according to Sir Christopher Wren's direction and Mr Tompson's model' (*Wren Soc.* XVII, 76–7). The London mason John Tompson was therefore almost certainly responsible for the design.

160 Willis and Clark II, 532.

161 *Wren Soc.* V, Pls. xiii–xiv.

162 ibid. Pls xv, xviii–xxi. Palladio, *Quattro Libri* (1570) II. 19. The Greek Cross design for St Paul's (1672) was also indebted, as its sloping roofs betray (Fig. 9), to the Rotonda.

163 Mostly at All Souls (*Wren Soc.* V, Pls xxii–xxvi, p. 44; IX, Pl. 43). The sheet of details is at Trinity College (Downes, *Wren*, Fig. 6). The letter is printed in *Wren Soc.* V, 32–4, and Willis and Clark II, 534–7. The drawings show a building 2 ft longer than executed.

164 H. M. Fletcher, 'Sir Christopher Wren's Carpentry', *RIBA Jnl.* 3/XXX (1923) 388–91; Downes, *Wren*, Fig. 8. For the restoration see D. W. Insall, *The Care of Old Buildings Today* (London/New York 1972) 177–82. A low opinion of the hidden supports was expressed by Peter E. Locke ARIBA in a paper to the Society of Antiquaries on 25 November 1971.

165 *Parentalia*, 283.

166 This was the last appearance of an outside portico giving effective shelter; as built, the portico appears to the visitor to be part of the whole front and to some extent already part of the interior. But by the time it was built the secular business had long since moved away into the coffee-houses, which the availability of the new non-alcoholic beverage made an acceptable place to businessmen of whatever persuasion.

167 *Wren Soc.* I, Pl. ix.

168 ibid. Pls. x–xiii.

169 *Burlington Mag.* CIII (1961) 83–9.

170 *Wren Soc.* I, Pls xix, xxii lower, xxiii lower, xxiv, xxv (subsequently altered); XIV, Pl. ix.

171 The same dome design appears in a half-section-elevation with two quarter-plans (*Wren Soc.* III, Pl.xxix right) which is in Woodroffe's characteristic hand. This identification was communicated *en passant* by Sir John Summerson in a discourse to the Royal Institution in 1952. Later in the 1950s, discussion between him, Dr Margaret Whinney and myself centred on quite different evidence in relation to the complete elevation. In reviewing the problem, it is a pleasure to be able, in the face of my previous conclusions, to acknowledge both the accuracy and the appropriateness of Summerson's observation.

172 The structural function of the screen walls was discussed by Somers Clarke in *Bicentenary Memorial Volume* (1923) 73–82; its temporary nature was suggested to me by Robert Crayford.

173 Drawings – admittedly surveys, not designs – of Greenwich (*Wren Soc.* VI, Pls vi, vii, xxv).

174 *Wren Soc.* IX, Pl. 23.

175 *Parentalia*, 331–2; *Wren Soc.* V, 52–4, Pls xli–xliii. See n.247.

176 *De Re Aedificatoria*, VIII.v.

177 *Wren Soc.* IX, Pl. 23.

178 *Parentalia*, 293.

179 Scaffolding of this type is shown in Sutton Nicholls's print of 1695 of the choir under construction (*Wren Soc.* XIV, Pl.l). The print was ephemeral and is rare; the Guildhall has a nineteenth-century forged version. Two early attempts to show the new building to the public are reproduced by Fuerst, *Wren*, Figs 112, 114. The first,

added to the 1676 and later editions of Godfrey Richards's *First Book of Palladio*, resulted from grafting the Great Model on to the basement piers and windows of the newly begun building. (The plaster model on which Fuerst speculates (n.430) is a chimaera.) The second image, one of the illustrations at the top of the 'Ogilby and Morgan' 1682 map of London (engraved late 1680–early 1681) follows the building for the lower storey; William Morgan added the rest 'according to the last information we could get, hoping it may not be very unlike when finish'd' (Morgan's prospectus, Guildhall Broadside 7.160, quoted by Ralph Hyde in the introduction to the Guildhall's facsimile reprint of the map).

180   Dean, *The Royal Hospital, Chelsea* (1950); *Wren Soc.* XIX. The building records are not complete.

181   Whinney and Millar, 217 n.1. These were perhaps the drawings in lot 41 of the Wren sale, 4/6 April 1749 (*Wren Soc.* XX, 79).

182   E. Hatton, *A New View of London* (1708) [II] 737.

183   *Walpole Soc.* XXXI (1946) Pl.xxi. This arrangement, without the portico, could also be found earlier in Wadham, Wren's college.

184   *Wren Soc.* XVI, 56.

185   *History of the King's Works*, V, 310.

186   Besides the account in *History of the King's Works* see A. Cook, 'Wren's Design for Winchester Palace' in H. Colvin and J. Harris eds, *The Country Seat* (1970) 58–63. The print in Milner's *Winchester* (Plate 160 here) is only approximate.

187   *History of the King's Works*, V, 285–90.

188   *Burlington Mag.* CXX (1978) 167.

189   'Some great sash-windows of the banquetting-house have been torn from the frames, and blown so as they have never been found nor heard of' (William Congreve, *Letters*, ed. J. C. Hodges (1964) 26 (30 Nov. 1703).

190   *Wren Soc.* XIX, 113–14. See also D. Howse, *Greenwich Observatory* (1975) III, who cogently suggests (p. 4) that the summer-houses (so called in a plan of 1676)

were last-minute additions to the design.

191   W. D. Caröe, *Tom Tower* (Oxford 1923) 31–2.

192   Since its restoration as part of the National Maritime Museum the Observatory's simple functional nobility has been largely recovered. Bricks from Tilbury Fort and other old materials were re-used in the structure: Charles II could not afford ostentatious patronage of the sciences on the scale of Louis XIV evidenced by the massive Paris Observatory begun in 1667 to the design of Claude Perrault.

193   Caröe, loc. cit.

194   ibid. 23.

195   *Parentalia*, 302.

196   H. M. Colvin, *Architectural History* XXIV (1981) 21–31. Drawings for a tower for St Michael, Cornhill, not as carried out but probably in Dickinson's hand (*Wren Soc.* X, Pl. 9), show a similar style to the towers of St Sepulchre and St Christopher. Drawings for the latter are probably also by Dickinson (BM K.124.51–2). Hawksmoor on the other hand made most of the surviving drawings for a rebuilding project at St Mary, Warwick, in 1694–7 (*Wren Soc.* X, Pls 15–18; see K. Downes, *Hawksmoor* (1959) 54–5). This church was carried out in 1698–1704 by Sir William Wilson of Sutton Coldfield, without reference to the earlier project which is probably the 'Designs . . . not executed' listed in *Parentalia*, 342. Also mentioned there is a design for the tower, 'erected after an unsuccessful Attempt in Execution of a defective prior Design by other Hands'. Wilson's tower failed but the present one, built 1700–04, is usually attributed to him. Christopher III retired to Wroxall near Warwick and would have been in a position to know whether the masses and outline (but not the surface detail) of the tower were his father's work. The case made for this (K. Downes, *English Baroque Architecture* (1966) 122–3) rests.

197   *Diary*, IV, 392–3.

198   M. I. Batten, *Walpole Soc.* XXV (1937) 89–90.

199   E. Croft-Murray, *Decorative Painting in England*, I (1962) 221.

200   R. M. Laporte-Payne, *St Mary*

Abchurch (1946).

201   Evelyn, IV, 543–5; *History of the King's Works*, V, 290–3.

202   ibid. 274–5; *Wren Soc.* V, Pl.XLIV (as Hampton Court).

203   *History of the King's Works*, V, 294–6.

204   In the Soane Museum: *Wren Soc.* IV, Pls IV, XI, XII; Whinney, *Wren*, Fig. 142. See also K. Downes, *English Baroque Architecture* (1966) Figs 12, 13. See n.214.

205   *Burlington Mag.* XCII (1950) 229. The drawing bears the name (not the signature) of Daniel Marot and the date 1689, which is several years too early.

206   *Parentalia*, 352.

207   e.g. Jean Marot, *Recueil des Plans, Profils et Elevations* – the 'Petit Marot', c. 1654–60. Although the Fountain Court is twelve bays each way, the design conceals a difference of about 7 feet between adjacent sides. Moreover, the southern corners are unsquare by about 1 degree.

208   *Parentalia*, 326–7.

209   By A. T. Bolton in *Wren Soc.* IV, 20, and unaccountably resurrected by Whinney, *Wren*, 173.

210   *Wren Soc.* I, Pl.XVII.

211   In the past I have referred to the fruits in the wreaths of these roundels as oranges (for William of Orange). The accounts refer only to laurels, but it is worth noting that orange trees became popular in England after the Revolution of 1688.

212   *Wren Soc.* IV, 58–9, Pls XXXII, XXXV, XXXVI.

213   *History of the King's Works*, V, 164–6.

214   Whinney, *Wren*, Fig. 142. The drawing is All Souls II. 116*. The scoring is invisible in most reproductions. A similar grid is recommended by Scamozzi (*Architettura* (1615) I, 48) and scored grids can be seen in some of Webb's Whitehall plans (*Walpole Soc.* XXXI (1946) Pl. x). 15 feet is approximately the bay width of the Great Hall.

215   K. Downes, *Hawksmoor* (1959) 65–6; *History of the King's Works*, V, 190 as Wren; the case argued there would in any event refute that made by W. Kuyper,

Dutch Classicist Architecture (Delft 1980) 123–4, for an attribution to Jacob Roman c. 1690.

216   K. Downes, *Hawksmoor* (2nd ed. 1979) 274. The construction of a conduit for water supply in 1694 is likely to have preceded the start of the main house. The arguments offered by H. M. Colvin, *Country Life* CXLVIII (1970) 968–71, cannot be sustained. For Wren's relationship to Fermor see n.7.

217   According to his letter of that year to Fermor (see n.41). See also n.248.

218   K. Downes, *Hawksmoor* (London 1969), Fig. 10.

219   Documents in *Wren Soc.* XVII, 54–75.

220   *Wren Soc.* VIII.

221   *Parentalia*, 334.

222   *Cal. Treasury Books 1693–6*, 796–7; *Wren Soc.* VI, Pl.x right shows the extent of land granted.

223   *Cal. S.P. Dom. 1696*, 152 (29 April 1696). This formalized several decisions made early in the year (*Wren Soc.* VI, 32–3).

224   *Wren Soc.* VI, 32.

225   *Wren Soc.* XVIII, 111 (4 Oct. 1694; office copy of lost original) in reply to letter from Henry Guy, 21 Sept. (*Cal. Treasury Books 1693–6*, 770). Travers had made a survey of Greenwich Park before May 1694 (*Cal. Treasury Papers 1557–1696*, 364).

226   *Wren Soc.* VI, 83 left, Pl.XXI upper; VIII, Pls XVIII, XIX. A design close in spirit was probably made at about the same time, for a domed Greek cross church in the centre of Lincoln's Inn Fields. A wooden model was made, but only prints and drawings survive of the project (*Wren Soc.* IX, Pl. 31; XVIII, Pl. VIII).

227   *Wren Soc.* VI, Pl.x left; VIII, Pl.XXI. The south edge of the granted site is shown on the first drawing.

228   *Wren Soc.* VI, Pls XXIV, XXV; VIII, Pl.XXII.

229   *Wren Soc.* VI, Pl.XXVI.

230   *Parentalia*, 292. Evelyn's dedication to Wren of his *Account of Architects and Architecture*, 1697. He had used the word of the whole city in 1666 (*Diary and Correspondence* (1894) III, 188).

231 The apocryphal reference to a 'damned box of whistles' has neither the force nor the elegant richness of Wren's genuine 'edging' remark (p. 20). The screen was removed in 1861 and the organ, split into two, re-mounted against the sides of the chancel arch in 1872. An anonymous broadside of *c*. 1700, *Questions about St Paul's Organ* (BM 816.m.9(93)) suggested that Wren would have liked 'a free and airy Prospect of the whole length of the church' (*Camden Soc.* n.s. XXVI (1880) 165). The suggestion was repeated by H. H. Milman, *Annals of S. Paul's Cathedral* (1869) 435, on the basis of a drawing by Grinling Gibbons for a *choir organ* case within one of the side arches of the choir (*Wren Soc.* III, Pl.xxxvII) and the opinion of Milman's architect F. C. Penrose that the piers in the crypt below the organ screen were an afterthought. But it was normal to build crypt vaults last of all. By this date it was assumed that the interior of St Paul's needed not restoration but 'completion' by coloured decoration. See G. L. Prestige, *St Paul's in its Glory* (London 1955) and J. M. Crook, *Antiquaries' Jnl.* LX (1980) 285–307. The latter should not, however, be relied on for Wren's intentions; see in particular my notes 232–4, 241.

232 References in accounts. The need for uniformity was increased by the amount of patching carried out because of cracks that had appeared during construction.

233 'as . . . in the Cupola of St Peter's in Rome' (*Parentalia*, 292, note (a)). However, the drawing cited in n.171 shows that in 1675 Wren had considered a dome painted with figures and sky.

234 *Wren Soc.* XIII, Pls xxxi (with Latin reference to the horse's pedestal), xxxii; Downes, *Hawksmoor* (1959) Pl. 10b.

235 *Wren Soc.* XV, 173 (information from Robert Crayford).

236 *Wren Soc.* III, Pls xxxi, xxxii; XIII, Pl.xxxiii. Also designs for a baptistery or chapter house, III, Pls xxiii, xxiv.

237 *Wren Soc.* III, Pl.xv upper. The drawing in II, Pl.xviii (Whinney, *Wren*, Fig. 98) is not by Hawksmoor and is neither inscribed nor dated.

238 *Parentalia*, 287–8. On the supply of Portland stone see J. H. Bettey, *Archaeol. Jnl.* CXXVIII (1971) 176–85.

239 *Burlington Mag.* CXXIII (1981) 35–6. That the lack of large blocks affected abutment and projection rather than the entablature spans is confirmed by a remark of Roger North, *Of Building* (ed. H. Colvin and J. Newman, Oxford 1981) 22, xvii–xviii. North also commented on Wren's use of flat arches in the transept ends of St Paul's (ibid. 120).

240 *Wren Soc.* XIV, Pls vi, ix–xii; XV, 84, 94, 96.

241 *Wren Soc.* XIV, Pls vii, xiii–xvii, xxxvi–xxxvii.

242 St Paul's Collection (Sotheby sale 23 May 1951, f. p. 4).

243 *Commons Jnl.* XI, 665, 680 (18 and 28 Jan. 1697); Act 8/9 William III, *c*. 14.

244 Balance account (Guildhall MS.25541/4). Hawksmoor was not paid after Aug. 1701. He had earlier made designs for a 'lantern' for St Augustine (*Wren Soc.* IX, Pl. 36, K. Downes, *Hawksmoor* (1969) Fig. 16) and it is tempting to see his influence in the peculiarly square scrolls at the top of St James Garlickhythe.

245 A copy of the 1684 Perrault edition of Vitruvius signed *Nich Hawksmoor at Sir Christopher Wren's in Scotland Yard* (Canadian Architectural Centre, Montreal) confirms Wren's residence and implies that Hawksmoor lived in his household in the mid 1680s.

246 A north portico figures in the earliest drawings for St Stephen Walbrook; the 1679 design is documented but not extant.

247 The parliamentary Bill funding the mausoleum failed a second reading in the Commons. A minor regal monument, no doubt related in the King's mind, was erected at this date: Wren designed the white marble tablet, carved by Joshua Marshall and set up in Westminster Abbey in 1678, to the 'Princes in the Tower', Edward V and Richard Duke of York (*Parentalia*, 333; *History of the King's Works*, V, 455).

248 William III dined at Tring on 4 June 1690 (Luttrell II, 52).

LIST OF WORKS

This list is a guide to those buildings either wholly or substantially carried out to Wren's designs and thus forming the essence of his architecture. It does not include all unexecuted projects, minor alterations or fittings, autonomous works by his subordinates, or attributions which in the writer's opinion are improbable. A fuller list, based on different criterions, is to be found in H. M. Colvin's *Biographical Dictionary of British Architects*. Dates are generally those of significant periods of construction. For brevity, documentary references are omitted.

St Paul's Cathedral. 1675–1710, with minor later works. For convenience the following preliminary stages are listed.

1663. 18 April. Commission for repair.
1666. [7] May. Wren's report.
        5 August. Drawings for crossing.
        27 August. Site meeting.
        2 September. Great Fire.
1668. 25 April. Sancroft requests re-submission of earlier drawings.
        25 July. Order to demolish tower and choir.
1670. March. First Model finished.
1672. Before 25 March. Wren paid £100 for [Greek Cross] drawings.
        June (or earlier). First Model returned from Whitehall.
        2 November. Hooke 'Saw model . . . approved by the King', i.e. Greek Cross.
        9 November. 'Curious Model' rather bigger than old foundations (*Wren Soc.* XIII, xviii).
1673. 8 February. Hooke told by Wren of 'Addition of Library Body and portico on the west'.
        12 July. Pratt's criticism of First Model.
        Summer. Scaffold and standard to set out centre of dome.
        22 September. Wren and Woodroffe scaling up drawings for Great Model.
        12 November. Warrant for rebuilding commission, with approval of Great Model design.
1674. 21 February. Hooke walked through Great Model.
        8 August. Hooke saw Great Model finished.
1675. 14 May. Warrant for Warrant Design.
        15 July. Mason's contracts for Definitive Design.

City Churches rebuilt

St Alban, Wood Street. 1682–7; tower finished 1697. Gutted 1940 and demolished except tower.

All Hallows, Lombard Street. 1686–94. Demolished 1939, tower rebuilt and fittings installed at All Hallows, Twickenham.

All Hallows the Great, Thames Street. 1677–82. Demolished 1876–94.

All Hallows, Watling Street (Bread Street). 1677–84; tower completed 1698. Demolished 1877.

St Andrew-by-the-Wardrobe. 1685–94. Gutted 1940 and restored. Because of the poverty of the parish the furniture was paid for from the coal tax. The altarpiece has wrongly been attributed to Hawksmoor because he witnessed the contract.

St Anne and St Agnes, Gresham Street. 1676–81. Gutted 1940 and restored.

St Antholin, Budge Row. 1678–83, the spire built by contract 1686–7. Demolished 1875–6.

St Augustine, Watling Street. 1680–6; spire 1695–6. Gutted 1941; tower remains with reconstructed spire.

St Bartholomew, Exchange. 1674–81. Demolished 1841.

St Benet Fink. 1670–81. Demolished 1846.

St Benet, Gracechurch Street. 1681–7. Demolished 1876.

St Benet, Paul's Wharf. 1677–85.

St Bride, Fleet Street. 1670–4; steeple 1702–03. Gutted 1940, rebuilt and rearranged.

Christ Church, Newgate Street. 1677–87. Spire 1703–04. Gutted 1940; tower and steeple remain.

St Christopher-le-Stocks. Repaired and re-roofed 1670–1. Tower completed 1712, church rebuilt 1712–14. Demolished 1781–6.

St Clement, Eastcheap. 1683–7.

St Dionis Backchurch. 1670–7. Tower completed 1685. Demolished 1878.

St Dunstan-in-the-East. Repaired 1668–71, probably not by Wren. Restored 1695–1702. Tower and spire 1695–8. Destroyed except tower and spire.

St Edmund, Lombard Street. 1670–6. Spire 1706–07.

St George, Botolph Lane. 1671–9. Demolished 1903–04.

St James Garlickhythe. 1676–82. Tower finished 1685, steeple 1714–17. Damaged 1941 and restored.

St Lawrence Jewry. 1670–81. Gutted 1940 and restored.

St Magnus, London Bridge. 1671–8. Tower finished 1684, steeple 1705–06. West end shortened 1762–8, north windows made circular 1782.

St Margaret Lothbury. 1686–92; spire completed 1699.

St Margaret Pattens, Rood Lane. 1684–7. Spire completed 1702.

St Martin Ludgate. 1677–86.

St Mary Abchurch. 1681–7. Damaged 1940 and restored.

St Mary Aldermanbury. 1670–4. Gutted 1940, reconstructed 1964–9 at Fulton, Missouri.

St Mary Aldermary. 1679–82. Tower recased 1701–03.

St Mary-le-Bow. 1671–5. Tower and spire finished 1680. Gutted 1941 and restored.

St Mary-at-Hill. 1670–2; lantern 1695. Interior rebuilt and refitted 1827–49.

St Mary Somerset. 1686–94. Demolished 1871 except tower.

(St Mary Woolnoth. Repaired 1670–5, probably not by Wren. Subsequently rebuilt by Hawksmoor.)

St Mary Magdalen, Old Fish Street. 1683–7. Demolished 1886–90.

St Matthew, Friday Street. 1681–6. Demolished 1885.

St Michael Bassishaw. 1676–9. Steeple 1708–12. Demolished 1900.

(St Michael, Cornhill. Restored 1670–2, probably not by Wren. Tower 1718–24 by Hawksmoor.)

St Michael, Crooked Lane. 1684–7. Tower finished 1698, spire 1709–14. Demolished 1831.

St Michael, Queenhythe. 1676–80. Tower and spire 1685–7. Demolished 1876.

St Michael Royal. 1686–94. Steeple 1713–17. Damaged 1944 and restored.

St Michael, Wood Street. 1670–3; lantern on tower 1687. Demolished 1897. The leaded spire was a later addition.

St Mildred, Bread Street. 1681–7. Damaged 1941 and demolished.

St Mildred, Poultry. 1670–7. Demolished 1872.

St Nicholas, Cole Abbey. 1671–8. Gutted 1941 and restored.

St Olave, Old Jewry. 1670–9. Demolished 1887 except tower.

St Peter, Cornhill. 1677–81. Steeple finished 1685.

(St Sepulchre, Holborn. Restored 1667–71, probably not by Wren. Ornaments, pinnacles and windows of tower rebuilt 1712–13, probably by Dickinson.)

St Stephen, Coleman Street. 1674–7. Gutted

1940 and demolished.

St Stephen Walbrook. 1672–8. Tower finished 1680, spire 1713–17. Damaged 1941 and restored.

St Swithin, Cannon Street. 1677–81. Spire finished 1686. Gutted 1941 and demolished.

St Vedast, Foster Lane. Repaired 1671–2. Rebuilt 1695–1700. Spire 1709–12. Gutted 1940 and restored.

Other churches

St Andrew, Holborn. Rebuilt 1684–92. Tower rebuilt 1704. Gutted 1941 and restored.

St Clement Danes. Rebuilt 1680–2. Gutted 1941 and restored. Steeple by James Gibbs 1719.

St James, Piccadilly. 1676–84. Gutted 1940 and restored. The authorship of the spire, now reconstructed, is uncertain.

(?) Warwick, St Mary. Tower. 1700–04.

University and Secular

Cambridge, Pembroke College Chapel. 1663–5. East end extended 1880.

Oxford, Sheldonian Theatre. 1664–9. Re-roofed 1802, cupola rebuilt 1838. Refaced 1959–60.

Oxford, All Souls College Chapel, screen. 1664. Remodelled by Thornhill 1716.

Cambridge, Emmanuel College. Chapel and gallery. 1668–73.

Oxford, Trinity College. Garden quadrangle. North wing 1668, west and south wings added 1682, 1728. Attic added 1802. Refaced 1958–65.

London, Custom House. 1669–71. Destroyed 1718.

Oxford, St John's College Chapel, screen. *c.* 1670. Destroyed 1843.

(?) London, Temple Bar. 1670–2. Moved to Theobalds Park 1878.

Hampton Court. South-east corner. 1670.

Destroyed 1689. East side of chapel court converted 1670–4. Chapel altarpiece 1676.

Oxford, Merton College Chapel, screen. 1671–3. Partly reinstated 1960.

Salisbury Cathedral, bishop's throne and stalls. 1671–3. Destroyed.

London, The Monument, Fish Street. 1671–6.

Oxford, The Queen's College, Williamson Building. 1671–4. Top storey added *c.* 1730. Only the north end retains its original appearance (Plate 7).

London, Drury Lane Theatre. 1672–4. Rebuilt 1791.

Greenwich, Royal Observatory. 1675–6.

Cambridge, Trinity College Library. 1676–84.

London, Middle Temple, Pump Court Cloisters. 1680–1. Destroyed 1940 and partially reconstructed.

Oxford, Christ Church, Tom Tower. 1681–2.

London, Chelsea, Royal Hospital. 1682–92. Sash windows installed in the 18th century.

Winchester Palace. 1683–5, unfinished. Destroyed 1894.

London, Whitehall Palace. Range containing Privy Gallery, Council Chamber and Roman Catholic Chapel. 1685–7. Destroyed 1698.

Tring Manor, Hertfordshire. *c.* 1687–90. Carcase survives inside the late Victorian house.

London, Whitehall Palace. Queen's Apartment and terrace garden. 1688–93. Destroyed 1698.

Hampton Court. South and east ranges. 1689–1700.

London, Kensington Palace. New ranges. 1689–96.

Greenwich, Royal Hospital. Begun 1696.

Winslow Hall, Bucks. 1699–1702.

BIBLIOGRAPHY

Most people think a book should have a bibliography; how useful it is depends on the user as well as on its content and arrangement. Since the proper place for individual references is in the notes, and since most of the works cited have their own bibliographies, this one is intended for two functions. One is to indicate the *principal* sources for the study of Wren's architecture; the other is to identify works cited in the notes in shortened form. Entries, by author or keyword, are in alphabetical order.

Batten (M. I.) 'The Architecture of Robert Hooke'. *Walpole Soc.* XXV (1937) 83–113.

Bennett (J. A.) 'Christopher Wren: the Natural Causes of Beauty', *Architectural History* XV (1972) 5–22.

Bicentenary Memorial Volume. *Sir Christopher Wren*. Published under the Auspices of the Royal Institute of British Architects (London 1923).

Caröe (W. D.) *Tom Tower* (Oxford 1923).

Cobb (G.) *The Old Churches of London* (London 1942).

Colvin (H. M.) *Biographical Dictionary of British Architects 1600–1840* (London 1978).

Davies (J. H. V.) 'The Dating of the Buildings of the Royal Hospital at Greenwich'. *Archaeol. Jnl.* CXIII (1956) 126–36.

Dean (C. G. T.) *The Royal Hospital, Chelsea* (London 1950).

Dick (O. L.) *Aubrey's Brief Lives* (London 1962).

Downes (K.) *Christopher Wren* (London 1971).

Downes (K.) 'Wren and Whitehall in 1664'. *Burlington Mag.* CXIII (1971) 89–92.

Downes (K.) *English Baroque Architecture* (London 1966).

Elmes (J.) *Memoirs of the Life and Works of Sir Christopher Wren* (London 1823).

Evelyn (John) *Diary*, ed. E. S. de Beer (Oxford 1955).

Fuerst (V.) *The Architecture of Sir Christopher Wren* (London 1956).

Gunther (R. T.) *The Architecture of Sir Roger Pratt* (Oxford 1928).

Hatton (E.) *A New View of London* (London 1708).

History of the King's Works, ed. H. M. Colvin. Vol. V. 1660–1782 (London 1976).

Hooke (Robert) *Diary* (London 1935).

Lang (J.) *Rebuilding St Paul's* (London 1956).

Little (B.) *Sir Christopher Wren, a Historical Biography* (London 1975).

Luttrell (N.) *A Brief Relation of Historical and State Affairs* (Oxford 1857).

Lynton (N.) 'A Wren Drawing for St Paul's'. *Burlington Mag.* XCVII (1955) 40–44.

Parentalia, or Memoirs of the Family of Wrens [by Christopher Wren] (London 1750; facsimile reprint London 1965).

Pepys (Samuel) *Diary* (various eds).

Poley (A. F. E.) *St Paul's Cathedral Measured, Drawn and Described* (London 1927; 2nd ed. 1932).

RCHM (Royal Commission on Historical Monuments, England) *City of Cambridge*

(London 1959) and other vols.

Reddaway (T. F.) *The Rebuilding of London after the Great Fire* (London 1940).

Sekler (E. F.) *Wren and his Place in European Architecture* (London 1956).

Sprat (T.) *History of the Royal Society* (London 1667).

Summerson (J.) *Architecture in Britain 1530–1830* (London 1953 and later eds).

Summerson (J.) *Sir Christopher Wren* (London 1953).

Summerson (J.) *Heavenly Mansions* (London 1949): pp. 51–86, 'The Mind of Wren'.

Summerson (J.) 'Drawings of London Churches in the Bute Collection'. *Architectural History* XIII (1970) 30–42.

Summerson (J.) 'The Penultimate Design for St Paul's'. *Burlington Mag.* CIII (1961) 83–9.

Survey of London (published by the London County Council; later by the Greater London Council. Various vols).

Vanbrugh (J.) *Letters*, ed. G. F. Webb (London 1928).

Watkin (D.) ed. *Sale Catalogues of Libraries of Eminent Persons 4. Architects* (London 1972).

Weaver (L.) *Sir Christopher Wren* (London 1923).

Webb (G. F.) *Wren* (London 1937).

Whinney (M. D.) *Wren* (London 1971).

Whinney (M. D.) and Millar (O.) *English Art 1625–1714* (Oxford 1957).

Willis (R.) and Clark (J.) *The Architectural History of the University of Cambridge* (Cambridge 1886).

Wren Society. The First . . . Twentieth Volume (Oxford 1924–43).

INDEX

Notes are in parentheses. Plate numbers are in *italic*. The List of Works is not indexed.

PLATES

1 Edward Pierce. Sir Christopher Wren. *Ashmolean Museum, Oxford.*

2   Project for Whitehall (doubled). 1664. *All Souls, Oxford.*

3   William Arnold (?) Oxford, Wadham College. Hall and Chapel.

4 Inigo Jones. The Banqueting House, Whitehall.

5 Oxford, Sheldonian Theatre. East side. 1664–9.

6   Oxford, Sheldonian Theatre. North end. Engraving by David Loggan.

7   Oxford, The Queen's College. Williamson Building.
1671–4.

8   Oxford, Divinity School. North Doorway. 1669.

9 Oxford, Sheldonian Theatre. South front.

10 Oxford, Trinity College. North side of Garden Quadrangle. 1668.

11   Cambridge, Pembroke College. Chapel. West front. 1663–5.

12   Cambridge, Emmanuel College. Chapel and gallery. 1668–73.

13   Cambridge, Emmanuel College. Chapel arcade.

15 Cambridge, Emmanuel College. Chapel.

14 Cambridge, Pembroke College. Chapel with organ removed.

16 Cambridge, Pembroke College. Chapel. Capital.

17 Oxford, Sheldonian Theatre. Corinthian capital.

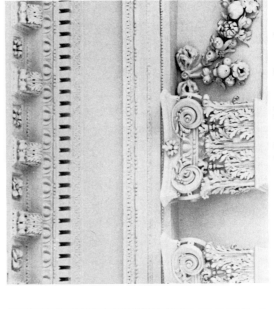

19 Cambridge, Trinity College. Library. Composite capital.

18 Cambridge, Emmanuel College. Corinthian capital.

20   St Paul's. Pre-Fire Design. 1666. *All Souls, Oxford.*

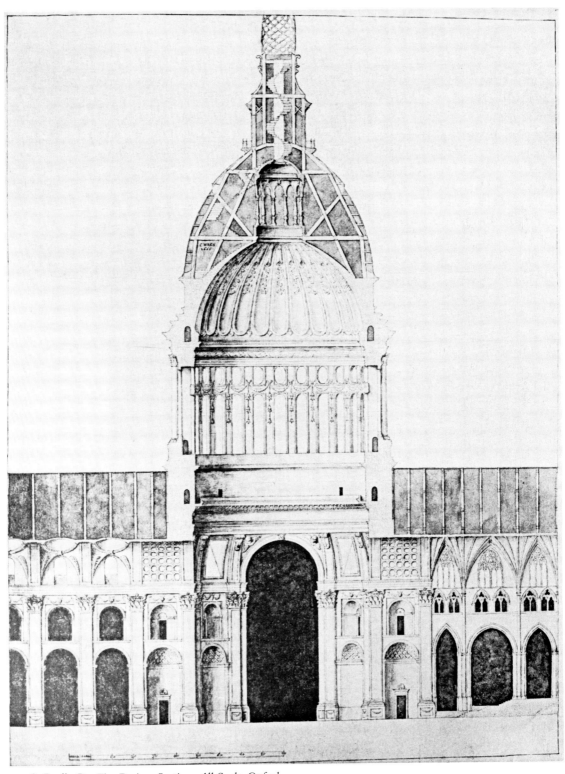

21 St Paul's. Pre-Fire Design. Section. *All Souls, Oxford.*

22   The Custom House. 1669–71 (demolished). Engraving by J. Harris. *British Museum.*

23   Theobalds Park, Herts. Temple Bar. 1670–2.

24 St Olave, Old Jewry. 1670–9 (demolished).

25 St Mildred, Poultry. 1670–7 (demolished).

26 St George, Botolph Lane. 1671–9 (demolished).

27 St Bartholomew, Exchange. 1674–81 (demolished).

28 St Dionis Backchurch. Interior. 1670–7 (demolished).

29 St Bartholomew, Exchange (demolished). Interior.

30 St Dionis Backchurch (demolished). Exterior. Tower completed 1685.

31 St Dionis Backchurch (demolished). East front.

32 St Lawrence Jewry. Interior. 1670–81. After restoration.

33 St Lawrence Jewry. Exterior from south–east.

34 St Michael, Wood Street.
1670–3 (demolished). East front.

35 St Michael, Wood Street (demolished). Interior.

37   St Bride, Fleet Street. Interior looking west (before rebuilding).

36   St Bride, Fleet Street. 1670–4. Spire 1702–3.

38 St Bride, Fleet Street. Interior looking east (before rebuilding).

40 St Nicholas, Cole Abbey. 1671–8.

39 St Mary-le-Bow. 1671–5. Spire 1676–80.

42   St Magnus. Interior. 1671–8.

41   St Mary Aldermanbury. Interior. 1670–4 (demolished).

43 St Stephen Walbrook. Dome. 1672–8.

44   St Stephen Walbrook. Interior looking south.

45 St Paul's. Great Model. Crossing looking east. 1673–4.

46 St Paul's. Great Model from north-west.

47   St Paul's. Great Model. Portico.

48   St Paul's. Great Model. North side.

49   St Paul's. Great Model. Interior from west end.

50 St Paul's. Great Model. North transept.

51 St Paul's. Great Model. View into choir.

52   St Paul's. Crossing looking south-east. 1675–1700.

53 Greenwich. Royal Observatory from north. 1675–6.

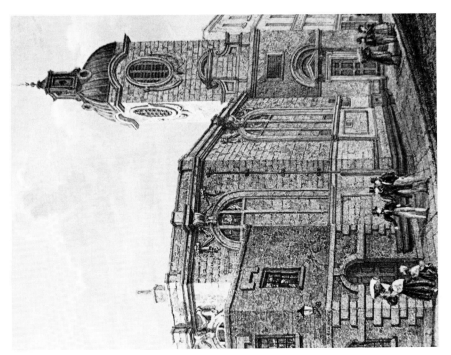

55 St Benet Fink. 1670–81 (demolished).

54 Greenwich Observatory. Octagon.

56 St Paul's. Warrant Design. South elevation. 1675. *All Souls, Oxford.*

57 St Paul's. Warrant Design. Section. *All Souls, Oxford.*

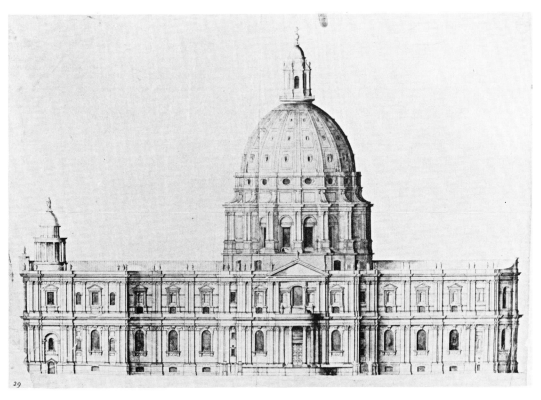

58 St Paul's. Definitive Design. South elevation. 1675. *All Souls, Oxford.*

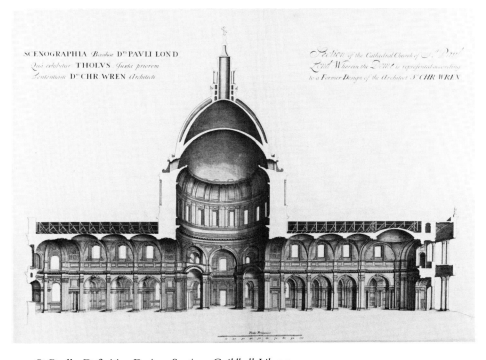

59 St Paul's. Definitive Design. Section. *Guildhall Library.*

60   Cambridge, Trinity College. Library. East front. 1676–84.

61   Cambridge, Trinity College. Library. West front.

62   Cambridge, Trinity College. Library. Centre of West front.

63 Cambridge, Trinity College. Library from south end.

64 St James, Piccadilly. North aisle and gallery. 1676–84.

65   St James, Piccadilly. Interior looking south-east.

66   Oxford, Sheldonian Theatre. Interior looking south.

67   Oxford, Sheldonian Theatre. Interior looking north.

68 St Clement Danes. Interior. 1680–2. After restoration.

69   Chelsea Hospital. Chapel. 1682–5.

70 Christ Church, Newgate Street. Interior looking west. 1677–87 (demolished).

71 Christ Church, Newgate Street (demolished). Interior looking east.

72 St Paul's. South aisle.

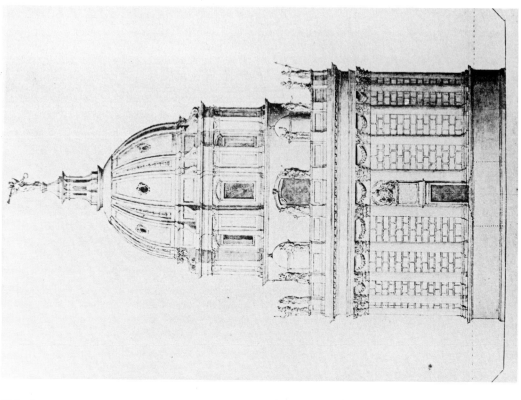

74   Design for a mausoleum for Charles I. 1678. *All Souls, Oxford.*

73   St Mary Magdalen, Old Fish Street. 1683–7 (demolished).

75 St Paul's from south. 1675–1710.

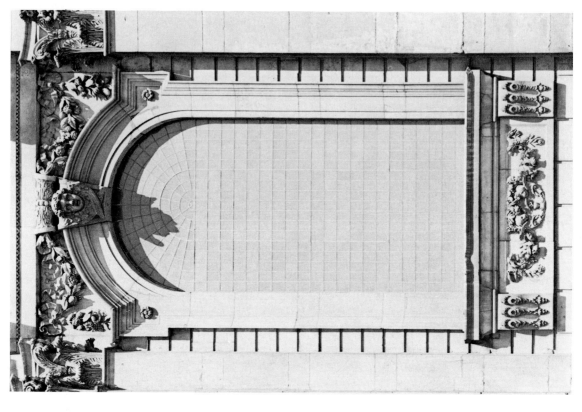

78 St Paul's. Nave window.

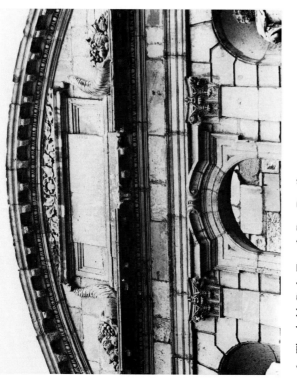

76 Theobalds Park. Temple Bar. Detail.

77 St Clement Danes. Doorhead on west front.

79   St Paul's. South transept gable end.

80 St Paul's. South transept and dome.

81 St Paul's. Aedicule on south transept.

83   The Monument. 1671–6.

82   St Paul's from north-east.

84   St Paul's from south-east with tower of St Augustine, Watling Street (1680–96, reconstructed).

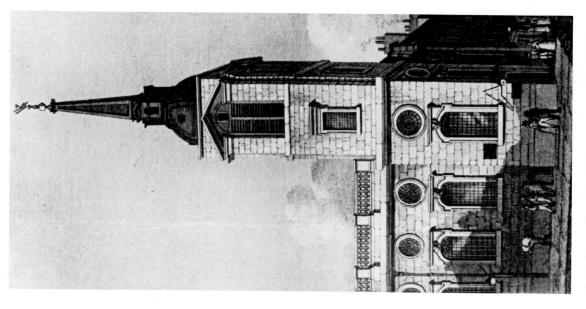

86 St Benet, Gracechurch Street. 1681–7 (demolished).

85 St Mary-le-Bow. West door to tower.

88 St Peter, Cornhill. Interior.

87 St Peter, Cornhill from east. 1677–85.

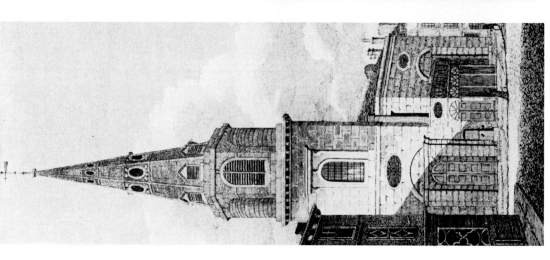

89   St Antholin. 1678–87 (demolished).

90   St Anne and St Agnes. 1676–81.

91   St Antholin (demolished). Interior.

92   St Anne and St Agnes. Interior after rebuilding.

94 St Michael, Queenhythe. 1676–87 (demolished).

93 St Swithin. 1677–81 (demolished).

96 St Michael Bassishaw (demolished). Interior looking west.

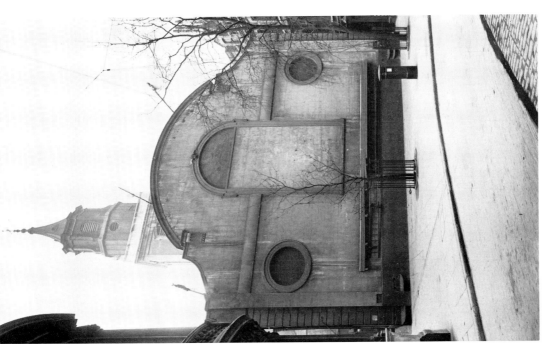

95 St Michael Bassishaw. 1676–9. Spire 1708–12 (demolished).

98 St Martin Ludgate. Interior looking east.

97 St Martin Ludgate. South front. 1677–86.

100 St Mary Abchurch. South front. 1681–7.

99 St Benet, Paul's Wharf, from north-east. 1677–85.

101   All Hallows, Bread Street. Interior looking west. 1677–84 (demolished).

102   St Benet, Paul's Wharf. Interior.

103 St James Garlickhythe. 1676–82. Interior after restoration.

104 St Mary Abchurch. Interior.

105 St Andrew, Holborn, from north-east. 1684–92. Tower 1704.

106 St Andrew-by-the-Wardrobe. 1685–94. Interior before reconstruction.

107 St Margaret Lothbury. 1686–92. Screen from All Hallows the Great.

108 St Mildred, Bread Street. Interior. 1681–7 (demolished).

109 St Mildred, Bread Street (demolished) from west.

110 All Hallows, Bread Street (demolished).

111 All Hallows the Great. 1677–82 (demolished).

112   Chelsea Hospital. First floor ward.

113   Chelsea Hospital. North-east range.

114   Chelsea Hospital. Figure Court.

115   Chelsea Hospital. Frontispiece on east side of court.

117   St Michael Royal. 1686–94. Steeple 1713–17.

116   St James Garlickhythe. 1676–82. Steeple 1714–17.

119   St Mary Aldermary. Exterior. Tower 1701–03.

118   St Mary Aldermary. Interior. 1679–82.

122   St Mary Somerset. Tower. 1686–94.

121   St Alban, Wood Street. Tower. 1682–97.

120   Oxford. Christ Church. Tom Tower. 1681–2.

125 St Edmund, Lombard Street. 1670–6. Spire 1706–07.

124 St Margaret Pattens. 1684–1702.

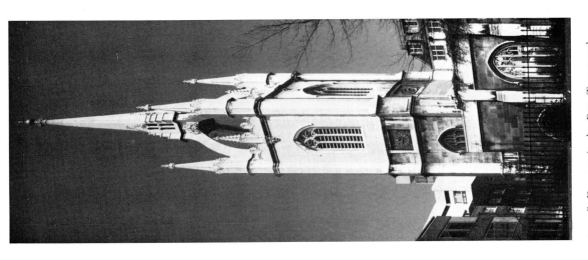

123 St Dunstan-in-the-East. Tower and spire. 1695–8.

128   St Vedast. Steeple. 1709–12.

127   Christ Church, Newgate Street. Steeple.
1703–04.

126   St Mary-le-Bow. Steeple. 1676–80.

131 St Michael, Crooked Lane. Steeple 1709–14 (demolished).

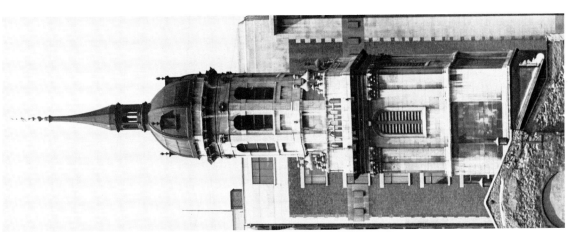

130 St Magnus. Tower 1671–84. Steeple 1705–06.

129 St Stephen Walbrook. 1672–8. Steeple 1713–17.

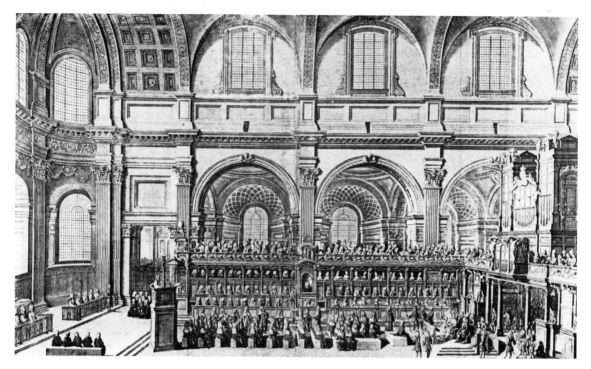

132 St Paul's. Choir in 1706.

133 St Paul's. Crossing and choir *c.* 1880.

134 St Paul's. Choir. North side and stalls.

135   St Paul's. West end, north side.

136 St Paul's from west end.

137 St Paul's. West front.

138 St Paul's. West front.

139 St Paul's. Impost capitals in nave.

140 St Paul's. West front, lower frieze.

141 St Paul's. South transept door made from organ screen.

142 St Paul's. Crossing c. 1750.

144   St Paul's. South-west tower and library.

143   St Paul's. Nave roof and south-west tower.

146   St Paul's. South-west tower. Dean's Door.

145   St Paul's. Detail of peristyle.

147 Hampton Court. East frontispiece. 1689–95.

148 Hampton Court. Colonnade in Clock Court.

149   Hampton Court. South front.

150　Hampton Court. Fountain Court.

151 Hampton Court. Window in Fountain Court.

152   Hampton Court. Exedra on east of Fountain Court.

153   Hampton Court. Vestibule on east front.

154 Chelsea Hospital. Colonnade.

155 Cambridge, Trinity College. Library. Stoa.

156 Hampton Court. Detail of east front.

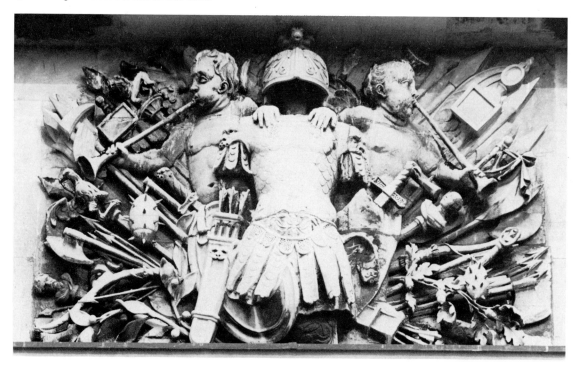

157 Hampton Court. Trophy on south front.

158   Hampton Court. Royal arms on south front.

159   Hampton Court. Door hood on east front.

160 Winchester Palace. 1683–5 (demolished).

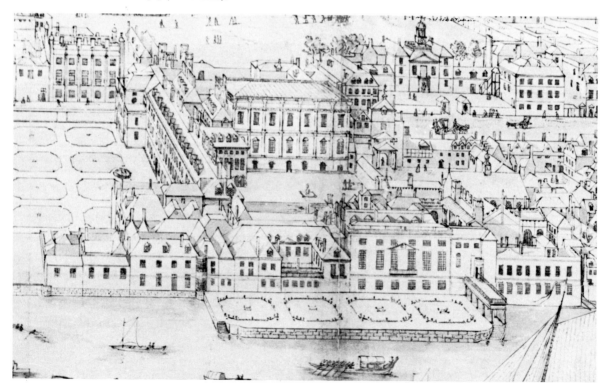

161 Whitehall Palace (demolished). Privy Gallery (left). Queen's apartment and terrace (right).

162 Kensington Palace. Clock Court. 1689–92.

163 Winslow Hall. 1699–1702.

164 Hampton Court. South and east fronts.

165 Whitehall project. Detail. 1698. *All Souls, Oxford.*

166 Greenwich Hospital. View from river terrace.

167 Chelsea Hospital. Vestibule to Hall and Chapel.

168   Greenwich Hospital. Vestibule to Painted Hall.

169   Greenwich Hospital. Painted Hall.